Inside The **World's**

Development Finance Institutions

William A. Delphos

THOMSON

™

Australia · Canada · Mexico · Singapore · Spain · United Kingdom · United States

THOMSON

SOUTH-WESTERN

Inside The World's Development Finance Institutions
William A. Delphos

VP/Editorial Director:
Jack W. Calhoun

VP/Editor-in-Chief:
Dave Shaut

Acquisitions Editor:
Steve Momper

Production Editor:
Darrell E. Frye

Production Manager:
Patricia Matthews Boies

**Manufacturing
Coordinator:**
Charlene Taylor

Senior Designer:
Mike Stratton

Production House:
Argosy

Printer:
Transcontinental
Quebec, Canada

2961848

54111023

ADDITIONAL TITLES BY
WILLIAM A. DELPHOS

Inside Washington, 2004 (4th edition of this popular resource, coming March 2004)
Inside the World's Export Credit Agencies, 2003
Inside the World Bank Group: The Practical Guide for International Business Executives, 1998

For more information about these publications or additional titles, please contact Delphos International at +1.202.337.6300 or visit our website at www.delphosinternational.com

TABLE OF CONTENTS

ACKNOWLEDGMENTS

It is impossible to mention everyone who contributed to the book, but its publication would not have been possible without the dedication and cooperation of the many talented individuals at Delphos International. I would like to particularly thank the following people for their untiring efforts: Linda Habgood, Tsewang Namgyal, Jennifer Daines, Svetoslav Gatchev, Todd Morath, Ksenia Serbryanikova, Suzi Sidek, Briana Fichtner, Melissa Faubert, Elena Batalla, Tara Dempsey, and Nicolas Nannetti. Our diligent and dedicated research team spent many hours working to compile and present the most up-to-date, comprehensive information possible.

William A. Delphos
November 2003
Washington, DC

PREFACE

While the 1990s ushered in a global trade and commercial environment that dramatically affected the way many companies operated, the following decade is filled with even more international opportunities for companies that know and understand the many facets and intricacies of the global economy. As the international business world grows smaller and economies become more closely tied, companies must take advantage of opportunities in "emerging markets." The developing world poses endless possibilities to companies willing to make investments in underdeveloped regions. As a result, development finance institutions (DFIs) willing to facilitate, finance, and support these endeavors continue to grow. DFIs offer a variety of financial products and services and actively work with private businesses to create sustainable growth. Technical assistance, training, and improved procurement procedures also make projects funded by these organizations a multi-billion dollar opportunity few companies can afford to pass up.

Finance is the lubricant of commerce. Without financing, in all of its varieties (i.e., project finance, short-term trade credit, letters of credit, medium- and long-term capital equipment loans, equity investments, political risk insurance, and so on), companies would have difficulty capitalizing on most international ventures. Often times, private sector companies find that a commercial infrastructure must be put in place before a private physical infrastructure project can be contemplated. Financing forms a bridge allowing innovative dreams to become a viable business reality.

This book is a practical guide to the institutions providing these essential services. *Inside the World's Development Finance Institutions* provides a resource on who these organizations are, what products and services they offer, and how they can be contacted. In addition, a number of case studies are included throughout the main text of the book to help you take full advantage of business opportunities worldwide. Many business executives are unaware of the numerous resources available for development in emerging markets. All too often programs are underutilized because companies are generally unaware of the types of assistance at their disposal. The goal of this book is to make information about private sector financial assistance more accessible to the international business community.

While it would be an exaggeration to suggest that this publication is comprehensive, every effort has been made to include detailed descriptions of each of the major DFIs existing at the time of publication. We also provide specific contact information so interested executives can follow up directly with the agencies for next-step advice. If your company is actively operating in emerging markets, we are confident this book will become a valuable one-stop shop for financing sources.

William A. Delphos
November 2003
Washington, DC

INTRODUCTION

DFIs, ECAs, bilaterals, multilaterals, aid, tied-aid, sovereign and subsovereign loans, grants, technical assistance, private sector initiatives, and so on, sound like the kind of gobbledygook you would expect to come out of Washington, DC. Certainly, the typical U.S. business executive wouldn't think that this esoteric world could have any application to the world of business. However, as the globalization of the world's economies continues, choosing to limit business opportunities to the so-called safe markets of the United States, Euroland, Japan, and Korea is no longer a realistic option for dynamic growth-oriented businesses. This book is designed to expose executives to funding sources and risk mitigation tools for direct foreign investment in emerging markets. Furthermore, it serves as a guide for negotiating the maze of acronyms and new terms.

BACKGROUND

Countries' efforts to rebuild after World War II resulted in the genesis of institutions that today help to carry aid from rich countries to poor countries. In the United States, the Marshall Plan had a far-reaching and timeless impact in establishing how governments thought about aiding other countries. Although the Marshall Plan was self-described as an interim plan for rebuilding Europe after the War, "an emergency tool for assistance," it did spawn at its conclusion in 1951 the Mutual Security Agency, in 1953 the Foreign Operations Administration, and in 1954 the International Cooperation Administration. All of these institutions were established with the goal of consolidating economic and technical assistance on a worldwide basis, but none were given the autonomy necessary to effectively execute a coordinated global development plan. It wasn't until 1961 and the passing of the Foreign Assistance Act under President John F. Kennedy that U.S. foreign aid was revised and refocused toward nonmilitary aid. It was then that the United States Agency for International Development (USAID) was born. USAID unified already existing efforts and organizations, but more importantly, it embodied the U.S. recommitment to overseas development through programs and risk capital that could help countries become self-supporting. To focus on supporting private investment in developing economies, the Overseas Private Investment Corporation (OPIC) was established within USAID and then later spun off in 1975.

Organizations similar to USAID and OPIC were established in all parts of the world throughout the latter half of the twentieth century, and new ones are created every year. Some of these so-called development agencies were born of post-war development theories, and some were based on post-colonization concepts. All are surprisingly similar in mandate, however, seeking to support the economic and social development of their global "neighborhood" by providing risk capital and transferring business and technical know-how.

Prior to the creation of the International Bank for Reconstruction and Development, the original institution of the World Bank Group, in 1946, there were no multilateral organizations—and only a handful of bilateral (or one-country) agencies—focused on economic development through the financing of enterprises and projects in the world's lower- and medium-income countries. Indeed, some institutions included in this book were established as early as 1921. Three of these frontrunners focused on social progress and economic development through financial assistance within their own borders, but one serves as the first true global development finance institution— Agence Francaise de Developpement (AfD). Established a full 5 years prior to IBRD, AfD was established as, and remains today, a bilateral institution providing loans, equity, and technical assistance to public institutions and private companies in an effort to increase per capita income in less-developed countries. AfD continues to make its mark on the international finance scene, funding approximately 130 projects per annum from its network of 45 offices in 60 countries. In the 62 years since AfD was established, the field of development finance institutions (DFIs), has grown exponentially.

WHAT IS A DFI?

For purposes of this publication, DFIs are defined as the multilateral or bilateral institutions providing the risk capital (debt and equity) guarantees, technical assistance, and/or insurance and that enable flows of foreign direct investment into less-developed or emerging markets. It is important to note from this definition the focus on *private investment.* Certainly, quite a few of the major DFIs, such as the International Bank of Reconstruction and Development (IBRD), the Inter-American Development Bank (IADB), and the Asian Development Bank (ADB), exist primarily to provide governments with capital. However, even though the dollars dedicated to private funding are small, the impact is often of similar magnitude to public funding dollars. This is because private sector activities typically focus on playing a catalytic role—investing the first dollar (or peso or baht), guaranteeing against political risks, and being paid back last so private sector players are entering as opposed to leaving their money on the sidelines or more often in investment-grade countries. This book focuses on the role DFIs play in relation to the private sector and their involvement in emerging markets. So although IBRD, IADB, and ADB programs are discussed at length, their public sector activities are not addressed.

COMMONALITIES OF DFIS

DFIs, multilateral and bilateral alike, described in this book are widely disparate in terms of capitalization, membership base, breadth of mandate, location, age, and revenue. However, there are also many similarities, as follows.

- DFIs have an interest in a "greater good." Although programs vary in "packaging," all focus largely on reducing unemployment, improving the environment, enhanced trade flows, and social and economic development.
- DFIs play a catalytic role in increasing capital flows. Although they lend on market terms, they work very hard not to compete with, but rather complement, private capital. Most DFIs invest in projects that meet their individual investment criteria but that cannot get financing and/or technical expertise elsewhere at reasonable terms.
- Transactions benefit from the halo effect that a DFI, as a government-owned or government-supported institution, offers. A DFI's presence in a transaction is beneficial from a financial as well as a technical and political standpoint. Foreign investors seek DFI participation because of their business expertise in developing countries and because of their excellent relationships with developing-country governments. A DFI's status as an independent international organization reassures both foreign investors and host countries and can provide added comfort by helping companies and sponsors negotiate with host governments.
- DFIs have an appetite for supporting venture and greenfield transactions and are accustomed to the inherent risks. To mitigate risks, DFIs have a structured way of lending and are rigorous in the due diligence they perform. Most lending to venture or greenfield projects is done as project financing with a long-term loan being made to a special purpose vehicle (SPV) whose cash flows in and out are very predictable, for example, because of the presence of off-take contracts. Project

finance lenders require a security interest (and assignment of all project contracts) in highly controlled cash mechanisms and as much mitigation as possible of foreign exchange risks.

- DFIs have a clear commercial perspective on risk and return. DFIs rarely offer grants or subsidized loans, but charge market rates for services and capital. The benefits lie in a DFI's ability to consider a 15-year or more tenor and in its ability to attract additional capital into a deal.

- Most DFIs are initially capitalized with government and/or IBRD monies. However, they are expected, over time, to become self-sustaining through their ability to raise large sums in the global capital markets. For this reason, most DFIs maintain investment-grade risk ratings from the major international rating agencies (Standard & Poor's, Moody's, and/or Fitch). Therefore, DFIs must focus on portfolio balance and credit quality. And because they rarely act alone, DFIs must be cognizant of the risks that the rest of the market (i.e., their co-lenders) is willing to undertake on a given transaction.

- DFIs understand and accept political risks, but require compensation for shielding other project participants from them.

- Due to government ownership or sponsorship, many DFIs occasionally use their programs to accomplish the political mandates of their shareholders, but unlike ECAs, are not primarily interested in promoting exports. Even in these isolated cases, however, the loans still have commercial terms and a clear expectation of repayment.

DFIs generally offer great advantages to companies and individuals embarking on projects in less-developed economies, but there are also some drawbacks, or "costs," to doing business with a DFI. They include the following:

- *Timing.* Because of the governmental nature of these institutions and, particularly within a multilateral institution, the number of constituents' objectives that need to be met, it can take a substantial amount of time to close a transaction with a DFI. Companies may consider hiring a consulting firm that specializes in procuring government resources to help run the gauntlet.

- *Policy.* Environmental standards are a good example of policy requirements that DFIs must adhere to that commercial lending institutions often do not. Enterprises supported by a DFI need to comply with the higher of World Bank or local environmental standards and must prove compliance up front and on an ongoing basis.

- *Eligibility.* All DFIs have certain eligibility requirements that are often above and beyond the typical credit checklist of a pure commercial institution. Requirements often relate to the number of jobs an enterprise can offer or restrictions on certain types of businesses (such as the manufacturing of arms or the operation of casinos). In some instances, whole industries may be ineligible for support because it is perceived that other sources of capital are available or that the business itself is not politically correct.

HOW TO USE THIS BOOK

This book was created to aid and guide international business executives investing in emerging markets. Because commercial and institutional sources of funding ebb and flow with the changing tides of the world economy and shifting views of credit officers, the constancy of the resources housed within DFIs can be invaluable to those seeking advice, insight, risk capital, and/or technical assistance. This book can also be a useful resource to those seeking procurement opportunities. Many of the DFIs described herein offer online information about projects that are being supported. Each project that receives DFI support creates jobs. Projects require equipment, contractors, consultants, technical advisers, insurance brokers, lawyers, and more in order to be realized. Check out the web sites in a methodical fashion to make sure you don't miss any procurement opportunities, but keep in mind that even if you overlook an opportunity to work for the DFI, the sponsor of a project may still be in need of assistance.

WHICH DFI IS FOR YOU?

DFI programs can be organized into concentric circles, so those seeking support from institutions must make sure that they approach the correct agency based on industry, region, risk capital type, sponsor nationality, degree of interest, or ability to participate. Remember, not all DFIs have the same policy guidelines.

This book is organized into chapters corresponding to these circles. DFIs with the broadest mandates and, correspondingly, the largest circle is discussed first, followed by those with more refined mandates, and so on. Generally, the size of a DFI's circle is determined by whether its charter restricts it to focusing on particular countries and whether its membership (or ownership) restricts it to considering only "member-sponsored" or "member-benefiting" projects. This is because, for the most part, DFIs do not restrict their support of transactions according to sectoral criteria. From a policy perspective, DFIs have traditionally been most adept at financing infrastructure projects, but often consider projects in most sectors as long as doing so results in a greater good; that is, more jobs, less pollution, cheaper services to locals, and so on. (See previous section for mention of a few exceptions to this "greater good" rule.)

As a brief introduction to these DFIs, the goal of this Introduction is to accomplish the following:

- Discuss the categories of DFIs that exist in today's global marketplace
- Briefly introduce each of the DFIs covered in this book
- Highlight the products offered by DFIs
- Enlighten the readers, presumably investors, as to the eligibility criteria for DFI support
- Describe the process for obtaining DFI support

Chapter 1 focuses on multilateral DFIs with a global focus. The large majority of the DFIs in this category are members of the World Bank Group (WBG), which supports investments across sectoral lines in any of the 183 member countries. Institutions covered in this chapter include the following:

- *International Bank for Reconstruction and Development (IBRD)*—IBRD is the largest source of market-based loans to developing countries and is the original institution of the WBG.
- *International Finance Corporation (IFC)*—Headquartered in Washington, DC, this member of the WBG promotes development by encouraging the growth of productive enterprise and efficient capital markets.
- *United Nations Development Program (UNDP)*—As the global development network of the United Nations, UNDP aims to reduce global poverty by providing financing, development advice, and advocacy.

Chapter 2 covers bilateral DFIs (BDFIs). These single-member development financial institutions support projects in most global emerging markets under the philosophy that sponsor countries benefit from a more prosperous global economy. For example, AfD might support a project in Botswana even if there is no apparent direct French benefit—no French sponsor, no French contractor or adviser—and even if there is no existing trade between France and Botswana. Of course, the project must be beneficial to the social and economic development of Botswana and be financially viable taking into account credit supports offered by project participants. Many of these bilateral DFIs have been in existence for several decades, and they are generally very active in the international finance scene. However, most consider themselves primarily finance participants and prefer to lend to transactions that have World Bank, IADB, ADB, or similar support taking comfort from a "stamp of approval" provided by these other organizations.

- *Agence Francaise de Developpement (AfD)*—Established in 1941, AfD was one of the first DFIs. It now continues to increase per capita income in less-developed countries by encouraging development projects, supporting trade associations, and participating in the restructuring of financial systems.
- *CDC Capital Partners*—This organization was created by the government of the United Kingdom in 1948 to assist commercial and industrial development around the world.
- *German Investment and Development Company (DEG)*—A subsidiary of Kreditanstalt für Wiederaufbau (KfW), this organization was set up to establish and expand private enterprise structures within developing countries.
- *Netherlands Development Finance Corporation (FMO)*—Established in 1970, FMO provides financing to the infrastructure sector and to projects aimed at promoting micro, small-, and medium-sized enterprises (MSMEs) in developing countries.
- *German Agency for Technical Cooperation (GTZ)*—This German development corporation was founded in 1975 to promote international cooperation through sustainable development around the world.

In Chapter 3, the bilateral DFIs highlighted are those providing assistance when there is a clear linkage to the sponsor's national interests. This linkage can be established by a citizen of the sponsor country having a minimum ownership interest in the project or by a contractual relationship the project has with a company of the same nationality as the sponsor.

- *Portuguese Agency of Support for Development (APAD)*—Recently established, APAD promotes Portuguese investment, supports social and economic infrastructure, and fosters the private sector in projects with a Portuguese interest.
- *Belgian Corporation for International Investment (BMI-SBI)*—The BMI-SBI provides financing to Belgian companies through the creation of new joint ventures or subsidiaries and the acquisition, restructuring, and development of existing companies.
- *Compañía Española de Financiación del Desarrollo (COFIDES)*—Headquartered in Madrid, Spain, COFIDES encourages

Spanish companies to invest in projects related to transportation infrastructure, capital goods, electronics, and agribusiness in developing countries

- *Ducroire/Delcredere (Delcredere)*—Founded in 1921 after the First World War, this Belgian organization provides financing and insurance products to support the expansion, creation, and improvement of Belgian industry.
- *Export Development Canada (EDC)*—Established in 1995, EDC has grown considerably, having closed more than 100 transactions in over 30 countries by providing trade finance services to Canadian investors and exporters.
- *Finanzierungsgarantie-Gesellschaft (FGG)*—Originally founded in Austria in 1969, FGG bears the risk of long-term financing to Austrian countries.
- *Finnfund*—Headquartered in Helsinki, this Finnish development finance company provides long-term risk capital for private projects in developing countries.
- *Danish International Investment Funds (IFU)*—Through this group of funds, the Danish Parliament supports growth in emerging markets through project financing, loans and guarantees. There are four funds: IFU, IFV, IØ, and MIØ. These funds provide assistance to specific countries based on per capita income and region.
- *Japan Bank for International Cooperation (JBIC)*—Created through a merger of the Export-Import Bank of Japan and the Overseas Economic Cooperation Fund, JBIC was established in 1999 to support development efforts in developing countries, to promote stability in international financial markets, and to promote Japanese export and economic activities overseas.
- *Kreditanstalt für Wiederaufbau (KfW)*—This German organization was created to distribute U.S. Marshall Plan aid. Today it provides loans to finance investment goods and related services, primarily to developing countries.
- *Nordic Development Fund (NDF)*—Established to promote economic and social development in developing countries, NDF provides financial support to activities with an interest in the Nordic region.
- *Nordic Investment Bank (NIB)*—Operating primarily in the Nordic countries, NIB offers services to promote growth in these countries through the long-term financing of projects in the public and private sectors.
- *Overseas Private Investment Corporation (OPIC)*—Established in 1971 by the U.S. government, OPIC provides services to U.S.

businesses looking to expand into foreign countries and emerging markets.

- *Societa Italiana per le Imprese all'Estero (SIMEST)*—Created by the Ministry of Foreign Trade in 1991, SIMEST supports Italian entrepreneurs in all aspects of international business.
- *Swedfund International (Swedfund)*—This investment banking organization was established to help create profitable Swedish companies in order to stimulate economic growth.
- *United States Agency for International Development (USAID)*—for more than 50 years, USAID has been the principal U.S. government agency providing assistance to countries recovering from disaster, trying to escape poverty, and engaging in democratic reforms.

Chapter 4 covers the subset of DFIs that are multilateral organizations whose mission it is to support development by participating in projects in member countries. Often the membership base of these particular DFIs includes a combination of developed capital-providing countries and developing recipient countries. Initial capital is often provided by membership institutions that sit on voting boards, with a goal of maintaining very high credit ratings (A+ and above) so future funding requirements can be met through global debt issuance. Increasingly, these DFIs are involved in providing capital to local financial institutions to broaden their reach. This chapter is organized according to the regions these particular DFIs support.

AFRICA
- *African Development Bank (AfDB)*—To break the cycle of poverty in the African region, AfDB promotes the flow of external and domestic resources and investment and provides policy assistance and technical service to the region.
- *Banque Ouest Africaine de Developpement (BOAD)*—Established in 1973 by the West African Monetary Union, BOAD promotes regional economic development and integration within its eight member states.
- *Industrial Development Corporation (IDC)*—The South African parliament established the IDC in 1940 to foster economic growth, industrial development, and economic empowerment in the region.
- *Eastern and Southern African Trade and Development Bank (PTA Bank)*—Located in Kenya, the PTA promotes economic prosperity to its members primarily by providing project and trade finance.

ASIA

- *Asian Development Bank (ADB)*—ADB is dedicated to reducing poverty in Asia and the Pacific region by providing assistance in the form of loans, technical assistance, grants, guarantees, and equity investments.

LATIN AMERICA

- *Banco Latinoamericano de Exportaciones (BLADEX)*—Established in 1977 in Panama, BLADEX serves the Latin American and Caribbean regions by providing integrated solutions for exports.
- *Central American Bank for Economic Integration (CABEI)*—Located in Honduras, CABEI is committed to improving social and economic development by providing resources and technical assistance to South America.
- *Andean Development Bank (CAF)*—Established in 1970 in Caracas, Venezuela, CAF serves to implement economic integration measures and to coordinate policies among participating countries in the areas of trade, industry, finance, and technical cooperation.
- *Caribbean Development Bank (CDB)*—Created in response to requested assistance from the United Nations Development Program, CDB finances regional development projects that benefit member countries as well as the region as a whole.
- *Inter-American Development Bank (IADB)*—Headquartered in Washington, DC, the IADB is the oldest and largest regional multilateral development institution, financing economic and social development as well as infrastructure projects that serve to reduce poverty and improve social equity, competitiveness, modernization of the state, regional integration, and the environment.
- *Inter-American Investment Corporation (IIC)*—As part of the IADB, the IIC provides financing and consulting services to private Latin American and Caribbean enterprises.
- *North American Development Bank (NADB)*—Spurred by the North American Free Trade Agreement, NADB seeks to facilitate economic and social development through the development of an environmentally sound infrastructure.

EASTERN EUROPE

- *Black Sea Trade and Development Bank (BSTDB)*—Established in Greece in 1998, BSTDB fosters development and promotes business through the support of regional trade and financing projects.

- *European Bank for Reconstruction and Development (EBRD)*—Located in the United Kingdom, the EBRD is the largest single regional investor in Central and Eastern Europe. It provides financing for banks, businesses, industries, and investments.
- *European Investment Bank (EIB)*—As the multilateral financing institution for the European Union (EU), EIB provides assistance to small- and medium-sized enterprises (SMEs) by offering venture capital, loans, and guarantees.

MIDDLE EAST

- *Arab Fund for Economic and Social Development (AFESD)*—Created by the League of Arab States in 1974, AFESD eliminates development constraints and fosters economic integration and cooperation among member countries.

Chapter 5 covers the national DFIs (NDFIs), which are government-owned, funded, and supported development institutions that were created to lend or invest in developmental projects within their national boundaries. Almost every developing country has an NDFI, so depending on the location of a project, the resources available from the relevant NDFI should be explored. This chapter provides detailed information on NDFIs in 11 of the largest emerging markets: Brazil, China, India, Indonesia, Korea, Mexico, Poland, Russia, South Africa, Taiwan, and Turkey. In some instances, several institutions provide assistance. Mexico has two and India has four; Argentina, on the other hand, relies on the programs of the IADB and has not established a developmental agency of its own. Appendix B includes information about other NDFIs around the globe.

BRAZIL

- *Brazilian Development Bank (BNDES)*—Established in 1952, BNDES is the primary source of long-term funding for Brazilian development projects in the private sector.

CHINA and TAIWAN

- *China Development Bank (CDB)*—CDB is committed to narrowing the economic development gap between China's coast and its central and western regions by providing finance instruments for the construction of an infrastructure and industry.

INDIA

- *Industrial Development Bank of India (IDBI)*—Established in 1964, IDBI provides financial assistance for greenfield projects, expansion, modernization, and diversification purposes.

- *Industrial Investment Bank of India (IIBI)*—Established in 1956, IIBI provides financial assistance to the Indian region through loans, equity, credit, and capital market investment and provides technical assistance.
- *Small Industries Development Bank of India (SIDBI)*—As an institution designed to support small industry, the SIDBI provides assistance in the areas of export, industrial manufacturing, transportation, health care, and tourism.

INDONESIA
- *Bank Mandiri*—In response to the Asian crisis of 1997, Bank Mandiri was formed to provide comprehensive financial services to SMEs in Indonesia.

KOREA
- *Korea Development Bank (KDB)*—As the bilateral development bank of Korea, KDB seeks to act as a leader in Korean international finance.

MEXICO
- *Bancomext*—Operating for over 65 years, Bancomext promotes the international competitiveness of Mexican businesses and attracts foreign investment and joint ventures.
- *Nacional Financiera (NAFIN)*—As Mexico's largest development bank, NAFIN is dedicated to the modernization and economic development of Mexico through policies that strengthen and support business owners, economic sectors, companies, the development of financial markets, and the growth of underdeveloped regions.

POLAND
- *BRE Bank*—The primary purpose of BRE Bank is to provide services to SMEs. It is heavily involved in foreign trade transactions and services.

RUSSIA
- *Russian Regional Development Bank (RRDB)*—Since its establishment in 1996, RRDB has grown to become one of the largest Russian banks, having a presence in all segments of the financial markets and offering various foreign currency instruments.

SOUTH AFRICA
- *Development Bank of Southern Africa (DBSA)*—Established in 1983, DBSA serves to improve the socioeconomic conditions

and quality of life within the region through investments in an infrastructure and development.

TURKEY

- *Development Bank of Turkey (DBT)*—DBT provides funding and operational support to enterprises in order to foster economic development.
- *Turkiye Sinai Kalkinma Bankasi (TSKB)*—Established in 1950 with support from the World Bank, TSKB provides assistance to the private sector, fosters the participation of private and foreign capital, and assists with the development of the capital market in Turkey.

Chapter 6 discusses the region-to-region DFIs. These DFIs are a relatively new phenomenon. BADEA and ISDB were the first to be established in 1975, and others have been created since as particular regional groups of countries identified a need to support projects that (for environmental, fiscal, or national security reasons, among others) foster improved social and economic stability.

- *Arab Bank for Economic Development in Africa (BADEA)*—Established in Sudan in 1975, BADEA serves to strengthen economic, financial, and technical cooperation between Arab and African countries by financing economic development, stimulating Arab capital contributions, and providing technical assistance.
- *Islamic Development Bank (ISDB)*—Headquartered in Saudi Arabia, the ISDB assists member countries economically and socially in accordance with Islamic law.
- *Nordic Environment Finance Corporation (NEFCO)*—Established in 1990 by the five Nordic countries, NEFCO facilitates the implementation of environmentally beneficial projects in neighboring Central and Eastern Europe.
- *Nordic Southern African Development Fund (NORSAD)*—This Nordic operation was founded in 1991 to support economic and industrial development by promoting and financing sound business cooperation between private sector enterprises.

Chapter 7 discusses a few important DFIs that now have a significant amount of private sector ownership. Most of them started out as traditional NDFIs, but over time, they acquired or merged with other commercial or investment banking groups. As a result, today they have a much broader product offering and only minority stakes owned by a government. They are referred to as quasi DFIs.

- *Development Bank of Singapore (DBS)*—In addition to providing long-term project financing, DBS has also developed into a fully operational commercial, retail, and investment bank.
- *Société Internationale Financiere pour les Investissements et le Developpement en Afrique (SIFIDA)*—Headquartered in Switzerland, SIFIDA actively contributes to the development of the African private sector through structured trade finance, equity, and financial engineering.
- *Sri Lanka National Development Bank (NDB)*—Established in 1979, NDB seeks to achieve long-term economic growth for Sri Lanka by focusing on developing private capital from local and international markets.

DFI PRODUCTS

The products that are most frequently offered by DFIs are risk capital and technical assistance. Risk capital comes in a variety of forms, including long-term debt project financing, equity investment, and working capital loans. The type of capital offered by a DFI depends on the characteristics of the project in question. To a large extent, DFIs support greenfield development of infrastructure projects, often in the context of a privatization, brownfield expansion of an existing infrastructure or manufacturing enterprise or the banking industry. For greenfield development, DFI loans typically take the form of project finance with limited recourse to the sponsor's balance sheet. Project financing offers long-term debt capital to support up to 75 percent of the project costs, depending on the economics of the transaction. Less frequently, DFIs lend to existing enterprises that are seeking to expand their operations in an emerging market. Most of the DFIs described in this book will also consider an equity investment. Equity investments made directly by a DFI or by a fund partially capitalized by a DFI (see Appendix C) are on a passive (i.e., a noncontrolling interest) basis and typically do not account for more than 25 percent of the total equity provided by private parties. Risk capital products have also been tailored by DFIs to meet the specific needs of the banking industry. By "on-lending," or guaranteeing a certain portion of a loan to a local enterprise, a DFI can play a catalytic role in stimulating flows of debt capital into a marketplace.

Risk Capital Products

Limited or Non-Recourse Project Finance

Traditional finance is corporate finance, where the primary source of repayment for investors and creditors is the sponsoring company, backed by its entire balance sheet, not the project alone. Although creditors usually seek to assure themselves of the economic viability of a project (so it is not a drain on the corporate sponsor's existing pool of assets), an important influence on their credit decision is the overall strength of the sponsor's balance sheet, as well as the sponsor's business reputation. Depending on this strength, creditors still retain a significant level of comfort in being repaid even if the individual project fails. In corporate finance, if a project fails, its lenders do not necessarily suffer, as long as the company owning the project remains financially viable. In project finance, if the project fails, investors and creditors can expect significant losses.

On the other hand, lenders seek comfortable levels of equity on a nominal as well as a percentage basis to ensure that the sponsors are committed to the project. Lenders generally require the project company or third-party equity participants to contribute a significant portion of the capital invested in the project, with an alternative or a supplement to equity being subordinated debt. Sponsors may prefer to contribute subordinated debt rather than equity for tax and corporate finance reasons. However, a DFI generally requires that subordinated debt from a project's sponsors act from a legal perspective just like equity; that is, it foregoes rights to accelerate debt and to exercise other remedies against the project, including foreclosure.

Contracts are central to the project finance transaction since they set out and define each party's role, making the liabilities clear and helping to define the apportionment of risks between participants. The agreements need to be designed to fit within the legal framework of the project's host country and must deal with methods of construction, financing and operation of the facility, procedures to be implemented in the event of default and/or failure to complete construction, standards to be achieved during the operational period, and plans in case of unforeseen events (e.g., war and natural disasters). Security packages are also created and comprise the various contractual arrangements, including the key agreements, contracts, and government undertakings that enable a project to be realized.

Because of the lack of a balance sheet to support a project finance loan, the laws and regulations of the project's host country should be clearly explained and enforced. If laws and/or regulations are changed or not enforced, potential financial burdens may affect investors and creditors.

Equity and Quasi-Equity

A large number of DFIs offer equity capital as well as debt. More than half of the DFIs described in this book will make a direct equity investment, while many have the ability to invest in projects through funds to which they have contributed debt or equity capital. DFIs don't invest in projects of emerging markets to have a controlling interest. DFIs prefer a passive stake, and often combine an equity investment with a loan.

To complement private and public sources of capital, special DFI-supported investment funds have been established. And despite having been in existence for less than 15 years, these funds are quite numerous. In most cases, these funds have specific development goals that permit them to assume a higher level of risk without charging unreasonable rates of return. As with direct equity investors, DFI-supported funds are managed by investors who also prefer to play a passive role in the management of the enterprise. (See Appendix C for a list of active DFI-backed funds.)

Increasingly, many DFIs lend on a corporate basis, especially to emerging-markets firms, but the opportunities are not prevalent. A large majority of the enterprises needing capital from DFIs are venture or greenfield projects that are capital-intensive and lacking a preexisting balance sheet to secure a loan.

Project finance benefits primarily sectors or industries in which a project can be structured as a single-purpose separate entity, apart from its sponsors. A case in point is a stand-alone production plant that can be assessed in accounting and financial terms separately from the sponsor's other activities. Generally, such projects tend to be relatively large because of the time and other transaction costs involved in structuring and include considerable capital equipment that needs long-term financing. Traditionally, in developing countries at least, project finance techniques have shown up mainly in the mining and oil and gas sectors. Projects in these sectors depend on large-scale foreign currency financing and are particularly suited to project finance because their output has a global market and is priced in hard currency. Since market risk greatly affects the potential outcome of most projects, project finance tends to be more applicable in industries where the revenue streams can be defined and rather easily secured. In recent years, private sector infrastructure projects under long-term government concession agreements with power purchase agreements (PPAs) that assure a purchaser of the project's output have been able to attract major project finance flows. Regulatory reform and a growing body of project finance experience continue to expand situations in which project finance structuring makes sense; for example, in the case of merchant power plants, which have no PPAs but sell into a national power grid at prevailing market prices.

Project finance can be applied over a fairly broad range of nonfinancial sectors, including manufacturing and service projects such as privately financed hospitals or wherever projects can stand on their own and where risks are clearly defined. Although the risk-sharing attributes of a project finance arrangement make it particularly suitable for large projects requiring hundreds of millions of dollars in financing, DFIs' experience—including textile, agribusiness, and hotel projects— also shows that the approach can be employed successfully in smaller projects in a variety of industries.

The amount of project financing offered depends heavily on size and predictability of the cash flows of the new enterprise. If the expected cash flows can handily cover the debt service on an 80 percent leveraged company, then a DFI may require the shareholders to invest "equity" of only 20 percent into the SPV. The required amount of equity to be contributed varies widely. For instance, very strong projects with strong and dependable cash flows and low risk can be structured 20 percent equity and 80 percent debt. However, this proportion can rise to 50 percent equity and 50 percent debt depending on the perceived risk and other credit factors. It is in the best interest of the sponsors to minimize equity contributions since equity commands a higher rate of return and, thus, is more expensive than debt.

Technical Assistance

The technical assistance offered by DFIs includes a diverse range of services, including feasibility study funding, technical assistance funding, agricultural business development assistance, R&D funding, and training services. All of these services are offered to allow a company or business executive to evaluate the commercial feasibility of an export or investment opportunity in a foreign market while staying within the confines of a development budget. In many cases, the technical assistance is provided by a DFI on a cost-share basis and can cover all aspects of a feasibility analysis, including travel costs, costs related to the issuance of a request for proposal (RFP) for consulting services, financial modeling, environmental impact assessments, consulting fees, and business plan formulation, as well as all types of engineering analysis.

In unusual circumstances, business executives may find grant money to help cover assessment and start-up costs. This is unusual, though, as most DFIs prefer to partner with the investor/developer and receive assurance from him or her that the project, if feasible, will be realized.

Specialized Product Offerings

As market weaknesses are identified over time, DFIs are quite effective at structuring new products to bridge the gaps and renew flows of capital into particular markets and/or specific sectors. A good example is the creation of new products to support the local capital markets in emerging markets and to offer new sources of liquidity and training programs to local financial institutions.

Capital Markets

Capital market development in emerging markets encompasses a wide range of activities, including building institutions, developing new instruments and mechanisms, and creating and improving legal and regulatory frameworks. On the institutional side, capital market development involves areas such as commercial and investment banking, insurance and pension funds, rating agencies and bond insurance companies (financial guarantors), private equity and venture capital, structured finance, derivatives, securitization, and securities markets. To support the development of local capital markets, several DFIs have developed tools to assist, including debt instruments, guarantees, advisory and technical assistance work, equity, and quasi equity.

By supporting transactions in local capital markets, DFIs can help build confidence in the integrity of the system, the liquidity of the market, and the creditworthiness of the issuers. Transactions have a high demonstration effect and can contribute to consolidating market reforms by transferring financial structuring know-how and market instruments from major markets to developing markets.

By deploying a variety of credit enhancement instruments (mentioned below), certain DFIs expect to be able to structure deals for which there is a market demand and that embody the institutions' developmental perspective. The objective is to help develop domestic local currency debt markets for corporations, banks, private sector utility companies and other local issuers. The main focus is to lengthen the tenor of locally issued instruments and broaden the available investor base by absorbing risks found unacceptable by capital markets players.

Some of the capital markets products offered by DFIs include:

- Direct credit enhancement through guarantees of domestic long-term debt issues (e.g., corporate, infrastructure project, financial institution and mortgage bonds), as well as medium-term debentures and short- and medium-term note programs (e.g., commercial paper).
- Direct credit enhancement through guarantees of domestic securitization instruments (e.g., most types of asset-backed securities, including mortgage-backed securities).
- Loans for commercially viable market-making mechanisms, risk management and underwriting facilities, and financial guarantee facilities (e.g., bond insurers).
- Subordinated debt (quasi equity and mezzanine financing) for country and regional private equity funds and secondary mortgage market institutions.

Liquidity Instruments for Local Financial Institutions
Many DFIs work closely with local financial institutions in emerging markets to empower the bank to lend to local and international businesses. The support provided encompasses partial guarantees of loans made to certain sectors, training, and shorter-term lines of working capital. These DFI products are "behind the scenes" from most business executives' perspective, but it is valuable to be aware of the initiatives. As a result, in some markets, local banks are going to be able to provide more support to foreign investors.

Political Risk Insurance (PRI)

In addition to sources of capital and technical assistance, a number of DFIs provide PRI for lenders and equity investors. By providing protection from these risks, DFIs act in another way to facilitate the flow of funds into certain higher-risk jurisdictions. PRI is available to insure against inconvertibility/transfer restrictions, political violence, and expropriation.

Inconvertibility/Transfer Restrictions

If local currency revenues cannot be converted by a borrower to repay a loan or to make a dividend payment or if conversion takes place but the hard currency cannot be repatriated (in other words, transferred out of the country into the hands of the obligee), then a claim under a PRI policy can be made. However, inconvertibility/transfer coverage does not protect against depreciation or devaluation of a currency.

Political Violence

The risks covered here include war, revolution, and insurrection. If a lender purchases PRI, an insurer will pay the insured portion of the principal and interest payments in default as a direct result of (1) damage to the assets necessary for the project caused by war and civil disturbance or (2) interruption of operations that are, among others, the result of violent activities in the area or conscription of the workforce. Keep in mind, however, that political violence coverage does not typically cover losses due to labor strife or student unrest without a political objective.

Expropriation

Expropriation coverage protects lenders and equity investors against (where appropriate) forced loan reschedulings, confiscation, expropriation, nationalization, and other actions by the host government that would prevent or reduce payments to the obligee. In addition to explicit acts of nationalization and confiscation, PRI also protects a lender or an equity investor from the effects of discriminatory legislative actions, cancellation of rights under a permit, and other host government actions more informally referred to as "creeping expropriation." However, expropriation coverage does not cover losses related to legitimate actions by a host government (such as taxation) that have a negative commercial impact on the economics of a project.

PRI is offered by some DFIs (OPIC, World Bank through the Multilateral Investment Guarantee Agency [MIGA], and IADB) and also by fully private providers, such as AIG and various Lloyd's syndicate members. (See Appendix D for a listing of providers.) The export credit agencies also provide PRI to cover the risk of nonpayment by a government buyer for noncommercial reasons.

In addition to these explicit sources of PRI, a project or an investment can benefit from implicit PRI in various ways. Included in this category are government-sponsored programs such as these:

- U.S. Trade and Development Agency to support pre-financing feasibility studies
- U.S. Department of Commerce Advocacy resources
- B Loan programs offered by a number of multilateral DFIs (MDFIs) through which commercial lenders fund loans but a multilateral is the lender of record

Through these government-backed programs, a lender or an equity investor increases assurance that its funds will be treated with special care because the implications of defaulting on multilateral debt are significantly more grave than defaulting on a commercial lender or withholding payment from a private independent investor. Utilizing these services and programs can offer a project an implicit "government seal of approval" that translates into a plethora of qualitative benefits ranging from assistance during dispute resolution to reversal of a contemplated act of expropriation.

PROCESS FOR OBTAINING DFI SUPPORT

When considering applying for support from a DFI, one should check in advance the specific eligibility requirements for each agency. Each DFI description included in this book includes an outline of eligibility requirements, including type of project, nationality of sponsor, level of support, and so on.

For your reference, Appendix E includes an outline of a project information memorandum that should be prepared and submitted as part of the application package to each DFI. Below is a process flowchart indicating the process an application is subject to before funds are made available.

EXPORT CREDIT AGENCIES

Export credit agencies (ECAs) sometimes perform functions similar to development finance institutions, for example, extending limited recourse loans to private projects in emerging markets. However, ECAs have been generally excluded from this book for two important reasons: (1) ECAs can, under Organization for Economic Co-operation and Development (OECD) rules, provide financing for a direct investment, but their primary focus is supporting domestic employment through exports, and (2) Delphos International, Ltd., recently published another book, *Inside the World's Export Credit Agencies,* to cover the topic of these ECAs. That said, a couple of institutions included in this book also appear in the above-mentioned book—EDC, BLADEX, and KfW. However, this book describes these institution's non-OECD

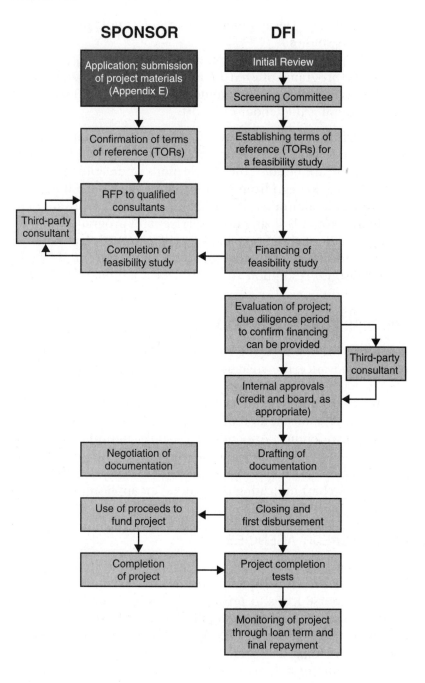

based mandates to support foreign investment in emerging markets, whether it be through trade finance, project finance, guaranties, insurance, equity investment, or technical assistance.

For further reference, the ECAs not included in this book do provide project financing that may be useful as a co-financing source alongside one (or more) of the DFIs. As expected, the project finance terms that an ECA can provide are highly dependent upon the OECD arrangement. Per OECD rules, an ECA project finance loan can cover:

- Financing of interest accrued during construction related to the ECA tranche.
- Allowance of up to 15 percent eligible foreign content in the components sourced from the ECA's locality.
- Financing of the host country's local costs of up to 15 percent of the exporter's contract value.

The rules outlined by the OECD Arrangement allow the ECAs to provide flexible loan repayment terms to match a project's revenue stream. Thus, project finance transactions can be structured with tailored repayment profiles, more flexible grace periods, and more flexibile total repayment terms.

An individual ECA can implement these flexibilities on a case-by-case basis for qualifying project finance transactions. Generally, extended grace periods or repayment terms must be justified by project cash flows or project considerations specific to certain industry sectors. For example, extended grace periods and back-ended repayment profiles may be justified for telecommunications projects, but they may not be appropriate for power plants.

The new rules allow for the following:

- Full flexibility for setting a project's grace period, repayment profile, and maximum repayment term, subject to a maximum average life of 5.25 years
- The extension of a project's average life up to 7.25 years, subject to constraints for setting a maximum grace period of 2 years and a maximum repayment term of 14 years

The new flexible terms are subject to the following additional constraints and/or considerations:

- If a project's repayment term extends beyond 12 years, 20 basis points are added to the Commercial Interest Reference Rate (CIRR) for direct loans.
- Interest cannot be capitalized post-completion.

- The flexible terms are offered in high-income OECD markets only, with additional constraints.
- The average life allowed under the new flexible terms is taken into consideration when meeting the Minimum Premium Benchmark fees required as of April 1, 1999.

AGENCY ACRONYMS

ADB	Asian Development Bank
AfD	Agence Francaise de Développement (French Development Agency)
AfDB	African Development Bank
AFESD	Arab Fund for Economic and Social Development
APAD	Portuguese Agency of Support for Development
BADEA	Arab Bank for Economic Development in Africa
BLADEX	Banco Latinoamericano de Exportaciones
BMI-SBI	Belgium Corporation for International Investment
BNDES	Brazilian Economic and Social Development Bank
BOAD	Banque Ouest Africaine de Developpement (West African Development Bank)
BSTDB	Black Sea Trade and Development Bank
CABEI	Central American Bank for Economic Integration
CAF	Andean Development Bank
CDB	Caribbean Development Bank
CDB	China Development Bank
COFIDES	Compañía Española de Financiación del Desarrollo
DBS	Development Bank of Singapore
DBSA	Development Bank of Southern Africa
DBT	Development Bank of Turkey
DEG	German Investment and Development Company
EBRD	European Bank for Reconstruction and Development
EDC	Export Development Canada
EIB	European Investment Bank
FGG	Finanzierungsgarantie-Gesellschaft
FMO	Netherlands Development Finance Corporation
GTZ	German Agency for Technical Cooperation
IADB	Inter-American Development Bank
IBRD	International Bank for Reconstruction and Development
IDBI	Industrial Development Bank of India
IDC	Industrial Development Corporation
IFC	International Finance Corporation
IFU	Danish International Investment Funds
IIBI	Industrial Investment Bank of India
IIC	Inter-American Investment Corporation
ISDB	Islamic Development Bank
JBIC	Japan Bank for International Cooperation
KDB	Korea Development Bank
KfW	Kreditanstalt für Wiederaufbau
NADB	North American Development Bank

NAFIN	National Financiera
NDB	Sri Lanka National Development Bank
NDF	Nordic Development Fund
NEFCO	Nordic Environment Finance Corporation
NIB	Nordic Investment Bank
NORSAD	Nordic Southern African Development Fund
OPIC	Overseas Private Investment Corporation
PTA Bank	Eastern and Southern African Trade and Development Bank
RRDB	Russian Regional Development Bank
SIDBI	Small Industries Development Bank of India
SIFIDA	Société Internationale Financière pour les Investissements et le Développement en Afrique
SIMEST	Societa Italiana per le Imprese all'Estero
TSKB	Türkiye Sinai Kalkinma Bankasi
UNDP	United Nations Development Program
USAID	United States Agency for International Development

Global Multilateral DFIs (MDFIs)

This chapter covers multilateral development finance institutions (MDFIs) with a global focus. Most DFIs in this category are members of the World Bank Group (WBG). World Bank institutions support investment across sectoral lines in any of its 183 member countries.

INTERNATIONAL FINANCE CORPORATION (IFC)

I. INTRODUCTION

The IFC, a member of the World Bank, was established in 1956. IFC's focus is to promote development by encouraging the growth of productive enterprise and efficient capital markets in its member countries. IFC aims to stimulate private investment by limiting investments to 25 percent of the total project cost.

Since its inception, IFC has made a profit every year. It has a staff of almost 2,000, of whom about 70 percent work at headquarters in Washington, DC, and about 30 percent are stationed in over 80 IFC field offices. It is the largest multilateral source of loan and equity financing for private sector projects in developing countries and uses its own funds to provide clients with a variety of financial products.

II. PRODUCTS

IFC operates on a commercial basis. It invests exclusively in for-profit projects and charges market rates for its products and services.

Loans and Guarantees

- *A-Loans*—IFC offers fixed- and variable-rate loans from its own account to private sector projects in developing countries. They are used to finance greenfield companies and expansion projects in developing countries. IFC also makes loans to intermediary banks, leasing companies, and other financial institutions through credit lines for further lending. Credit lines are often targeted at small- and medium-sized enterprises (SMEs) or at specific sectors. Most A-loans are issued in leading currencies, but local currency loans are also provided.

Terms

To ensure the participation of other private investors, A-loans are usually limited to 25 percent of the total estimated project costs for greenfield projects or, on an exceptional basis, to 35 percent for small projects. For expansion projects IFC may provide up to 50 percent of the project cost, provided its investments do not exceed 25 percent of the total capitalization of the project company. Generally, A-loans range from USD 1 million to USD 100 million.

Repayment

The loans typically have maturities of 7–12 years at origination. Grace periods and repayment schedules are determined on a case-by-case basis in accordance with the borrower's cash flow needs. If warranted by the project, IFC provides longer-term loans and longer grace periods. Some loans have been extended to as long as 20 years

- *B-Loans*—In the syndicated loans, also called B-loans, participating banks provide their own funds and take their own commercial risk, while IFC remains the lender of record. Mobilizing funds for private sector projects in developing countries from other investors and lenders is one of IFC's most essential functions. IFC actively seeks partners for joint ventures and raises additional financing by encouraging other institutions to make investments in IFC projects. The cornerstone of IFC's finance mobilization efforts is the loan participation program. The program arranges syndicated loans from commercial banks, providing additional financing to IFC-financed projects in developing countries.

Guarantees

IFC offers credit enhancement structures for debt instruments (bonds or loans) in the form of partial credit guarantees. These structures allow IFC to use its AAA credit rating to help clients diversify their funding services, extended maturities, and obtain financing in their currency. A partial credit guarantee covers creditors irrespective of the cause of default. However, the amount IFC pays out under the guarantee is capped at an agreed-upon amount; for example, 40 percent of the initial principal or one year of debt service. The guaranteed amount may vary over the life of the transaction, based on the borrower's expected cash flows and creditor's concerns, and may be used to cover any debt-servicing shortfalls. Client companies may issue bonds with the partial guarantee to attract local currency in their domestic capital market or foreign currency in the international capital market. Alternatively, they may use the partial guarantee for loans to attract financing from local and international financial institutions.

Equity and Quasi Equity

IFC takes equity stakes in private sector companies and other entities, such as financial institutions, and portfolio and investment funds in developing countries. IFC is a long-term investor and usually maintains equity investments for a period of 8–15 years.

Specifications

To ensure the participation of other private investors, IFC generally provides between 5 and 15 percent of a project's equity. IFC is never the largest shareholder in a project and does not normally hold more than a 35 percent stake. IFC's equity investments are based on project needs and anticipated returns. IFC does not take an active role in company management. IFC risks its own capital and does not accept government guarantees, however, to meet national ownership requirements, IFC shareholdings can be treated as domestic capital or local shares.

IFC also offers a full range of quasi-equity products with debt and equity characteristics to private sector projects in developing countries. These products are called C-loans. Among other instruments, IFC provides convertible debt and subordinated loan investments, which impose a fixed repayment schedule. IFC also offers preferred stock and income note investments, which require less rigid repayment schedules. Quasi-equity investments are made available whenever necessary to ensure that a project is soundly funded. IFC operates on a commercial basis.

III. ELIGIBILITY AND APPLICATION PROCESS

To be eligible for IFC funding, a project must meet a number of IFC criteria:

- The project must be located in a developing country that is a member of IFC.
- The project must be in the private sector.
- The project must be technically sound.
- The project must have good prospects of being profitable.
- The project must benefit the local economy.
- The project must be environmentally and socially sound, satisfying IFC environmental and social standards as well as those of the host country.

A company or an entrepreneur, foreign or domestic, seeking to establish a new venture to expand an existing enterprise can approach IFC directly by submitting an investment proposal. After this initial contact and a preliminary review, IFC may proceed by requesting a detailed feasibility study or business plan to determine whether to appraise the project.

IV. CONTACTS

Headquarters:
International Finance Corporation
2121 Pennsylvania Avenue, NW
Washington, DC 20433
Tel: (202) 477-1234
Fax: (202) 944-4327
Internet: www.ifc.org
Email: info@ifc.org

Latin America and Caribbean Department
Bernard Pasquier, Director
Tel: (202) 473-0736

Sub-Saharan Africa Department
Haydee Celaya, Director
Tel: (202) 473-0319

Middle East and North Africa Department
Sami Haddad, Director
Tel: (202) 473-6864

Southern Europe and Central Asia Department
Khosrow Zamani, Director
Tel: (202) 473-5650

East Asia and Pacific Department
Javed Hamid, Director
Tel: (202) 473-0400

Agribusiness Department
Jean-Paul Pinard, Director
Tel: (202) 473-0517

Health and Education Department
Guy Ellena, Director
Tel: (202) 473-2689

Global Financial Markets Group
Karl Voltaire, Director
Tel: (202) 974-4374

Global Information and Communication Technologies Group
Mohsen Khalil, Director
Tel: (202) 473-6786

Infrastructure Department
Declan Duff, Director
Tel: (202) 473-9779

Oil, Gas, Mining, and Chemicals Department
Rashad Kaldany, Director
Tel: (202) 473-6787

Power Department
Francisco Tourreilles, Director
Tel: (202) 473-0814

Private Equity and Investment Funds Department
Teresa Barger, Director
Tel: (202) 473-8801

Small and Medium Enterprises Department
Harold Rosen, Director
Tel: (202) 473-8841

UNITED NATIONS DEVELOPMENT
PROGRAM (UNDP)

I. INTRODUCTION

The UNDP is the global development network of the United
Nations. It provides development advice, advocacy, and support
through grants. The main objective of UNDP is to help world
leaders achieve their goal of cutting poverty in half by 2015. This
goal was developed at the United Nations Millennium Summit in
September 2000. There are six main target areas of the UNDP:
democratic governance, poverty reduction, crisis prevention and
recovery, energy and environment, information and communications technology, and HIV/AIDS. Additionally, it has fostered
strategic partnerships with many of the world's development
banks.

II. PRODUCTS

United Nations Capital Development Fund (UNCDF)

UNCDF is a part of the UNDP that provides local development
programs as well as microfinance operations. The resources
behind the UNCDF are contributions from member states and
co-financing from governments and international organizations,
as well as from the private sector.

Through its microfinance programs, UNCDF supports a variety of initiatives that facilitate the provision of financial services
to the poor. To facilitate coordination between the different
microfinance initiatives in the UNDP Group, a joint unit between
UNDP and UNCDF was established in 1997, called the Special
Unit for Microfinance (SUM). SUM is now fully integrated into
UNCDF and is considered the lead technical unit on all matters
pertaining to microfinance in the UNDP Group. Some of the
programs offered by SUM include these:

- *Capital Investments* provide financial support and technical
  assistance to microfinance institutions. Selected investments
  support policy objectives and operating principles, using finan-

cial mechanisms including grants to fund start-up costs and operational expenses, and provide capital for lending.

- *MicroStart Programme* supports young, promising microfinance operations to expand their operations in a sustainable way through a combination of technical and microcapital grants.
- *Technical Advisory Services (TAS)* assist UNDP offices in reviewing microfinance portfolios, developing microfinance strategies, appraising institutions, and designing, developing, and evaluating microfinance operations.
- *Capacity Building and Best-Practice Dissemination* opens the world of microfinance principles and practices to donor organizations that want to become more familiar with the industry. Activities include developing training programs, coordinating with donors and practitioners to mainstream best donor practices, and documenting and analyzing UNDP's and UNCDF's work in microfinance to make policy recommendations.

United Nations Development Fund for Women (UNIFEM)

UNIFEM is a fund through the United Nations designed to provide technical and financial assistance to programs that aim to promote the human rights of women as well as political participation and economic security. Created in 1976, UNIFEM now operates in over 100 countries worldwide.

Thematic Trust Funds

This type of aid is provided through donors who make additional contributions to the practice areas of UNDP. This includes a "multiyear funding framework," including a compact made between donors, the UNDP, and the governments of the host countries to implement results-oriented programs. These programs are designed at the global, regional, and country levels.

III. ELIGIBILITY AND APPLICATION PROCESS

Contact company headquarters for more information.

IV. CONTACTS

Headquarters:
United Nations Development Program
One United Nations Plaza
New York, NY 10017

Tel: (212) 906-5558
Fax: (212) 906-5364
Internet: www.undp.org
Email: enquiries@undp.org

Liaison Offices:
European Office at Geneva
Palais des Nations CH-1211
Genève 10, Switzerland
Tel: (41-22) 917 8542
Fax: (41-22) 917 8001

UNDP Liaison Office in Brussels
United Nations Office/UNDP
14 Rue Montoyer, 1000
Brussels, Belgium
Tel: (32-2) 505 4620
Fax: (32-2) 505 4729

UNDP/Inter-Agency Procurement Services Office (IAPSO)
Nordic Liaison Office
Midtermolen 3, P.O. Box 2530
Copenhagen 0, Denmark
Tel: (45-35) 46 71 54
Fax: (45-35) 46 70 95

UNDP Tokyo Office
UNU Building, 8th Floor
5-53-70 Jingumae Shibuya-ku
Tokyo 150-0001, Japan
Tel: (813) 5467 4751
Fax: (813) 5467 4753

UNDP Liaison Office in Washington, DC
1775 K Street, NW, Suite 420
Washington, DC 20006
Tel: (202) 331-9130
Fax: (202) 331-9363

THE WORLD BANK GROUP

I. INTRODUCTION

The International Bank for Reconstruction & Development (IBRD) is the original institution of the World Bank. It opened its doors for business in 1946. Today it is the largest source of market-based loans to developing countries and is a major catalyst of similar financing from other sources. IBRD lends, guarantees, or provides developmental assistance to governments and public or private entities to middle-income and creditworthy lower-income countries. It is funded mainly through member contributions and borrowings on international capital markets.

In 2001, IBRD disbursed USD 10.5 billion for 91 new operations in 36 countries. Its cumulative lending is no less impressive—USD 360 billion. IBRD has earned a net profit since 1948. Earnings are used to finance and expand its working capital for new projects, and its funds come from member countries. The level of economic strength or level of contribution to IBRD determines each member country's voting rights and, therefore, its position of power.

IBRD was originally conceived in Bretton Woods, New Hampshire, after the Second World War. Its original objective was to reconstruct Europe, but its current focus is on reducing global poverty. Forty percent of IBRD staff work from the region in which they are based, and 66 percent of the country directors are based in the field to ensure that project implementation runs smoothly and fairly, as planned. IBRD makes loans only to those lacking the ability to obtain financing on market terms. IBRD and the International Development Association (IDA) offer softer terms than those of the market, although they do not offer grants as some other multilateral agencies do.

II. PRODUCTS

IBRD has two basic loan programs, investment loans and adjustment loans, and three guarantee programs. Investment loans are designed for long-term projects (5–10 years) to finance goods, works, and services, while adjustment loans are designed for short-term projects (1–3 years) needing quick disbursement to support policy or reform initiatives. Loans can be used in combination for a customized finance package or alone to match a particular need.

Investment Lending

This product is not structured for any particular sector, but rather suits a wide range of enterprises that build infrastructure and sustain development. IBRD currently believes that assisting private sector institution building, social development, and public policy infrastructure provides the longest lasting and most successful solutions for alleviating poverty. Private sector development boosts economic independence and social development. Investment loans have accounted for 75 to 80 percent of IBRD lending for the past 20 years. IBRD offers a number of investment loan types:

- *Specific investment loans* support the creation, rehabilitation, and maintenance of infrastructure. The loan is also used to finance consultant services, management, and training so policies affecting the productivity of the investment can be reformed.
- *Sector investment and maintenance loans* are designed for public programs in certain sectors. These loans usually involve the participation of multilateral or bilateral donors.

Indonesia Sumatra Region Roads Project

IBRD made a loan of USD 234 million to improve the efficiency and accessibility of road transportation within the eight provinces of Sumatra. The loan financed over 60 percent of the total cost of the project. The Indonesian government financed about 30 percent of the project and contributed USD 135.3 million.

The project concentrates on building the management and planning of transportation infrastructure institutions. As traffic demand grew but transportation infrastructure did not grow as quickly, traveling in the region became chaotic, untimely, and environmentally harmful. The project integrated transportation management and planning across four regions. The project aims to, among other things, lower freight and passenger transportation costs, boost the transportation industry, prevent physical and social inconveniences of road works, increase trade and development, and connect villages to provincial and national networks.

- *Adaptable Program Loans (APLs)* are designed for long-term projects with more than one phase. APLs can be adapted and evolve according to lessons learned so the World Bank can continue its support of a long-term project. Between each phase, the project and financing terms are reviewed. These loans can be used in the health, power, water, education, and natural resource management sectors, where time is required for consensus and reformation.

- *Learning and Innovation Loans (LILs)* are designed to support small pilot-type investment and capacity building projects. If the pilot is successful, the LIL could lead to increasing the scale of the project. These projects should not exceed USD 5 million or have an implementation time exceeding 2 or 3 years. They are used to test new approaches or new borrowers, build trust, and act as pilot projects in preparation for larger projects and to support locally based development initiatives.
- *Technical Assistance Loans (TALs)* finance outside and/or local consultants to strengthen organizations in preparation for public sector reform. These loans help consultants build institutional capacity before implementing public sector reform. These loans often complement an investment or adjustment operation.
- *Financial Intermediary Loans (FILs)* are designed to develop financial sector policies and institutions. Specifically, IBRD aims to improve the efficiency of institutions, promote sound business practices, encourage private investment, and improve credit terms for households and enterprises. Financing goes to financial intermediaries, but is routed to fill the needs of real sector investment. The financial institution does, however, assume a credit risk with each subproject.
- *Emergency Recovery Loans (ERLs)* are designed for assets and production levels immediately after a civil disturbance, war, or natural disaster. The loans can be used for investment and productive activities, making recurring emergencies such as floods or expected crises such as droughts most appropriate for ERLs.

Terms
The terms of a project loan are up to 25 years.

Eligibility
Borrowers must not be in arrears with the World Bank and they must be eligible IBRD and IDA borrowers.

Disbursement
Loans are awarded and disbursed for specific foreign or local functions that are funding investment projects. Projects include pre-identified equipment, materials, civil works, technical and consulting services, studies, and incremental recurrent costs.

Loan agreement most likely includes conditions of disbursement to stipulate allocation of funds to specific project components.

Cost

IBRD charges a front-end fee of 1 percent of the loan amount, payable upon loan effectiveness. Lending rates depend on the product being financed and vary with the currency in Fixed-Spread Loans (FSLs) and Variable-Spread Loans (VSLs). The commitment fee on the undisbursed balance varies with the type of loan: for FSLs the fee is 0.85 percent in the first 4 years and 0.75 percent thereafter. All other loans have a commitment fee of 0.75 percent, but for all loans, a partial waiver may apply. For borrowers paying on a timely basis, a partial waiver may apply to disbursed and outstanding loan balances.

Guarantees

World Bank guarantees partially cover risks so the private sector will also take on risks it would not normally be able to manage or absorb. All guarantees are partial guarantees of private debt.

There are two types of guarantees: project-based guarantees and policy-based guarantees. Project-based guarantees mobilize private sector financing for individual projects, while policy-based guarantees mobilize private resources for sovereign entities.

- *Project-based partial risk guarantees* ensure payment to private lenders on specific items or services in the case of sovereign or political risks, such as breach of contract, foreign currency exchange and availability, changes in law, and expropriation and nationalization.
- *Project-based partial credit guarantees* cover anything contributing to nonpayment for a specified part of financing. They are commonly used for extending maturity since this guarantee can be arranged for the later years of financing. Most users are government agencies or government-associated agencies in need of new sources of debt financing and longer maturities. Four structures can be arranged: principal cover for a bullet maturity; single rolling coupon and principal cover for bullet maturity; rolling zero-coupon; and amortizing syndicated loan.
- *Policy-based guarantee (PBG)* is similar to the project-based partial credit guarantee, but finances sovereign borrowings for the purpose of supporting structural and social policies and reforms. These guarantees improve the World Bank's access to private foreign financing and are offered only to countries

with a strong credit history, a satisfactory macroeconomic policy framework, and a coherent strategy for attaining access to international financial markets.

Coverage
Guarantees cover sovereign and political risk or credit risk.

Eligibility
World Bank guarantees are available only to IBRD borrowers.

Special Development Initiatives

The World Bank also supports targeted development projects in regions that often lack resources or development in specific areas such as health, education, or infrastructure. The following are some of these initiatives:

- Asia Development Forum
- Brazilian Rain Forest
- Early Childhood Development in Africa
- Immunization in India
- Indigenous Knowledge
- Middle Income Countries Task Force Report
- Nile Basin Initiative
- Small States
- Social Development Initiative for South East Europe
- South Caucasus Regional Initiatives
- South East Europe Reconstruction
- Transport Policy Program for Africa

III. ELIGIBILITY AND APPLICATION PROCESS

Projects looking to receive both IBRD and IDA financing must be in a host country where the average annual per capita income does not exceed USD 885. Special cases are made for projects in transitional and island economies.

IV. CONTACTS

Headquarters:
The World Bank
1818 H Street, NW
Washington, DC 20433
Tel: (202) 473-1000
Fax: (202) 477-6391
Internet: www.worldbank.org

Europe
Vice President for Europe
66 Avenue d'Iéna
75116 Paris
Tel: 331 (1) 4069-3010
Fax: 331 (1) 4069-3064

United Kingdom, New Zealand
New Zealand House, 15th Floor
Haymarket
London SW1 Y4TE
Tel: 44 (207) 930-8511
Fax: 44 (207) 930-8515

Belgium
Special Representative to the EU Institutions
10 Rue Montoyer
B-1000 Brussels
Tel: 32 (2) 552-0052
Fax: 32 (2) 552-0025
Internet: www.worldbank.org/eu

Germany
Representative of the World Bank Group
Bockenheimer Landstr. 109
D-60325 Frankfurt am Main
Tel: 49 (69) 7434-8230
Fax: 49 (69) 7434-8239

Switzerland
Special Representative and the Head of Office
3 Chemin Louis Dunant
C.P. 66
CH-1211 Geneva 10
Tel: 41 (22) 748-1000
Fax: 41 (22) 748-1030

Toyko
Director
Fukoku Seimei Building, 10th Floor
2-2-2 Uchisawai-cho
Chiyoda-Ku, Tokyo 100

Tel: 81 (3) 3597-6650
Fax: 81 (3) 3597-6695

East Timor, Papua New Guinea, and Pacific Island Operations
East Asia and Pacific Region
Country Director
Level 18, CML Building
14 Martin Place
Sydney
NSW 2000
Australia
Tel: 61 (02) 9223-7773
Fax: 61 (02) 9223-2533

2

Global Bilateral DFIs (BDFIs)

This chapter covers bilateral DFIs, those single-member development financial institutions that support projects in most global emerging markets. BDFIs were established under the philosophy that the sponsor country will benefit from a more prosperous global economy. Of course, projects need to be beneficial to social and economic development and need to be financially viable, taking into account credit supports offered by project participants. Many of these BDFIs have been in existence for several decades and are generally very active in the international finance scene. However, most consider themselves primarily finance *participants*. They like to lend to transactions that also have World Bank, IADB, or ADB support, and they take comfort from a "stamp of approval" provided by these other organizations.

AGENCE FRANCAISE DE DÉVELOPPEMENT (AfD)

I. INTRODUCTION

The AfD is a public institution established in 1941 to increase per capita income in less-developed countries by encouraging development projects, supporting trade associations, and participating in the restructuring of financial systems. AfD funds approximately 130 projects each year from a network of 45 offices operating in over 60 countries.

AfD has formed several subsidiaries that perform various functions aimed at productive public and private projects. Additionally, AfD provides government-allocated structural adjustment aid. One subsidiary, Proparco, handles private sector financing through loans and equity investments, while CEFEB, another subsidiary, provides technical training for managers and officers of developing countries.

Proparco

Established in 1977 as a limited company wholly owned by the AfD, Proparco was mainly concerned with risk capital. In 1990, it converted to a financial company and now has over EUR 142.6 million in capital. This AfD subsidiary specializes in financing and developing the private sector through loans or equity investments by working directly with companies or working through local financial institutions. In overseas departments/territories, only long-term financing is available. Start-up companies, privatization, restructuring, and development programs are eligible for financing in all "productive sectors."

II. PRODUCTS

Loans

Several types of long-term loans, denominated in euros or U.S. dollars, are available through Proparco. Typically, loans are available for up to 15 years with a grace period of up to 5 years. Loans offered directly to investors may be subject to bank guarantees or mortgages or limited rights of recourse, while loans offered to banking institutions take many forms and are adapted to the needs of the market and the institution's specific requirements.

Special Funds

Proparco has access to the following special funds:

- *European Community Investment Partners (ECIP)* is a financial instrument designed to promote enterprise creation with European partners. This instrument, which covers Latin America, Asia, and the Maghreb, is used in the Maghreb, in South Africa, and in Southeast Asia. The ECIP offers four instruments to assist in the creation and development of a business. The first instrument serves to identify the project and the partners, while the other three instruments involve the subsequent stages of creation: feasibility studies, equity and quasi-equity investment, and technical assistance and training.
- *European Community Finance Institutions (ECFIs)* offer a line of risk capital financing through the European Investment Bank. ECFIs complement Proparco's equity investments in private companies in the member countries of the Lome Convention. Investments range from EUR 20,000 to EUR 2,000,000, thus doubling Proparco's input.

- *Centre de Développement Industriel (CDI)* works closely with Proparco to co-finance training and technical assistance and to consolidate the start-up or development of companies supported by Proparco.
- *Africa Management Services Company (AMSCO)* supports African private enterprise under an original concept aimed at associating qualified and experienced managers in the management of these companies, with a view to transfer of know-how. These managers also coordinate training programs for national staff.
- *Compagnie Française D'assurance pour le Commerce Extérieur (COFACE)* is an agreement between Proparco and the French Credit Insurance Company to improve the use of political risk insurance facilities, especially in the Proparco geographical area of businesses.
- *The Fund for the Preparation of Private Projects (F3P)* was set up by the AfD to finance part of the cost of pre-investment studies, whether it is related to the creation, development, diversification, rehabilitation, or privatization of private manufacturing or service companies. The amount granted is limited to EUR 23,000 per operation, covering up to 70 percent of the cost of the study, with the promoter being responsible for the remainder. Financing is provided in the form of an interest-free loan in euros. Co-financing in the form of a subsidy from the Centre for Industrial Development (European Union) is also available subject to certain conditions.

Guarantees

Proparco has substantially expanded its guarantee products and with other partners and enterprises, actively promotes new formulas and financing schemes. Proparco provides a guarantee of liquidity and facilitates mobilization of local currency resources by private sector operators (credit institution and private sector), guaranteeing repayment of the capital and related interest. More than Proparco's other products, loan guarantees require the establishment of a close professional relationship with the clients to evaluate jointly the scale and extent of the risks to be covered.

- *Guarantie des Investissements Prives en Afrique de l'ouest (GARI)* is a fund established for private investment in West Africa to cover economic risks, excluding all political risks. The fund guarantees financing to private companies located in the 16 member countries of the Economic Community of West African States (ECOWAS). It guarantees up to 50 percent of the amount of loans between EUR 150,000 and EUR 3.7 million of national financing or international investment in productive sectors. Where there is simultaneous recourse to other guarantee funds, the cumulative cover ceiling is 60 percent of the principal balance of the loan.

Equity/Quasi-Equity Investments

By means of its equity and quasi-equity operations, Proparco hopes to contribute to the emergence and stimulation of financial markets. Proparco's investments are minority shareholdings. They are intended for transfer to other shareholders, or sale on the financial market in the case of negotiable securities, after an average period of 6 years, when the company has reached a sustainable level of maturity. The project's internal rate of return must be at least 15 percent to ensure a reasonable return on the capital invested and thus facilitate the liquidity of the shares held. Proparco engages in all forms of long-term investment, including shareholders' current accounts, convertible bonds, participating loans, and junior debt.

Financial Engineering

Proparco advises companies it finances and offers them various financial engineering services: legal and financial appraisal of the project, advice on legal and financial instruments for company mergers or takeovers, and arrangement of additional resources.

Centre d'Etudes Financieres, Economiques et Bancaires (CEFEB)

The AfD supports development through technical assistance and training programs. CEFEB was founded 35 years ago by the AfD to provide high-level technical training for senior officers and managers from developing countries and overseas France.

CEFEB offers three main services: an annual diploma course, specialized short-term seminars, and training missions. The purpose of these activities is to provide training for personnel from developing countries with current or future careers in senior positions in economic or financial services, financial development institutions, and public or private companies.

III. ELIGIBILITY AND APPLICATION PROCESS

A complete project proposal must be submitted, including a clear definition of study terms of reference, to local AfD branches or to headquarters, where the proposals are processed according to specific terms.

IV. CONTACTS

Headquarters:
Agence Francaise de Developpement
5 Rue Roland Barthes
75598 Paris Cedex 12
Tel: 33 (1) 53 44 31 31
Fax: 33 (1) 44 87 99 39
Telex: 281871F
Internet: www.afd.fr
Email: com@afd.fr

CDC CAPITAL PARTNERS

I. INTRODUCTION

In 1948, the government of the United Kingdom created the Commonwealth Development Corporation (CDC) to assist commercial and industrial development around the world. In 1999, with the Commonwealth Development Act, the CDC was changed from a statutory corporation into a public limited company named the CDC Group, which has since changed its name to CDC Capital Partners. This public/private partnership raises and manages public and private capital. Currently CDC Capital Partners remains completely owned by the UK government. When market conditions are right, the majority of the company will be sold to the private sector. The government will maintain a substantial minority shareholding (not below 25 percent) and any special shares to ensure that CDC keeps its focus on the development of poorer countries.

CDC Capital Partners seeks the development of pre-emerging and emerging markets through risk capital and, increasingly, through investment in private equities. It provides risk capital directly and through third-party funds. CDC is involved in a wide spectrum of activities, including financial services, telecommunications, power, transportation, retail, information technology, property, and tourism. CDC Industries, a subsidiary, manages over 30 businesses in industries such as palm oil, cement, sugar, juice processing, aquaculture, and horticulture. CDC Globeleq is a company in charge of managing and expanding CDC's assets in the power sector. The CDC has 32 offices around the globe and is invested in over 420 businesses in 54 countries.

The investment policy of CDC limits its investments to nations classified by the World Bank as low or middle income (based on 1996 data). The goal is for 70 percent of new investments to be made in countries with a gross domestic product (GDP) per capita below the weighted mean for lower-middle income countries, with 50 percent reserved for sub-Saharan Africa and South Asia. In 2001, CDC had a portfolio worth GBP 479 million (approximately USD 753 million) and made new investments worth GBP 122 million (approximately USD 192 million). Of the new investments, 51 percent were focused in Africa, 18 percent in South Asia, 17 percent in Asia Pacific, and 14 percent in Latin America. CDC is involved in the following industries: minerals, oil and gas, telecommunications and technology, consumer goods, financial institutions, power, health care, and infrastructure.

II. PRODUCTS

In 2001, CDC invested USD 40 million in MSI Cellular, the pan-African mobile phone service provider. It was CDC's third investment in MSI, after USD 22.5 million in 1998 and USD 25 million in 2000. The funds will aid MSI in further expansion of its services and in the exploration and evaluation of possible new Global System for Mobile Communication (GSM) licenses. CDC was the first backer of MSI in 1998 and has helped make MSI Africa's second-largest GSM operator. MSI provides GSM service in 12 African countries and has over 500,000 customers.

Equity Investments

The equity investments offered by CDC can be used for a variety of projects and purposes. Examples of the types of operations of interest to CDC include privatizations, business expansions, and management buy-outs. CDC has vast experience with privatization projects and has been involved in privatizations of telephone, cement, power, transport, mining, infrastructure, and consumer goods businesses across Latin America, Africa, and Asia. Business expansions, from the creation of new products to the penetration of markets, can be financed with the help of CDC equity investments. CDC also aids in management buy-out operations by supplying the majority of the needed capital, assisting in the negotiations, and working alongside management to develop the business.

CDC made a USD 33 million equity investment in Vancouver Airport Services (YVRAS), the investment and management subsidiary of Canada's Vancouver Airport. YVRAS owns and is pursuing the purchase of emerging market assets. It is currently negotiating projects in Jamaica and Egypt and has existing assets in Chile and the Dominican Republic. YVRAS is helping emerging markets develop by aiding in the improvement of international airports.

III. ELIGIBILITY AND APPLICATION PROCESS

Contact company headquarters for more information.

IV. CONTACTS

Headquarters:
One Bessborough Gardens
London SW1V 2JQ
England
Tel: 44 (0) 20 7828 4488
Fax: 44 (0) 20 7828 6505
Internet: www.cdcgroup.com
Email: info@cdcgroup.com

Main Africa Office—London
Paul Fletcher/Patrick Helson
Tel: 44 (0) 20 7963-3945
Fax: 44 (0) 20 7963-3677
Email: phelson@cdcgroup.com

Main Latin America Office—Miami
Jim Romanos/Ralph Patino
Tel: (305) 415-0000
Fax: (305) 415-0010
Email: miami@cdcgroup.com

Main South Asia Office—India
Donald Peck
Tel: (91 11) 469-1691
Fax: (91 11) 469-1693
Email: india@cdcgroup.com

Main Asia Pacific Office—Thailand
Robert Binyon
Tel: (66 2) 654-3770/5
Fax: (66 2) 654-3776
Email: thailand@cdcgroup.com

CDC Globeleq—London
Torbjorn Caesar
Tel: 44 (0) 20 7963-3998
Fax: 44 (0) 20 7963-3956
Email: torbjorn.caesar@cdcdglobeleq.com

GERMAN INVESTMENT AND DEVELOPMENT COMPANY (DEG)

I. INTRODUCTION

The DEG is a subsidiary of the KfW, which was set up to finance and structure the investments of private companies in developing countries. For over 40 years the mission of the DEG has been to establish and expand private enterprise structures within developing countries to create sustainable economic growth and a lasting improvement in the living conditions of the local population. DEG invests in all sectors of the economy, from agriculture to infrastructure and manufacturing to services. To date, DEG has worked with more than 1,000 companies, providing EUR 4.7 billion in finance with a total investment of over EUR 30 billion.

II. PRODUCTS AND SERVICES

DEG finances start-ups as well as expansion, rationalization, and modernization investments. It supports all types of long-term intercompany cooperation, particularly joint ventures with German and European enterprises.

Loans and Guarantees

The following are some of the financing types available from DEG:

- *Mezzanine Finance*—DEG provides this type of financing to project-specific arrangements with risk-oriented yield, subordinated security, and conversion rights.

- *Long-term loans*—DEG is willing to provide long-term loans, generally for a term between 4 and 10 years. Collateral security must be provided, and DEG's share of the finance may be as high as 35 percent. Interest rates may be fixed or variable, but they are market-oriented based on the project and country risks involved.
- *Guarantees*—DEG guarantees are available for the mobilization of long-term loans or bonds in local currency to reduce exchange-rate risks via loan repayment. Risk is typically shared with local banks.
- *Long-term loans for business start-ups*—DEG offers advice and long-term loans to foreign specialists who have acquired professional experience or completed training in Germany to set up their own business abroad. DEG promotes people whose know-how will make a special contribution to developing a healthy economic structure in its partner countries. This service aims to provide new jobs and developing structures for SMEs, to provide successful export of German knowledge, and to ensure the existence of start-ups.

Equity Investments

DEG is willing to participate in equity investments that generally range from 5 to 25 percent of the total investment and in certain cases may require voting rights and a seat on the board of directors in the company. Exit strategies must be clearly defined before investment occurs.

Technical Assistance

DEG also supports investment projects with consultancy services and practical measures that ensure success in every project phase, especially when things get difficult.

- *Project design assistance*—DEG holds intensive discussions with partners on all aspects of the project, settles any open questions, and helps find solutions to problems that might stand in the way of successful implementation.
- *Financial engineering*—DEG is thorough in assisting and determining the correct debt-equity ratio, designing the finance mix, and arranging possible additional financial contributions.
- *Project development*—To secure long-term success, DEG maintains continuous dialogue with partners throughout the project life cycle. This relationship is based on an agreed-upon reporting procedure.

- *Voting capability*—Through membership on the supervisory board as part of its equity stake, DEG can exert influence on basic business policy.
- *Political facilitator*—As a government corporation, DEG has access to local government agencies and authorities. It can liaise many different contacts for partners to facilitate project implementation.

Risk Management

Many investments in developing and transition countries entail risks that are difficult for investors to assess. By helping to manage risks, DEG helps make the most of business opportunities. DEG is also willing to get involved where commercial banks do not venture.

To identify the risks connected with a foreign investment, DEG has developed a risk management system to make an exact check and assessment of the following factors:

- *Situation in the investment country*—national economic development, political stability, general legal conditions, protection of foreign capital investments, and transfer of capital and earnings
- *Prospects of the project enterprise*—sales, procurement, production, technology, market, management/organization, personnel, site, finance, cost structure, earning power, environmental viability, and legal affairs
- *Partners*—quality of available technical know-how, industry experience, financial situation and personnel resources of partners, risk spread among partners, contractual obligations of partners, and possible conflicting interests

III. ELIGIBILITY AND APPLICATION PROCESS

DEG only provides commitments to projects that make an effective development policy impact, meet environmental standards, and comply with social principles. DEG is particularly committed to its developmental mandate and guidelines for social and environmental compatibility.

IV. CONTACTS

Headquarters:
German Investment and Development Company
Belvederestrasse 40
D-50933 Koln
Germany

Tel: (02 21) 49 86-0
Fax: (02 21) 49 86-2 90
Internet: www.deginvest.de
Email: businessrelations@deginvest.de

NETHERLANDS DEVELOPMENT FINANCE COMPANY (FMO)

I. INTRODUCTION

The FMO was established in 1970 by the Dutch government, which continues to hold a 51 percent stake. The remaining 49 percent is held by Dutch banks, employers' associations, and trade unions. FMO is divided into two departments: Finance and Investment Promotion. FMO Finance offers loans, equities, guarantees, and syndicated loans to businesses and financial institutions in developing countries. FMO Investment Promotion offers programs to assist Dutch businesses that are investing in developing countries. Programs include training, technical assistance, feasibility studies, and assistance with exporting and importing.

FMO currently has a portfolio of EUR 2 billion, making it one of the largest bilateral development banks worldwide. In 2001, FMO disbursed EUR 962 million in loans, invested EUR 104 million in equity, and served 325 clients. FMO concentrates its efforts in 40 developing countries.

FMO's mission is to actively engage the private sector in providing sustainable development solutions and economic growth in emerging economies. FMO has a AAA Standard & Poor's rating and is therefore able to attract private capital to developing countries in what are often seen as risky investments. FMO focuses on risk analysis and ensuring investors a healthy return on investment. The majority of FMO financing is in the infrastructure sector and in projects aimed at promoting MSMEs. For the MSME sector, FMO supports financial institutions in developing economies by providing venture capital, management support, and staff training. FMO also provides assistance to the financial sector of developing countries in the form of support for local banks and mortgage companies in addition to the development of local capital markets with the goal of increasing access to capital for local businesses. In the infrastructure sector, FMO partners with other multilateral development banks to attract commercial partners to invest in and develop the transportation, telecommunications, water, and electric sectors of developing countries. FMO also promotes the trade sector by financing companies with high export potential.

In April 2001, FMO, in conjunction with other financial parties, established the MFB (Microfinance Bank) in Yugoslavia to give MSMEs access to credit for expanding their businesses. MFB already has EUR 34.9 million in account balances, deposits, and savings. The bank has disbursed 1,200 loans, with 69 percent of the loans going to micro businesses and the remaining 31 percent to small- and medium-sized businesses. The rapid growth of MFB is a strong indicator of the lack of access to capital for MSMEs in Yugoslavia.

EUR 993,000 in technical assistance was also provided to MFB. The bank now has one main branch and three satellite branches. The technical assistance grant is being used to train local bank staff. In addition, three new branches opened in 2002.

II. PRODUCTS

Loans and Guarantees

FMO supports private enterprises and financial institutions through long-term capital in the form of project finance, corporate balance sheet finance, working capital facilities, mezzanine finance, guarantees, and medium- to long-term trade finance. FMO provides loans for up to 25 percent of the cost of a project or of the company's total balance sheet, which generally ranges from USD 1 million to USD 100 million. Loan maturities are 5–12 years. Typically, terms are only 3 years for trade financing. Grace periods and repayment schedules are determined by individual project needs based on cash flow estimates.

FMO also provides syndicated loans, or B loans, where it arranges loans with other banks at market rates for long-term capital required for larger projects in emerging markets. These syndicated loans are generally used for project financing and foreign exchange funding.

In 2001, FMO and ABN AMRO arranged a syndicated loan with a leading international bank for PoliBrasil, which is Brazil's largest producer of polypropylene. FMO's involvement was USD 25 million. The investment was used to open a new chemical production facility and incorporate the latest technology. The expansion and increased efficiency contributed to a significant cost advantage, making PoliBrasil more internationally competitive at a time when access to foreign capital in Brazil was declining.

Technical Assistance

The two major programs of FMO that provide technical assistance are IPTA (Investment Promotion and Technical Assistance) and TAEM (Technical Assistance Emerging Markets). IPTA is geared toward promoting cooperation between companies in developing and developed countries. Grants are provided for two main activities: feasibility studies that gather information necessary to make investment decisions and management support aimed at improving management, training, and advising. Grants cover up to 50 percent of the total project cost, with a maximum of EUR 275,000 for management assistance and EUR 80,000 for feasibility studies.

TAEM assists Dutch companies (particularly SMEs) in working with local companies in emerging markets. TAEM only provides support once a Dutch company has made an investment with a local company. The two types of activities covered under a TAEM grant are management support, which includes bringing in expertise in technology, marketing, sales, or other fields for temporary assistance with a project, and training, which includes internships, seminars, and on-the-job training. A TAEM grant also covers only 50 percent of a project cost, with a maximum of EUR 275,000 for management support and EUR 90,000 for training.

Equity Investments

FMO provides equity directly to companies and financial institutions seeking long-term risk capital and indirectly to private equity funds. Direct equity usually takes the form of a 10 to 35 percent FMO equity stake in a company with a maximum investment of EUR 3 million to EUR 5 million and an average commitment of at least 5 years. FMO also provides mezzanine financing with a combination of quasi equity and debt. In terms of indirect equity, FMO invests in local equity funds that stimulate MSMEs; it also invests in the NIMF (Netherlands Investment

Matching Fund). In the NIMF, FMO matches the investment of international companies in the amount of EUR 1 million to EUR 5 million in local companies with high growth potential in lower-middle income countries defined as having per capita of less than USD 3,000 a year. FMO also has a least developed country (LDC) fund that invests in infrastructure projects with equity and mezzanine financing.

FMO generally has a 5-year time horizon and looks for a well-defined exit strategy when entering into equity negotiations. Investment decisions are made with similar criteria used in making loan decisions: market analysis, investment plan, commitment of managers, and so on. After an equity investment is made, FMO continues to monitor the investment closely and provides managerial support when necessary.

III. ELIGIBILITY AND APPLICATION PROCESS

Private Sector Funding

Companies interested in private sector funding are encouraged to contact the local commercial area desk for the country in which they wish to do business, and speak directly with an FMO representative. Proposals are evaluated on a case-by-case basis. Some of the documents or procedures that may be requested include the following:

- Market analysis
- Investment plan
- Commitment of managers and other financiers
- Due diligence study
- Expected returns

The following criteria are evaluated when proposals are submitted to request private sector funding:

- Commercial viability
- Sound investment plan
- Feasibility study and market analysis
- Transparency and good corporate governance
- Sound environmental policy
- Execution by internationally socially acceptable standards
- Proven track record
- Management expertise and experience

Technical Assistance

To apply for technical assistance, a company must submit an application form, which is available on the FMO web site. Other requested documents include the following:

- Project plan
- Business plan
- Declaration of support
- Project budget
- Terms of reference or training program
- Curriculum vitae of managers
- Memos of association with emerging market companies
- Annual reports of all companies involved

The first round of applications are reviewed within 2–3 weeks to ensure that all necessary documentation is received. Companies are usually notified in writing of final decisions within 13 weeks in the form of a letter of subsidy, specifying grant amounts and disbursement terms.

IV. CONTACTS

Headquarters:
Netherlands Development Finance Company
Koningskade 40
2596 AA The Hague
The Netherlands
Tel: 31 (0) 70 314 96 96
Fax: 31 (0) 70 324 61 87

Mailing Address:
P.O. Box 93060
2509 AB The Hague
The Netherlands
Internet: www.fmo.nl
Email: info@fmo.nl

Private Equity
Birgit L. J. M. van de Reyt, Manager
Tel: 31 (0) 70 314 96 54

Micro and Small Enterprise
Emile H. J. de Groot, Manager
Tel: 31 (0) 70 314 96 54

Development Related Export Transactions
Jaap Wientjes, Manager
Tel: 31 (0) 70 314 98 14

Commercial Desk, Africa
Janos I. Bonta, Manager
Tel: 31 (0) 70 314 96 13

Commercial Desk, Asia
Gerrit M. van Kampen, Manager
Tel: 31 (0) 70 314 96 31

Commercial Desk, Europe and Central Asia
George A. M. Meltzer, Manager
Tel: 31 (0) 70 314 96 33

Commercial Desk, Latin America and the Caribbean
Wim J. M. Wienk, Manager
Tel: 31 (0) 70 314 96 47

GERMAN AGENCY FOR TECHNICAL COOPERATION (GTZ)

I. INTRODUCTION

GTZ, a German government-owned development corporation with international operations, was founded in 1975 and provides sustainable development assistance to partner countries. The countries that are eligible to receive assistance are wholly determined by GTZ on the basis of need and are not part of any internationally binding list. In recent years, GTZ has strengthened its operations in Eastern Europe and the former Soviet Republic. The German Federal Ministry for Economic Cooperation and Development (BMZ) is its principal source of funding. The goal of GTZ is to promote international cooperation through sustainable development around the world. The scope of work encompasses technical cooperation in the form of transfer of organizational and business expertise and transfer of technology (with a focus on priority areas such as civil society strengthening, environmental issues, energy, agriculture, land use, employment promotion and trade, appropriate technologies, health, and infrastructure). GTZ also provides consulting services, project management, and planning and advisory services to governments of emerging economies.

GTZ funds benefit the public sector primarily (88 percent of funds) on behalf of the Federal German Government. The remaining 12 percent of funds are commissions from international clients and financing institutions, which are financed by entities such as the World Bank, the European Union (EU), governments of the Gulf State, and the UNDP, as well as private sector enterprises. GTZ works closely with other development organizations, such as the DEG and KfW. GTZ is headquartered in Eschborn, Germany, but has approximately 10,000 employees in 130 countries in Africa, Asia, Latin America, and Eastern Europe.

GTZ employs private sector firms to implement its commissions. Consulting firms are used to produce expert reports and to implement complex projects. International suppliers are used to procure technical equipment and materials. Examples of the types of services offered by GTZ are economic, legal, and administrative reform and preparation for membership of the World Trade Organization (WTO); protection of natural resources; human rights and election monitoring; financial management and procurement of materials and equipment; organization of consulting associations for SMEs; and forestry and watershed management.

II. PRODUCTS

Financing

In recent years, GTZ implemented the Public Private Partnership (PPP) program to join the interests of corporations with development institutions to increase efficiency and reduce costs for both parties. Corporations provide training and technology transfer as well as new sources of capital, and development institutions provide specialized skills, international experience, and local contacts. In four years, GTZ has helped set up 250 partnerships in over 60 countries, with a particular focus on benefiting SMEs. Over EUR 100 million has been made available for PPP projects, with the share of public funds averaging around 40 percent.

PPP projects are financed for a term of 1–3 years at a maximum of EUR 200,000. The amount of financing depends on the level of development benefit of the project for the partner country. Projects are jointly financed and administered by the public and private parties involved. Project opportunities resulting from a partnership between public and private entities exist in the following areas:

- *Human resources development in industry*—Development at a micro level in terms of training local trainers and improving product quality from local suppliers and distributors, as well as human resources development at a macro level, including the support of trade associations, and strengthening of chambers of commerce
- *Capacity building in agriculture*—Transfer of environmentally friendly technology and marketing expertise, training for producer associations, and training for farmers
- *Vocational training*—Management training, development of specialized upgrading and training solutions, transfer of knowledge of production techniques, and established training systems
- *Environmental and social standards*—Full spectrum of internationally recognized environmental and social standards from introduction and awareness education to development, improvement, and implementation of in-company standards
- *Technology transfer*—Support of environmentally friendly technology and of pilot facilities and assistance to research institutions
- *Financial services*—Upgrading of banking infrastructure, including training and development of software for financial institutions
- *Infrastructure*—Reduction of company risk by ensuring business solutions that are culturally sensitive, in addition to training and raising of public awareness
- *Social initiatives/services*—Education in AIDS prevention and prevention of communicable diseases and introduction of employee health insurance and systems that support company health insurance

---

With subfreezing temperatures in Mongolia, a joint venture initiated by the German construction company Stahlbau Vietzke GmbH to introduce modern heat generation systems and insulation was very well received. However, Mongolia did not have properly trained technicians who could install the complex equipment. With the assistance of PPP, a heating technician training institute was formed in the capital of Mongolia by the Mongolian government and Stahlbau. A specialized curricula was developed for installation as well as customer service and support.

Consulting Services

Where applicable, GTZ contracts private sector enterprises to implement consulting projects, to perform project appraisal and evaluation, and to conduct feasibility studies. Contract awards under EUR 200,000 are provided in a direct award, whereas negotiations are entered into for awards above EUR 200,000. Consulting firms' bids are evaluated based on technical regional experience, appropriateness of concept, consideration of local resources, qualifications of personnel, and technical backstopping. After technical expertise is assessed and evaluated, firms compete on price, with the technical bid and price quote weighted by a ratio of 70:30.

III. ELIGIBILITY AND APPLICATION PROCESS

To be eligible for PPP financing, projects must be compatible with the directives of the German government's development policy. The contributions of the public and private parties must be complementary and assist in promoting development and increasing entrepreneurial success at a lower cost for both. The private partner must make at least a 50 percent contribution to the cost of the project, and PPP financing must be used for activities that are beyond the core functions of the private company involved.

PPP financing is open to all German and European companies and their affiliates in developing countries, as well as to trade associations and private business chambers. Companies of all size are eligible for PPP financing, but they must be able to solely finance all projects abroad. Project proposals do not have a strict format, but they should contain the following information:

- Brief description of the company and its business goals in the partner country
- Economic situation or the problem from the perspective of the company
- Preliminary idea of what the cooperation with GTZ might look like
- Estimate of costs and benefits for the company and for GTZ

Once an informal proposal is sent, GTZ notifies the company within 2 weeks whether to proceed with a concept. If the company is allowed to proceed, the concept is developed and an evaluation process occurs. An agreement is drawn up between GTZ and the public and private entities as to their respective roles and responsibilities; then a contract is created and signed by all parties.

Invitations to tender and contracts with consulting companies, in addition to all guidelines, can be downloaded online at www.gtz.de/bos/english/doku_i.htm. Applications are evaluated on the financial capabilities of the firm, human resources and backstopping capacity, experience in economic and technical cooperation, and technical and regional experience.

IV. CONTACTS

Headquarters:
GTZ
Dag-Hammarskjold-Weg 1–5
P.O. Box 5180
65726 Eschborn
Germany
Tel: 496 196/790
Fax: 632 636 2444
Internet: www.gtz.de/english
Email: international.services@gtz.de

Wolfgang Schmidt, Managing Director
Tel: 496196/792118

Dr. Bernd Eisenblatter, Managing Director
Tel: 496196/792109

PPP Financing
Karin Fiedler
Tel: 06196/79-7377

Director of the Centre for Cooperation with the Private Sector
Albrecht Graf von Hardenberg
Tel: 030/72614-210

Bilateral DFIs Supporting Sponsor Country Investors

The focus of this chapter is bilateral DFIs, which provide assistance when there is a clear linkage to the sponsor's national interests. This linkage can be established by a citizen of the sponsor country having a minimum ownership interest in the project or by a contractual relationship the project has with a company of the same nationality as the sponsor.

PORTUGUESE AGENCY OF SUPPORT FOR DEVELOPMENT (APAD)

I. INTRODUCTION

APAD was established in 2000 to promote Portuguese investment, to support social and economic infrastructure, and to foster the private sector in beneficiary countries. APAD promotes projects through direct investment of Portuguese companies, which contribute to development, particularly in African countries speaking the Portuguese language. APAD's efforts focus on projects that improve social and economic infrastructures, education and health, as well as those that provide incentives to the private sector.

II. PRODUCTS AND SERVICES

APAD provides a variety of products and services, including preferential loans, guarantees, equity, grants, and technical assistance. The amount of support is determined based on the merit of the initiatives and the available resources, not to exceed 50 percent of the project cost.

III. ELIGIBILITY AND APPLICATION PROCESS

Contact company headquarters for more information.

IV. CONTACTS

Headquarters:
Portuguese Agency of Support for Development
Tivoli Forum
Av. of the Freedom, No. 180-A
1250-146 Lisbon
Portugal
Tel: 21 317 73 00
Fax: 21 315 85 43
Email: apad@apad.pt

BELGIAN CORPORATION FOR INTERNATIONAL INVESTMENT (BMI-SBI)

I. INTRODUCTION

BMI-SBI was established in 1971 to provide long-term co-financing of foreign investments to Belgian companies. Specifically, its interests are oriented toward financing the creation of new joint ventures and subsidiaries worldwide and acquiring, restructuring, and developing existing companies. BMI-SBI typically serves medium-sized Belgian companies involved in international expansion in industrialized emerging or developing countries by providing financial resources, international expertise, and guidance throughout the project life cycle.

BMI-SBI's equity capital currently amounts to EUR 33 million. Its financial means can, in certain cases, be leveraged with external financing capacities from Belgian federal and regional entities. At present, BMI-SBI has a portfolio of 37 investments in 23 countries. Its income is generated mainly through dividends, capital gains, interests, and other revenues on participations.

In October 2001, Resilux N.V., a Belgian company specializing in the production and sales of PET (Polyethylene Terephthalate) preforms, initiated the start-up of a new production unit in Tuszér, Hungary. The total investment budget, which included a fourth production line scheduled in 2003, amounted to approximately EUR 6.5 million. To structure the project, Resilux Hungary Kft., a 100 percent Resilux N.V. daughter company, was founded. Resilux N.V. put in EUR 755,000 of share capital, while the Belgian Corporation for International Investment provided a subordinated loan amounting to EUR 745,000. Besides the financing, BMI-SBI offered Resilux a diversified network of contacts, which is of considerable value to the project.

II. PRODUCTS AND SERVICES

Equity Investment

BMI-SBI offers various co-financing arrangements for risk capital in the form of minority participations in equity or quasi equity (subordinated loans, profit-sharing loans, participating loans, convertible loans, and so on). This type of financing can range from EUR 500,000 to EUR 2.5 million usually for a period of 5–10 years. BMI-SBI operates at market conditions and carries out an in-depth pre-investment analysis to assess the eligibility, feasibility, and profitability of the project. Exit arrangements are flexible, but must be negotiated beforehand.

Technical Assistance

Support is provided to companies in the form of feasibility studies, joint venture capital requirements, training, and technical and management assistance. BMI-SBI also provides a variety of services to assist companies in all phases of the project life cycle:

- Identification of viable projects and partners (industrial, technical, and financial)
- Pre-investment analysis, including country and project analysis
- Financial engineering
- Corporate governance
- Intermediation for Belgian companies in obtaining complementary financing from governmental or supranational entities

III. ELIGIBILITY AND APPLICATION PROCESS

BMI-SBI supports Belgian companies seeking to invest abroad through the creation of a subsidiary or joint venture or through the acquisition, restructuring, privatization, and/or development of existing companies. To be eligible for assistance, companies must demonstrate the following:

- Feasibility of the project, including a strong financial structure and profitability of the project
- Quality of the Belgian partner company

- Size of the project
- Liquidity of the investment
- Economic interest for Belgium and the host country

Once the above information has been submitted to BMI-SBI, the proposal is reviewed for staff appraisal and submitted to the Investment Committee. Following project approval, the company is required to present legal documentation prior to project implementation.

IV. CONTACTS

Headquarters:
BMI-SBI
Avenue de Tevurenlaan 168/b.9
1150 Brussels
Belgium
Tel: 32 2 776 01 00
Fax: 32 2 770 66 38
Internet: www.bmi-sbi.be
Email: info@bmi-sbi.be

COMPAÑÍA ESPAÑOLA DE FINANCIACIÓN DEL DESARROLLO (COFIDES)

I. INTRODUCTION

COFIDES was established in 1988 to encourage Spanish companies to invest in developing countries. The objective of COFIDES is to improve development efforts in those countries, as well as internationalization of the Spanish economy. COFIDES has supported over 200 projects in more than 40 countries. The majority of projects are concentrated in Latin America and Morocco, although COFIDES is willing to support private investment projects in any developing country in Africa, Asia, Central and Eastern Europe, and Latin America. COFIDES supports projects related to transportation infrastructure, as well as capital goods, electronics, and agribusiness.

II. PRODUCTS AND SERVICES

Loans and Guarantees

Loans are granted to eligible projects at a minimum of EUR 250,000, have terms up to 10 years, and can be denominated in euros or other convertible currencies. Guarantees are determined on a case-by-case basis.

Equity Investment

COFIDES participates in equity investments, but will normally not assume more than 30 percent of capital. Participation is limited to Spanish investments. In cases where COFIDES acts as a co-financier in conjunction with other institutions or investors, this percentage may be increased. COFIDES participates only in the capital investment and is not involved in the daily management of the project.

In February of 2002, COFIDES became one of the lead shareholders in the Platinum Toll Highway project that will link the Maputo Harbor in Mozambique with the Walvis Bay in Namibia. This project brought more than R3 billion (approximately USD 379 million) into the economy and created about 3,000 jobs for the construction of South Africa's third largest toll road.

Technical Assistance

COFIDES offers a variety of technical services and is willing to obtain funds from different sources to provide financing for feasibility studies, training, and technical and management assistance.

III. ELIGIBILITY AND APPLICATION PROCESS

To apply, companies are required to submit a project proposal that includes the following:

- General project description, including project justification
- Present financial situation of the company and expected date of execution
- Detailed outline of support being requested
- Detailed information of the Spanish investor
- Market studies

Other information may be requested. Contact company headquarters for specific information.

IV. CONTACTS

Headquarters:
La Compañía Española de Financiación del Desarrollo
Príncipe de Vergara, No. 132, planta 12
28002 Madrid
Spain
Tel: 91 7454480 /91 5626008
Fax: 91 5610015
Internet: www.cofides.es
Email: cofides@cofides.es

DUCROIRE/DELCREDERE

I. INTRODUCTION

Ducroire/Delcredere, or Delcredere, was founded in 1921, after the First World War, by the Belgian government to create a public body that would insure political risks and revive exports. In 1939, the government granted autonomy to the institution while continuing to provide governmental guarantees. Delcredere continues to provide insurance products and financing instruments to support Belgian interests.

Delcredere provides a wide range of products and services. In general, for projects requiring assistance for less than 360 days, Delcredere provides comprehensive policies, SME policies, multinational policies, lendings for use and job work contracts, trade fairs and consignments, and confirmation letters of credit. For projects needing assistance for more than 360 days, Delcredere provides buyer/supplier credit, financial leasing, import pre-financing, project financing, foreign investment, discounting without recourse, framework agreements, operational leasing, other special transactions, guarantees, coverage for contracting equipment, exchange risk insurance, risk of revocation coverage, inconvertibility risk of local currency, and foreign exchange coverage.

II. PRODUCTS AND SERVICES

Loans and Guarantees

Delcredere participates directly in capital and provides loans and guarantees to overseas joint ventures as long as there is a Belgian investment interest. Repayment is based on cash flows generated by the project. Most risks affecting profitability of the project, which accordingly jeopardize the repayment of the credit, are borne by the shareholders, investors, and credit providers.

Build-Operate-Transfer (BOT) is a special form of project financing with many variants, including BOOT (Build-Own-Operate-Transfer), BOO (Build-Own-Operate), and BTO (Build-Transfer-Operate). Delcredere provides BOTs to supplement financial support. In the case of a BOT operation, the local authority (a state or a public organization) provides a concession to a private company to create and develop a public service at the latter's expense for a certain period. In general, primarily infrastructure projects (energy, telecommunications, and transport) are eligible as BOT projects.

Risk Insurance

Risk insurance provides exporters and supporting banks with coverage for political and commercial project risks. As a general rule, risks, particularly commercial risks, are shared among Delcredere, the exporter, and the bank. Risk sharing usually takes the form of a reduced covered percentage. Delcredere also provides coverage for the insurance of exchange rate risks the bank guarantees to be provided by the exporter (advance payment and performance guarantees) and for the contractor's material to be used by the exporter.

Insurance protects against the infringement to rights of ownership as the result of the following:

- Expropriation
- Transfer
- War
- Government action
- Breach of contract

In matters of overseas investments, Delcredere indemnifies investment losses due to expropriation, government actions, and wars. Delcredere also indemnifies investment losses when there is a shortage of foreign currency and when the capital or the product of the investment cannot be transferred to Belgium.

Insurance also protects against nonpayment. The waiting period in the event of nonpayment amounts to 6 months. This policy normally has a term of 15 years. After a minimum initial period (usually 3 years) that is established in the Special Conditions, the investor can cancel the policy each year.

All forms of Belgian investment are eligible for insurance. Delcredere is very flexible in creating tailor-made solutions to cover risks resulting from international commercial transactions as well as from overseas investments.

III. ELIGIBILITY AND APPLICATION PROCESS

Loans

Contact Delcredere headquarters for more information.

Risk Insurance

Delcredere only insures actual investments. The project must also have an economically justifiable purpose. Delcredere insures all investors who, due to the nature of their activity, are integrated in the Belgian economic community. There are no geographical restrictions with regards to transactions with medium- or long-term credits. In matters of short-term transactions (credits of less than 360 days), Delcredere covers political and commercial risks on all non-OECD countries as well as the Czech Republic, Hungary, Mexico, Poland, Slovakia, South Korea, and Turkey.

A request for insurance consists of information based on a list of questions Delcredere will forward upon request. Delcredere then evaluates the intensity of risks, the ability to properly transfer to Belgium the dividends or profits from the sale of the investment, and trade and cash flows resulting from the investment. Favorable decisions are communicated in the form of an offer of coverage, including a commitment by Delcredere to insure the investment according to the modalities (guaranteed proportion, waiting period, premium, and so on) and terms stipulated. Offers of coverage have a limited validity (usually 6 months) and are issued free of charge.

IV. CONTACTS

Headquarters:
Ducroire/Delcredere
Square de Meeûs 40
1000 Brussels
Belgium

Tel: 32 2 509 42 11
Fax: 32 2 513 50 59
Internet: www.ondd.be
Email: webmaster@ondd.be

Commercial contacts to insure credits of less than 360 days:
Richard Maroquin
Tel: 32 2 509 44 76
Email: r.maroquin@ondd.be

Commercial contacts to insure credits of more than 360 days:
Herman Christiaens
Tel: 32 2 509 42 66
Email: h.christiaens@ondd.be

Contact with Berne Union:
Karine Boussart
Tel: 32 2 509 43 83
Email: k.boussart@ondd.be

Contact with European Union and OECD:
Philippe Callut
Tel: 322 509 43 76
Email: p.callut@ondd.be

EXPORT DEVELOPMENT CANADA (EDC)

I. INTRODUCTION

EDC is a financial institution providing trade finance services to Canadian investors and exporters in over 200 markets, 130 of which are developing markets. Through its Project Finance Team, EDC specializes in complex limited recourse structured financing transactions for large-scale global infrastructure and industrial projects. Since its establishment in 1995, EDC's Project Finance Team has closed more than 100 transactions in over 30 countries, with EDC's total financing support exceeding USD 6.5 billion. The EDC also acts as a liaison for commercial banks and exporters to ensure success in the export market.

Approximately 90 percent of EDC's customers are small businesses. Support to companies is offered in the form of credit insurance, bonding, guarantees, political risk insurance, direct loans to buyers in other countries, limited recourse project financing arrangements, and joint ventures for projects involving long-term leasing arrangements and equity participation.

II. PRODUCTS

Loans

Direct loans are available for project financing through the Project Finance Team primarily in the areas of energy, diversified industries, and telecommunications. EDC also provides direct loans to people/organizations operating a business in Canada who wish to find financing for an export transaction that has a significant amount of Canadian content (usually 50 percent). The Loans require an additional exposure fee.

Lines of Credit

EDC provides lines of credit to foreign banks, institutions, or purchasers based on pre-arranged interest rates and repayment terms. These institutions, banks, and purchasers then use the line of credit to finance buyers of Canadian goods and services. A typical line of credit through EDC ranges from USD 50,000 to USD 5 million.

Equity Investments

EDC provides equity investments for medium-term capital. EDC invests in the following types of structures: a foreign company or project, a fund, or a Canadian exporter. However, EDC is only able to provide a maximum investment of between CAD 10 million or 25 percent of share capital, whichever is less. Among other criteria, EDC considers the competitive environment (i.e., sustainable competitive advantage), the financial position, the likelihood of a realistic and achievable exit (usually 4–6 years), and the amount of Canadian benefits (2 to 1 over the life of the investment). EDC may or may not seek a position on the board of the entity receiving financing.

Insurance

EDC offers several types of insurance policies:

- *Accounts receivable*—EDC covers 90 percent of the loss from nonpayment due to bankruptcy and default. It also covers delay of payment from fund blockage or transfer problems, as well as refusal of goods by the buyer. Furthermore, it covers war/hostilities in the buyer's country and cancellation/nonrenewal of export/import permits.

- *Political risk*—EDC's political risk insurance covers three main types of risk: transfer and inconvertibility of funds, expropriation, and political violence. To qualify, however, it must demonstrate benefits to Canada and the host country. Costs are determined on a yearly basis, during which time the insured can assess the risk for that year and request the corresponding amount of coverage.

- *Political risk insurance of loans*—This coverage is an expanded version of the political risk insurance. It, too, covers 90 percent of the loss due to the same three types of risk. However, it is designed to cover nonpayment of loans. The expanded coverage includes increased loan protection, a wider variety of solutions for investors and exporters, greater availability of commercial bank financing, as well as the potential to increase project capital.

III. ELIGIBILITY AND APPLICATION PROCESS

Individuals interested in accounts receivable insurance can apply directly through EDC's web site. For direct loans, information must be submitted about the company (including a detailed company profile), the buyer, the borrower, and the transaction itself (including the items to be exported). The contract price must also be submitted. To propose an equity investment, EDC requires the following information: a detailed business plan or memorandum, a copy of proposed investment terms and conditions, identification of other potential investors, and copies of relevant commercial documentation.

To apply for EDC financing or to propose an equity investment, contact an EDC regional office for appropriate details and forms. Regional offices are located in four regions of Canada, as well as in Mexico, Brazil, China, and Poland.

IV. CONTACTS

Headquarters:
Export Development Canada
151 O'Connor
Ottawa, Ontario, K1A 1K3
Tel: (613) 598-2500

Fax: (613) 237-2690
Internet: www.edc.ca
Email: export@edc.ca

FINANZIERUNGSGARANTIE-GESELLSCHAFT (FGG)

I. INTRODUCTION

In 1969, the FGG was founded in Austria under the name of Entwicklungs- und Erneuerungsfonds Ges.m.b.H. and served to close security gaps in investment loans by assisting companies with the aid of state-backed risk coverage. After being reorganized in 1977, FGG assumed a new name as well as the ability to issue guarantees for equity participations and junior loans. In 1981, FGG began to cooperate on restructurings with various institutions on a local and national level and provided a vehicle for the arrangement of financing for new technology-oriented companies.

FGG bears the risk of long-term financing of Austrian companies engaged in domestic and foreign projects. Therefore, FGG undertakes company-specific, individually structured guarantees. FGG also joined the umbrella organization of European Development Finance Institutions (EDFIs) and thus obtained access to the information network of the whole group. The Republic of Austria is the sole owner of FGG and acts as guarantor for all guarantees.

II. PRODUCTS AND SERVICES

FGG does not directly provide equity, but it can mobilize equity capital indirectly via its partners by means of capital guarantees facilitating the establishment of venture capital funds. Guarantees can also be given to financial investors acquiring shares in venture capital funds. Remuneration for FGG capital guarantees is calculated in such a way that the risk is covered by the fees charged and FGG can participate in the success of the venture capital fund (profit sharing). Capital guarantees thus protect the investors' money, thereby giving impetus to the founding of venture capital funds that provide equity for enterprises with a high level of technology orientation and good growth potential.

Guarantees

FGG offers a variety of guarantee products to facilitate direct investments to projects. The following are descriptions of these products:

- *Domestic investment guarantees* are offered to Austrian-based companies when the necessary collaterals for the financing institution would severely restrict the company's leeway for investment, which could prevent the company from benefiting from future opportunities. The FGG domestic guarantee secures up to 85 percent of the capital and interest compared to the lending bank. FGG provides guarantees to companies planning large-scale investments when the earnings performance and equity capital base of the company are solid and when extensive external financing for the investment makes sense and is feasible.

- *Foreign direct investments* support Austrian-based companies' activities abroad. Instruments focus primarily on direct investment, such as setting up subsidiaries and joint ventures. Guarantee instruments are designed to mobilize finance for direct investments abroad and to bear some of the potential economic risks for Austrian companies.

- *Direct guarantees* are tailor-made to the project-specific risk profile under the terms of which the company will get back part of its funds (up to 50 percent) if the investment project should fail. "Failure" must be defined beforehand and agreed upon by the company and FGG.

- *Financing guarantees* are provided when an Austrian company raises external funds from a bank to finance its foreign investment. FGG can provide security for up to 90 percent of the funds borrowed. This guarantee covers the insolvency risk with regard to the bank, as the FGG guarantee is regarded by the bank as a liability assumed by the Republic of Austria (AAA credit rating). However, this guarantee does not cover the risk in respect to the economic success of the project.

- *The FGG Study Fund* is an instrument used by Austrian-based companies for preparing direct investments in countries throughout the world. FGG bears up to 50 percent of the costs of a feasibility study or EUR 100,000 when support is not available from other European aid programs.

- *The East-West Fund* was created as an FGG guarantee facility for Austrian equity participation commitments abroad with a view of supporting the internationalization of Austrian companies and contributing to the economic transition in neighboring countries, particularly in Eastern Europe.

- *Capital guarantees* were developed to enable market-compliant risk capital generation via equity capital funds. These guarantees are used for SME financing companies as well as for other participation companies.

If, after disposal of the investment until the expiration of the fund, the value of the invested capital lies below its original value, FGG guarantees become effective and pay to the venture capital fund. If the value after disposal of investments exceeds the original value, FGG receives a part of the profit.

Technical Assistance

FGG supports Austrian enterprises with the planning, structuring, and financing of infrastructure projects at home and abroad, which are structured either as PPPs or as long-term operating models, and emphasizes the following areas: energy and energy efficiency, water supply, sewage disposal, and waste management. FGG actively supports Austrian enterprises in the implementation of construction projects in the infrastructure field as operating models and by these means strategically expands their business activities.

III. ELIGIBILITY AND APPLICATION PROCESS

FGG examines company organization and management, products and technologies, market and competitors, and marketing and distribution when determining eligibility. Once FGG determines that a project falls within its guidelines, it begins analysis of the proposed project. Examination of guarantee projects requires a fee. To apply, companies should contact the FGG directly or via the financing institution to discuss the planned project together.

IV. CONTACTS

Headquarters:
Finanzierungsgarantie-Gesellschaft mit beschränkter Haftung
Gasometer A, Guglgasse 6
1110 Vienna
Austria
Tel: 43 1 501 75 0
Fax: 43 1 501 75 360
Internet: www.fgg.at
Email: fgg@fgg.at

FINNFUND

I. INTRODUCTION

Finnfund is a Finnish development finance company providing long-term risk capital for private projects in developing countries. Since its inception in 1980, Finnfund has made 172 investment commitments valued at USD 326 million. With a mission of financing sustainable and profitable private sector enterprises in developing countries, FinnFund acts as a catalyst for other investors, attracting further financing with its involvement.

Finnfund originally financed only projects with a Finnish player, but in 2001, the fund gained greater flexibility and began financing projects with a Finnish interest as well. Apart from direct investments with Finnish companies or their partners, Finnfund also selectively finances the local private sector through intermediaries such as private equity funds. Shareholders include the Finnish government (79.9 percent), Finnvera Plc (20 percent), and Confederation of Finnish Industry and Employers (0.1 percent).

II. PRODUCTS

Financing is available to companies expanding internationally in manufacturing, service, and infrastructure, as well as finance and banking. Finnfund operates in the countries categorized as "developing" by the OECD Developing Aid Committee (DAC). The fund finances investment loans, minority equity investments, and mezzanine investments.

Investment Loans

Finnfund offers investment loans to start-ups, acquisitions, and expansions with a Finnish interest. The collateral policy is flexible, with the loan agreement specifying collateral in detail.

Terms

Investment loans are available for terms of 8–12 years, with an available grace period of 1–2 years. Finnfund can finance up to one-third of the project. The interest rate depends on collateral, as well as the grace period and repayment schedule. Funds are disbursed in the main convertible currencies or in a variety of currencies. An additional benefit is that many countries have granted Finnfund an exemption on withholding tax on loan interest payments.

Shanghai Eltete Packaging Technology Co., Ltd., was founded in 2000. The company is located in the Jiang Qiao industrial zone in Shanghai. The Finnish sponsor of the project is Loviisa-based Eltete TPM Oy, whose main line of business is the manufacture of transport packaging products and their related technology. The project company manufactures edge boards and other transport packaging products for China's domestic and export markets. The most important export countries are Japan, Korea, and Singapore. Production began in February 2001. The completed products are recyclable as is the raw material used. Eltete TPM Oy has delivered the production technology. The project company employs 30 people. Finnfund's share of the financing for Shanghai Eltete Packaging Technology Co., Ltd., is USD 600,000.

Equity Financing

Finnfund provides equity to companies on the same terms as other shareholders. Initial negotiations include signing a shareholder agreement, spelling out the involvement of Finnfund to the board of directors, and discussing shares of profits and exit terms.

Terms

Equity is available for up to 25 percent of the capital of the company being financed. Finnfund expects to be treated as a shareholder, with participation on the board of directors and the same access to profits. After operations have stabilized, Finnfund will exit the company in accordance with a shareholder agreement concluded during initial negotiations.

In June 2001, Finnfund's board of directors decided to participate in Nordea Bank Finland Plc's syndicated loan to EGE Haina. Finnfund's share was USD 4 million. The loan was used for meeting EGE Haina's local investment costs. The full amount of the syndicated loan was USD 80 million. The borrower was a Dominican Republic power utility that was half privatized in 1999.

The syndicated loan was be used to pay for a Wärtsilä-delivered floating power plant that has an electricity generating capacity of 150 MW. The power barge is one of the world's largest floating power plants. The electricity is supplied directly to the local distribution grid. The power plant has a very high efficiency ratio and is one of the world's most environmentally advanced plants thanks to its low noise level.

The power plant barge was built in Singapore, where nine diesel engines delivered by Wärtsilä were installed. It was transported ready for operation to the city of San Pedro de Macoris in the Dominican Republic. The floating power plant incorporates a good deal of other Finnish supplies in addition to the Wärtsilä engines. The inauguration of the power barge took place at the end of November 2001.

Mezzanine Financing

To best suit the capital needs of a project, Finnfund can arrange financing with mezzanine instruments. These include unsecured subordinated loans, preferred shares, and convertible bonds.

Co-financing

When the financing needs of a project exceed Finnfund's capacity to incur risk, the project may be financed in conjunction with other financial institutions. Finnfund is a member of EDFI and collaborates closely with its members. Finnfund also has had long-standing cooperation with the IFC, the EBRD, and other development banks, as well as commercial banks. Finally, Finnfund is an investor in a number of private equity funds active in developing countries.

III. ELIGIBILITY AND APPLICATION PROCESS

Projects should have an experienced sponsor strongly committed to the project. If the sponsor is not a Finnish parent company, some other link to Finnish interests must be demonstrated. The project must operate in a developing country or a country in transition, such as Russia. Projects in EU accession countries can be financed only in exceptional cases.

The basis of appraisal is the client's project plan. Format is flexible and early contact is advised. The following is a checklist of information required for application:

- Project sponsors and partners
- Financial information (annual reports from the past 3 years)
- Contact information
- Corporate strategy and the project's role in it

- Sponsors' and partners' experience and references in the sector, industry, and international markets
- Roles and responsibilities of partners

Documentation such as pre-feasibility studies, market surveys, lists of equipment, and information on comparable projects is also preferred.

IV. CONTACTS

Headquarters:
Finnfund
P.O. Box 391
FIN-00121 Helsinki
Finland
Tel: 358 (9) 348-434
Fax: 358 (9) 3484-3346
Internet: www.finnfund.fi
Email: finnfund@finnfund.fi

Regional Office:
Letter Box 146
UBN Tower, 17th Floor
10 Jalan P. Ramlee
50250 Kuala Lumpur
Malaysia
Tel: 60 (3) 2078-6355
Fax: 60 (3) 2078-6360
Email: finnfundkl@po.jaring.my

DANISH INTERNATIONAL INVESTMENT FUNDS (IFU)

I. INTRODUCTION

Danish International Investment Funds an organization comprised of four distinct funds: IFU, IFV, IØ, and MIØ. Each fund is operated separately to benefit specific countries based on per capita income and region.

- IFU operates in developing countries with a per capita income below the World Bank's upper limit for new loans (USD 5,225 in year 2002).

- IFV operates in developing countries with a per capita income above the World Bank's upper limit for new loans (USD 5,225 in year 2002).
- IØ operates in Central and Eastern Europe and in the Asian part of the former Soviet Union. IØ administers a special Environmental Investment Facility (MIØ) in cooperation with the Danish Ministry of the Environment.

IFU

IFU was established in 1967 by the Danish Parliament and operates in independent developing countries included in OECD'S DAC list with a gross national product (GNP) per capita below USD 5,225 (2002). IFU has invested more than DKK 4.5 billion (approximately USD 655 million) in 449 projects in 71 developing countries. IFU takes part not only in large investments, but also in SMEs, including pilot projects. IFU's policy is to withdraw from a project when the project has become self-supporting, normally 5–10 years after initiation.

IFV

IFV is the Danish Investment Fund for Emerging Markets. The Danish Parliament established this fund in 1996, with activities beginning in 1997 after being approved by the EU. The purpose of IFV is to assist Danish companies with investments in emerging markets and with strengthening the participation of Danish companies in globalization.

IFV offers financing support for large and small projects in developing countries. To be eligible, a project must be financed in part by a Danish business partner and not fall within the financial sector, the shipbuilding industry, the steel industry, the automobile industry, or the synthetic fiber industry. Greenfield projects, expansion of existing projects, and privatization of state-owned enterprises are eligible. IFV's policy is to withdraw from a project when the project has become self-supporting, which is expected to happen 5–10 years after project start.

IØ

The Investment Fund for Central and Eastern Europe (IØ) was established by the Danish Parliament in 1989, following the changes in Central and Eastern Europe. IØ offers to participate in Danish companies' investments specifically in Central and Eastern Europe and has invested in a total of 307 projects in 16 countries.

MIØ

The Environmental Investment Facility for Central and Eastern Europe (MIØ) was established in 1995 as a separate facility under the IØ. The purpose of MIØ is to create a better external environment and occupational health and safety conditions in Central and Eastern Europe by transferring and creating necessary environmental technology in the region.

MIØ is a flexible financial partner, but participates mostly as a share capital partner—holding a seat on the board of directors together with the Danish company investing in the project company. MIØ can provide share capital, loans, or guarantees. The financing of projects may include a combination of MIØ funds for environmentally related investments and IØ funds for broader purposes. Except for the specific environmental dimension, MIØ's operational rules and regulations generally follow those of IØ. Therefore, reference should be made to the rules and regulations for IØ.

II. PRODUCTS

IFU Products

Project Financing

Normally, IFU's total financial involvement in a project does not exceed 25 percent of the total investment, and the investment in any single project does not exceed 5 percent of IFU's equity capital plus reserves against losses. IFU normally provides up to 30 percent of the share capital of a project company, but can in certain cases subscribe up to 50 percent.

Loans

IFU can extend loans on commercial terms, usually for a period of up to 5 years. Equity, loans, and guarantees for loans from other sources may also be offered.

Guarantees

IFU can also issue guarantees for loans, which the project company can obtain from other sources.

To be eligible for IFU financing, the project must be wholly or partially owned by a Danish corporation. IFU usually participates for 6–8 years and contributes by sitting on the boards of project companies. When a project company is well consolidated, IFU sells its shares and injects the funds into new project companies.

IFV Products

Project Finance
Normally, IFV's total financial involvement in a project does not exceed 25 percent of the total investment, and the investment in any single project does not exceed 20 percent of IFV's equity capital plus reserves against losses. IFV's financial participation in a single project is generally not lower than DKK 3 million (approximately USD 436,000).

Loans
In certain cases, IFV can extend loans on commercial terms, usually for a period of up to 5 years.

IØ Products

Project Finance
IØ takes part in small, medium, and large investments and enterprises, including pilot projects. Generally, IØ's total financial involvement in a project does not exceed 25 percent of the total investment, and the investment in any single project does not exceed 5 percent of IØ's equity capital. IØ normally provides up to 30 percent of the share capital of a project company but can, in certain cases, subscribe up to 50 percent of the share capital. Project companies are established as joint ventures with the Danish company, a local partner, and IØ, forming a new limited liability company. In some cases, the Danish company may choose to make the investment without a local partner. IØ withdraws once the project company is well consolidated, usually after 6–8 years. Available funds can then be injected into new projects.

Loans
IØ can grant loans on commercial terms, usually for a period of up to 5 years.

Guarantees
IØ can also issue guarantees for loans, which the project company can obtain from other sources.

MIØ Products

Project Financing

MIØ operates specifically in Central and Eastern Europe countries. The countries bordering the Baltic Sea, however, are given highest priority.

To be eligible for MIØ financing, the projects must be commercially viable and contribute toward limiting the stress on the external environment, must improve the working environment, and/or must contribute to developing environmental technology in the project countries. MIØ exercises great flexibility regarding its financial participation in a given project. MIØ's facility capital amounts to DKK 450 million and had, by the end of 2001, co-financed 40 projects in nine Central and Eastern European countries.

Loans

Further, MIØ can grant loans on commercial terms, usually for a period of up to 5 years.

Guarantees

MIØ can also issue guarantees for loans, which the project company can obtain from other sources.

MIØ takes part not only in large investments, but also in SMEs, including pilot projects. Normally, MIØ's total financial involvement in a project does not exceed 25 percent of the total investment, and the investment in any single project does not exceed 5 percent of MIØ´s facility capital plus reserves against losses. MIØ normally subscribes up to 30 percent of the share capital of a project company but can, in certain cases, subscribe up to 50 percent of the share capital.

III. ELIGIBILITY AND APPLICATION PROCESS

IFU

To be eligible, projects must be partially financed by Danish-based firms. Additionally, projects should fall under the categories of greenfield projects, expansion of existing projects, or privatization of state-owned businesses and be commercially viable. Additionally, projects financed through IFU and IFV require that host countries of investment be listed under the OECD's DAC list of development aid recipients.

IFV

To be eligible, a project must be financed in part by a Danish business partner and must be considered a commercially viable project. Greenfield projects, expansion of existing projects, and privatization of state-owned enterprises are eligible. Host countries of investments must be on the OECD's DAC list of development aid recipients, and per capita income must exceed USD 5,225 (2002).

IØ

To be eligible, a project must be partially financed by a Danish business partner and must be considered a commercially viable project. Greenfield projects, expansion of existing projects, and privatizations of state-owned enterprises are eligible.

MIØ

Rules and regulations are typically similar to those of the IØ. Parties interested in financing should approach the IFU directly by submitting an investment proposal, available on the IFU web site. Following a preliminary review, a detailed feasibility study or business plan may be requested.

IV. CONTACTS

Headquarters:
IFU—Copenhagen Bremerholm 4
DK-1069 Copenhagen K, Denmark
Tel: 453-363-7500
Fax: 453-332-2524
Internet: www.ifu.dk
Email: ifu@ifu.dk

IFU—Beijing
Rm. 1815, China Travel Service Tower (CTST)
No. 2 Beisanhuan East Road
Beijing 100028, China
Tel: 861-064-609-797
Fax: 861-064-609-799
Email: ifubjs@public3.bta.net.cn

IFU—New Delhi
SPWD Building, 2nd Floor

14 A, Vishnu Digambhar Marg (Rouse Avenue Lane)
New Delhi 110002, India
Tel: 919-811-096-908
Email: ifudel@vsnl.net

JAPAN BANK FOR INTERNATIONAL COOPERATION (JBIC)

I. INTRODUCTION

JBIC was established in 1999 by merging the Export-Import Bank of Japan (JEXIM) and the Overseas Economic Cooperation Fund (OECF). JBIC operations fall into two major categories: International Financial Operations, which promotes Japanese exports and economic activities overseas, as well as stability in international financial markets, and the Overseas Economic Cooperation Operations (OECO), which supports self-reliant development efforts in developing countries. The International Financial Operations extends export loans, import loans, overseas investment loans, untied loans, and equity participations in overseas projects. In 2001, the amount of outstanding loans under International Finance Operations was 10,558.8 billion yen, or approximately USD 89 million (48.6 percent of outstanding loans), compared to 11,178.3 billion yen (51.4 percent) for its OECO. Official Development Assistance (ODA) loans, which support the activities of private companies in developing countries, are the major component under the OECO. In 2001, JBIC had a budget of 1.15 billion yen (USD 9.29 million) for its International Financial Operations and 760 billion yen (USD 6.14 billion) for its OECO.

II. PRODUCTS

JBIC does not provide short-term credit financing. Its products are targeted only at medium- and long-term repayment projects, typically 2–10 years. Some maturities, such as overseas investment loans for Japanese corporations investing in foreign corporations, may offer repayment terms of up to 15 years. ODA loans have repayment terms of 40 years.

Export Loans

Export loans finance Japanese exports to developing countries. Eligible borrowers must be Japanese exporters of products with a foreign content of up to 50 percent of the contract value. The maximum repayment term depends on the country to which the borrower is exporting. For exports to middle-income countries, the maximum repayment term is 5 years; for developing countries, it is 10 years.

Terms

The minimum down payment should be 15 percent of the contract amount, as required by OECD guidelines. The interest rate is the base rate (the interest rate for a Japanese treasury bond) plus a certain percentage, depending on the repayment terms of the export loan. For 5-year loans, the rate is 1.16 percent; for 5- to 8.5-year loans the rate is 1.5 percent; and for loans over 8.5 years the rate is 1.91 percent. The loan can be denominated in yen or dollars. JBIC does not finance the down payment portion.

Bolivia is a landlocked country in South America blessed with an abundance of natural resources. Its geographical isolation has meant that Bolivia has been slow in modernizing its transportation infrastructure, thereby hindering economic growth. In contrast, Bolivia's neighbor, Brazil, has a rapidly growing economy. A major economic issue in Brazil is how to respond to new energy demands. Bolivia has an abundance of natural gas, but had financial difficulty developing the supply routes. Brazil had an energy supply problem resulting from its rapidly growing economy. Out of this mutually beneficial situation, the Bolivia-Brazil gas pipeline project was born.

Petrobras (Petroleo Brasileiro) took responsibility for the construction and financing through JBIC of a 35 billion yen (USD 298 million) export loan. Japanese steel manufacturers received orders for 540,000 tons of steel pipes. Given the current recession in the steel industry, this total shipment of steel pipes accounted for some 20 percent of the annual export volume of major steel manufacturers.

ODA Loans

JBIC offers six types of ODA loans, each covering a different sector of development assistance.

- *Project loans* finance projects such as roads, power plants, irrigation, water supply, and sewerage facilities.

- *Engineering services (E/S) loans* typically include feasibility studies' reviews, project site surveys, detailed designs, and preparation of bidding documents.
- *Financial intermediary loans (two-step loans)* are used to aid in the implementation of policies, including the promotion of SMEs in manufacturing, agriculture, and other industries or facilities used to improve living standards.
- *SALs* are designed to aid recipient countries in the restructuring of their economic policies and to help implement the necessary structural adjustments of their economies as a whole. Typically, the funds are used for consulting services as well as the repayment of imported equipment and services.
- *Commodity loans* are designed to support the balance of payments and economic stability in developing countries. Usually, funds from these loans are utilized to import different types of commodities, such as industrial machinery, raw materials, fertilizer, pesticides, agricultural machinery, and other kinds of machinery. However, these are agreed upon beforehand between Japan and the government of the recipient country.
- *Sector program loans (SPLs)* support development policies in prioritized sectors of developing countries.

Untied Loans

Untied loans are designed to address economic problems in developing and transition economies, including trouble in servicing external debt, underdeveloped infrastructure and capital markets, lack of international competitiveness in certain key industries, and environmental pollution. These loans are not tied to the procurement of goods and services from Japan, but are utilized for the specific purposes designated for each loan.

Eligibility
The borrower is typically a sovereign government; however, in exceptional cases, these loans may be granted to public or private corporations. There are two major types of untied loans, project operation untied loans and program operation untied loans. The first type is typically used to finance a specific project; the latter is used to co-finance with another institution, such as the World Bank or the Inter-American Development Bank (IDB).

Terms
The repayment term is typically 10–20 years.

Private-Sector Investment Finance (PSIF)

This type of financing comes as part of JBIC's OECO. It seeks to provide economic cooperation through supporting private sector activities. Its mission is to improve living standards in developing countries by financing private enterprises, thereby generating employment in these regions, leading to technological improvements and the acquisition of foreign currency, among other benefits. This financing comes in the form of equity investments or loans.

Eligibility

PSIF loans are available to projects in the following sectors: prospecting, agriculture, forestry and fisheries, preparatory surveys and experimental implementation of development projects, and Private Finance Initiative (PFI) Infrastructure Projects. Additionally, in some cases, PSIF loans may be used for ODA loans as well as for projects unsuitable for financing from private sector financial institutions.

III. ELIGIBILITY AND APPLICATION PROCESS

The process for applying for financial assistance is as follows:

- *Project preparation*—Projects in developing countries are determined based on their objectives and strategies of medium- and long-term development plans. Then each project is investigated and analyzed from several aspects, such as economic, technical, and environmental.
- *Loan request*—At this stage, requests are made for a loan by the government of the developing country. These requests include the information gathered during the project preparation stage.
- *Examination/appraisal*—At this stage, many aspects of the projects are appraised and analyzed and the project site is visited and evaluated.
- *Exchange of notes/loan agreements*—At this stage, the loan amount is determined and the specific details and terms are arranged.

IV. CONTACTS

Headquarters:
Japan Bank for International Cooperation
4-1 Ohtemachi 1-chome
Chiyoda-ku, Tokyo 100-8144

Japan
Tel: 03 (5218) 3101
Fax: 03 (5218) 3955
Internet: www.jbic.go.jp

Representative Office in Beijing
3131, 31st Floor, China World Trade Center
No.1 Jian Guo Men Wai Avenue
Beijing 100004, The People's Republic of China
Tel: 86-10-6505-8989, 3825, 3826, 3827, 3828, 1196, 1197
Fax: 86-10-6505-3829, 1198

Representative Office in Hong Kong
Suite 3706, Level 37, One Pacific Place
88 Queensway
Hong Kong
Tel: 852-2869-8505, 8506, 8507
Fax: 852-2869-8712

Representative Office in Bangkok
14th Floor, Nantawan Building
161 Rajdamri Road, Bangkok, 10330
Thailand
Tel: 66-2-252-5050
Fax: 66-2-252-5514, 5515

Representative Office in Hanoi
6th Floor, 63 Ly Thai To Street
Hanoi, Vietnam
Tel: 84-4-8248934, 8248935, 8248936
Fax: 84-4-8248937

Representative Office in Jakarta
Summitmas II, 7th Floor
Jl. Jenderal Sudirman, Kav. 61-62
Jakarta 12190, Indonesia
Tel: 62-21-522-0693
Fax: 62-21-520-0975

Representative Office in Kuala Lumpur
22nd Floor, UBN Tower, Letter Box No.59
Jalan P. Ramlee 50250
Kuala Lumpur, Malaysia

Tel: 60-3-2072-3255, 2201, 2202
Fax: 60-3-2072-2115

Representative Office in Manila
31st Floor, Citibank Tower
Valero St., corner Villar St.
Makati, Metro Manila, Philippines
Tel: 63-2-848-1828, 63-2-752-5682
Fax: 63-2-848-1833, 1834, 1835

Representative Office in Singapore
9 Raffles Place, #53-01 Republic Plaza
Singapore 048619
Tel: 65-6557-2806
Fax: 65-6557-2807

Representative Office in Colombo
Level 13, Development Holdings 42
Navam Mawatha, Colombo 2, Sri Lanka
Tel: 94-1-300470, 300471, 300472
Fax: 94-1-300473

Representative Office in Dhaka
IDB Bhaban, 15th Floor
E/8-A, Begum Rokeya Sharani
Sher-E-Bangla Nagar Dhaka 1207, Bangladesh
Tel: 880-2-811-4081, 6700
Fax: 880-2-811-3336

Representative Office in Islamabad
5th Floor, Evacuee Trust Complex
Aga Khan Road, F-5/1
Islamabad, Pakistan
Tel: 92-51-2820119
Fax: 92-51-2822546

Representative Office in New Delhi
3rd Floor, DLF Centre
Sansad Marg, New Delhi
110001, India
Tel: 91-11-2371-4362, 4363, 7090, 6200
Fax: 91-11-2371-5066, 2373-8389

Representative Office in Sydney
Suite 2501, Level 25, Gateway
1 Macquarie Place
Sydney, N.S.W. 2000, Australia
Tel: 61-2-9241-1388
Fax: 61-2-9231-1053

Representative Office in Moscow
123610 Moscow
Krasnopresnenskaya Nab. 12
World Trade Center, Office No. 905
Russian Federation
Tel: 7-095-258-1832, 1835, 1836
Fax: 7-095-258-1858

Representative Office in Frankfurt
Taunustor 2,
60311 Frankfurt am Main, Germany
Tel: 49-69-2385770
Fax: 49-69-23857710

Representative Office in London
4th Floor, River Plate House
7-11 Finsbury Circus,
London EC2M 7EX, U.K.
Tel: 44-20-7638-0175
Fax: 44-20-7638-2401

Representative Office in Paris
21, Boulevard de la Madeleine
75038 Paris Cedex 01 France
Tel: 33-1-4703-6190
Fax: 33-1-4703-3236

Representative Office in Cairo
Abu El Feda Bldg, 16th Floor
3 Abu El Feda Street, Zamalek,
Cairo, Egypt
Tel: 20-2-738-3608, 3609
Fax: 20-2-738-3607

Representative Office in Nairobi
6th Floor, International House
Mama Ngina Street, P.O. Box 49526

00100 Nairobi, Kenya
Tel: 254-2-221420, 221637
Fax: 254-2-221569

Representative Office in New York
520 Madison Avenue, 40th Floor
New York, NY 10022
Tel: 212-888-9500, 9501, 9502
Fax: 212-888-9503

Representative Office in Washington, DC
1909 K St., NW, Suite 300
Washington, DC 20006
Tel: 202-785-5242
Fax: 202-785-8484

Representative Office in Bogota
Calle 114 No. 9-45 Torre B, Oficina 601
Teleport Business Park, Bogota, Colombia
Tel: 57-1-629-2436, 2437, 2438
Fax: 57-1-629-2707

Representative Office in Buenos Aires
Av. Del Libertador No. 498, Piso 19
1001
Capital Federal
Buenos Aires, Argentina
Tel: 54-11-4394-1379, 1803
Fax: 54-11-4394-1763

Representative Office in Lima
Av. Canaval Moreyra, No. 380
San Isidro, Lima 27
Peru
Tel: 51-1-442-3031
Fax: 51-1-440-9657

Representative Office in Mexico City
Paseo de la Reforma 265, Piso 16
Col. Cuauhtemoc
Mexico, D.F. 06500
Tel: 52-55-5525-67-90
Fax: 52-55-5525-34-73

Representative Office in Rio de Janeiro
Praia de Botafogo, 228- 801 B
Botafogo, Rio de Janeiro, RJ
CEP 22359-900, Brazil
Tel: 55-21-2553-0817
Fax: 55-21-2554-8798

Toronto Liaison Office
P.O. Box 493
2 First Canadian Place, Suite 3660
Toronto, Ontario, M5X 1E5
Tel: 416-865-1700
Fax: 416-865-0124

KREDITANSTALT FÜR WIEDERAUFBAU (KFW)

I. INTRODUCTION

The Federal Republic of Germany created KfW to distribute
Marshall Plan aid. Today it provides loans to finance investment
goods and related services, primarily in developing countries.
KfW provided EUR 39.7 billion in project and export financing
in 2002. DEG, a subsidiary of KfW, provides long-term corporate
and project finance. DEG has financed EUR 4.2 billion and
worked with nearly 1,000 companies seeking to expand the private sector in developing and transition countries. Although its
services are available to all private sectors of the economy, DEG
focuses on agriculture, manufacturing, infrastructure, and services. In 2001, 57 percent (EUR 1.5 billion) of all commitments
for the promotion of developing countries went to economic and
social infrastructure projects.

II. PRODUCTS

KfW works primarily with enterprises investing in developing
countries, offering project finance in its capacity as a part of
Germany's Official Export Financing Program and also acting as
a development bank. KfW's goal is to promote German investment in transition and developing economies. KfW's export
credit facilities are often used to extend developmental aid to
developing and transition companies.

Development Banking

KfW and its subsidiary, DEG, operate as the German Development Bank. Both entities offer loans, grants, and other financing to projects in developing and transition countries. Terms of loans are dependent upon the economic situation in terms of level of development. Financing is available from the German government and from KfW's commercial account. German budget funds may be offered to keep interest rates lower than the funds from KfW's own account, which place risk on the bank.

Terms

The least-developed countries, with an annual per capita income under USD 699, are eligible to receive grants. In addition, grants are extended to countries for measures aimed at self-help-oriented poverty reduction and the advancement of women, credit guarantee funds for SMEs, social infrastructure projects, and environmental protection projects. Countries above this level but with per capita incomes below USD 1,305 receive loans at IDA conditions. Terms of up to 40 years with a 10-year grace period and an interest rate of 0.75 percent are available. Finally, loans at normal conditions are offered to other developing countries. Terms of 30 years with a 10-year grace period and interest rates of 2 percent are also offered.

KfW will support China in the expansion of the use of renewable energies. Up to 170 villages in the Xinjiang and Yunnan regions will receive photovoltaic systems, making the power supply to these rural areas possible for the first time. KfW is providing approximately EUR 10.2 million for these projects. The funds will be provided from the budget of the German Federal Ministry for Economic Cooperation and Development. The loan agreement in the amount of EUR 5.1 million for the construction of solar energy systems in Yunnan was signed in Frankfurt by KfW and the Chinese Ministry of Finance.

The new solar systems will supply approximately 60,000 people with electricity. Large parts of the remote western provinces of Yunnan and Xinjiang have not been connected to the power grid until now. Both project areas are characterized by high solar radiation, which creates ideal conditions for the use of solar energy. In 1996, the Chinese government launched a program aimed at supplying electricity from renewable energies to regions not yet connected to the grid. The KfW projects will support this program.

Decentralized power generation from solar energy will improve living conditions of villagers in Yunnan and Xinjiang. In the future, these people will have electric light and access to information media. This power supply will also benefit village schools and rural health stations. Moreover, by supporting environment-friendly power generation, KfW contributes to the protection of the environment and natural resources in China.

Project Finance

Loans are granted for investment projects to economic entities that can produce their own profits. These loans are granted only to companies created for the specific purpose of carrying out the project. Insurance from Hermes under Germany's Official Export Insurance Scheme is available and strongly encouraged. KfW strongly encourages public-private partnerships in infrastructure projects, reducing pressure on state budgets while producing the needed groundwork for later growth. Specifically, KfW supports transportation and energy projects, among others. In addition to projects tied to Germany through exports or involvement of German corporations, KfW supports projects that are of German or European interest through its Untied Loans program.

Terms

Only projects with economic viability and technical potential are financed. Project finance is intended primarily for large-scale investment projects. Terms vary widely relative to the scale of the project. Basic agreements have been concluded with many foreign banks and buyers stating the general conditions of the financing, such as loan amount and terms of repayment.

Equity

KfW does not directly invest in any firm. Instead, it extends financing to investors of equity who use the funds to invest in an enterprise. Equity investment companies typically apply directly to KfW, though special circumstances may require them to file their application with a credit institution. Individuals and enterprises wishing to invest in another enterprise seeking KfW funding are encouraged to file their application with a bank of their choice.

Development Cooperation

Under this program, KfW provides financing for projects that help to expand social, economic, and industrial infrastructure and environmental protection in developing nations. In addition to financing, KfW also provides the expertise necessary to implement the projects.

Terms

To be eligible, applications must be submitted from a self-employed professional in Germany or by an enterprise that must reside and conduct business in Germany.

III. ELIGIBILITY AND APPLICATION PROCESS

To apply for funding, applicants must establish creditworthiness and security of the project and submit an application. KfW recommends that interested enterprises contact the closest office before submitting an application. Once received, the application is reviewed for eligibility. Applications should include the following information:

- Description of the planned project
- Copy of the pre-feasibility study or comparable preparatory study
- Estimated cost and financing information to include profitability and major risks
- Developmental impacts on host country
- Terms of reference
- Information on selected consultants
- Information on award of contract for subsequent project
- Financial situation of applicant

IV. CONTACTS

Headquarters:
Kreditanstalt für Wiederaufbau
Postfach 11 11 41
D-60046 Frankfurt
Germany
Tel: 49 (69) 74 310
Fax: 49 (69) 74 31 29 44
Internet: www.kfw.de
Email: kfw.asa@kfw.de

Berlin Branch
Charlottenstrasse 33/33a
10117 Berlin
Tel: 49 (0) 30 2 02 64-0
Fax: 49 (0) 30 2 02 64-5188

China
KfW Office Beijing
1170, Beijing Sunflower Tower
No. 37, Maizidian Street
Chaoyang District
Beijing 100026
Dr. Karl-Joachim Trede, Director
Tel: 86 (10) 85 27 51 71-3
Fax: 86 (10) 85 27 51 75
Email: kfwbeij@public3.bta.net.cn

India
KfW Office New Delhi
21, Jor Bagh
New Delhi 110003
Andrea Johnston, Director
Tel: 91 (11) 4 64 12 02, 71 13
Fax: 91 (11) 4 64 12 03
Email: kfwindia@vsnl.com

NORDIC DEVELOPMENT FUND (NDF)

I. INTRODUCTION

NDF was established in 1989 to promote economic and social development in developing countries by financing projects of interest to the five Nordic countries of Denmark, Finland, Iceland, Norway, and Sweden. NDF also provides financial support to private sector activities having an interest in the Nordic region. NDF only grants credits that are co-financed with other sources of funding—primarily other multilateral financial institutions such as the WBG and the major regional development banks. Co-financing is also undertaken with the NIB and with Nordic bilateral development assistance agencies. According to the agreement regarding the establishment of NDF, a project must be of Nordic interest to be considered for financing.

II. PRODUCTS AND SERVICES

NDF supports private sector development in cooperation with Nordic companies, Nordic/regional/international development institutions, and local partners. NDF provides the following finance instruments:

- Participation in joint ventures through extension of subordinated loans with equity features—priority is given to infrastructure projects with private sponsors in cooperation with the public sector, including privatizations
- Credit lines to subregional and national development banks for lending with focus on support to SMEs
- Participation as a shareholder in venture capital funds, extending financing to promote private and financial sector development

III. ELIGIBILITY AND APPLICATION PROCESS

To be eligible for NDF assistance, a project must have a Nordic interest to be considered. NDF only grants credits that are co-financed with other sources of funding. For information on how to apply, contact NDF headquarters directly.

IV. CONTACTS

Headquarters:
Nordic Development Fund
Fabianinkatu 34
P.O. Box 185
FIN-00171 Helsinki
Finland
Tel: 358 9 1800451
Fax: 358 9 622 1491
Internet: www.ndf.fi
Email: info@ndf.fi

NORDIC INVESTMENT BANK (NIB)

I. INTRODUCTION

The NIB operates primarily in the Nordic countries, along with the Baltic States, Poland, and northwest Russia. Although the bank focuses on this region, its products are available to projects in developing and OECD countries alike. Representing Denmark, Finland, Iceland, Norway, and Sweden, the NIB has financed over 1,000 projects since 1976, focusing on investment in energy, infrastructure, and research and development. The bank's primary mission is to promote growth in the Nordic economies through long-term financing of projects in the public and private sectors. NIB finances projects of interest to the Nordic countries and the borrower countries and will cooperate with or supplement other Nordic or international financiers. A secondary purpose of the bank is to act as a catalyst for cooperation between the Nordic countries.

II. PRODUCTS

NIB services are available worldwide, but investment is in the Nordic countries and adjacent areas. The bank focuses on assisting transition economies bordering the Nordic countries; being involved in infrastructure, energy, and environmental projects throughout Europe; and enhancing cooperation in the European Economic Area.

Nordic Loans

NIB grants loans within the Nordic countries across many sectors. Manufacturing, infrastructure, environmental, and research and development projects are financed most often; NIB is also involved in foreign investment in the Nordic countries. Loans for acquisitions, mergers, and expansion are offered within one country and across borders. Nearly 80 percent of NIB's lending is within the Nordic countries.

Terms

Nordic loans are medium to long term, with repayment made over 5–15 years. The loans are granted in most exchangeable currencies, with interest rates at fixed or variable commercial rates.

International Loans

Most international loans are project investment loans (PILs) used in projects that improve the environment or infrastructure or that foster economic development. Funds can be used to pay any project costs, including local costs. NIB offers loans in the OECD countries for investment, acquisitions, and joint ventures. PILs make up over 20 percent of the bank's lending.

Terms

These loans are long term and are available in most exchangeable currencies. Repayment periods are generally 10–15 years, and each loan is accompanied by as much as a 90 percent guarantee from the NIB's member countries. Most international lending is on a sovereign basis, but is sometimes offered without a government guarantee. Loans without a guarantee are generally used for private sector infrastructure projects.

Neighboring Loans

For countries in the neighboring Nordic region, NIB provides loans for projects that promote economic development of environmental improvement. Environmental protection loans are granted to projects in bordering countries in the public and private sector that prevent environmental degradation and cross-border pollution.

NIB committed a EUR 60 million (USD 59.5 million) loan to the state-owned Estonian energy company AS Eesti Energia to modernize power plants and ensure compliance with a bilateral environmental agreement with Finland. AS Eesti Energia plans to invest EUR 762 million (USD 755.1 million) from 2002 to 2006 to accomplish these goals, and EUR 150 million (USD 148.7 million) in financing has been secured from NIB and Germany's KfW. The package is one of the largest ever carried out in the Baltic region without a state guarantee and will ensure the company's competitiveness as well as improve the environment.

III. ELIGIBILITY AND APPLICATION PROCESS

Although the majority of projects are located in Nordic countries, NIB will consider any project that serves one of the following objectives:

- Promotes economic integration as well as environmental and infrastructural improvement within the Nordic region
- Contributes to the transition and economic development in the areas adjacent to the Nordic region, particularly in the field of environmental and infrastructural improvement
- Strengthens economic cooperation between countries outside of the Nordic region and the Nordic countries

For application information, contact the nearest NIB office directly.

IV. CONTACTS

Nordic Investment Bank Headquarters:
Fabianinkatu 34
P.O. Box 249
FIN-00171 Helsinki
Finland
Tel: 358 (9) 18-001
Fax: 358 (9) 1800-210
Internet: www.nibank.org
Email: info@nib.int

Denmark
Landgreven 4
DK-1301 Copenhagen K
Denmark
Tel: 45 (33) 144-242
Fax: 45 (33) 322-676

Norway
Dronning Mauds gate 15
N-0119 Oslo
Norway
Tel: 47 2201-2201
Fax: 47 2201-2202

Iceland
Kalkofnsvegur 1
IS-150 Reykjavík
Iceland
Tel: 354 (5) 699-996
Fax: 354 (5) 629-982

Sweden
Kungsträdgårdsgatan 10
P.O. Box 1721
S-111 35 Stockholm
Sweden
Tel: 46 (8) 5662-6590
Fax: 46 (8) 5662-6591

Singapore
Regional Representative Office
78 Shenton Way #16-03
Singapore 079120
Tel: 65 6227-6355
Fax: 65 6227-6455

OVERSEAS PRIVATE INVESTMENT CORPORATION (OPIC)

I. INTRODUCTION

OPIC was established in 1971 by the U.S. government to provide
services exclusively to U.S. businesses looking to expand into foreign countries and emerging markets. OPIC contributes substantially to the national and foreign policy interests of U.S. citizens
and works to strengthen and expand the U.S. economy by
improving U.S. competitiveness in the international marketplace.
OPIC also helps less-developed nations expand their economies
and become valuable markets for U.S. goods and services,
thereby increasing U.S. exports and creating U.S. jobs.

OPIC offers up to USD 400 million in total project support for
any one project, up to USD 250 million in project finance, and
up to USD 250 million in political risk insurance. OPIC covers
U.S. private investment in over 140 countries and across the
world and insures not only new investments, but also expansions
and modernizations. OPIC supports business projects in virtually
every industry and economic sector including agriculture,
energy, construction, natural resources, telecommunications,
transportation and distribution, banking, and services, among
others.

Since its founding, OPIC has supported USD 138 billion worth
of investments, generating USD 63.6 billion in U.S. exports and
creating nearly 250,000 U.S. jobs. OPIC projects have also helped

developing countries generate over USD 10 billion in host-government revenues and create nearly 673,000 host-country jobs. OPIC's profit in 2000 stood at USD 185 million, its reserves currently stand at more than USD 4 billion, and all guarantee and insurance obligations are backed by the full faith and credit of the United States.

II. PRODUCTS

OPIC assists U.S. investors by providing financing, insurance, and investments. All programs are designed to mitigate the risks associated with overseas investment.

Financing

OPIC provides financing through direct loans and loan guaranties that provide medium- to long-term funding to ventures involving significant equity or management participation by U.S. businesses.

- *Direct loans* are reserved for projects involving U.S. small businesses and cooperatives and generally range from USD 2 million to USD 30 million. OPIC carefully analyzes the economic, technical, marketing, and financial soundness of each project. There must be adequate cash flow to pay all operational costs, to service all debt, and to provide the owners with an adequate return on their investment.
- *Loan guarantees* are typically used for larger projects, ranging in size from USD 10 million to USD 250 million.

A $900,000 direct loan to a U.S.-owned small business in Guatemala, Jades S.A., is supporting the expansion of a jade processing and retail jewelry company. Jades trains its Guatemalan employees in various aspects of jewelry production and creates incremental employment through a growing "cottage industry" network of related jewelers and carpenters. Since OPIC first began supporting this project in 1992, Jades has added four new stores in Guatemala and Honduras.

OPIC can also provide financing on a project-finance or a corporate-finance basis. Rather than relying on sovereign or sponsor guaranties, project finance looks for repayment from the cash flows generated by projects. Therefore, OPIC carefully analyzes the economic, technical, marketing, and financial soundness of each project. There must be adequate cash flow to pay all operational costs, service all debt, and provide the owners or sponsors with an adequate return on their investments.

- *Project finance loans* can be extended to special-purpose companies with limited recourse to the project equity sponsor. This medium- to long-term financing is available only to projects that demonstrate stand-alone economic viability and that are substantially owned and managed by U.S. business partners. OPIC can support new investments and privatizations, as well as expansions and modernizations of existing plants sponsored by U.S. investors. The minimum amount for a project finance-style loan is generally USD 100,000, although OPIC has historically supported small businesses with loans over USD 1 million. Guarantees are available up to USD 250 million. To the extent that project financing is appropriate, sponsors need not pledge their own general credit beyond the required completion undertakings.
- *Corporate finance loans* are available to U.S. small- or medium-sized businesses or the overseas subsidiaries of such businesses. These loans are available to fund overseas investment, including permanent working capital, fixed assets, and expansion of facilities. Corporate finance looks to the credit of an existing corporate entity other than the project company to support debt repayment.
- *Small business center loans* help America's small businesses compete in the global marketplace. OPIC, together with the Small Business Administration (SBA) recently launched this initiative in order to increase opportunities for U.S. small businesses to expand into dynamic emerging markets. One value-added function of this product is that applications will be processed within a 60-day period. Any small business with annual revenues less than USD 35 million will be eligible. Loan amounts for overseas investments range from USD 100,000 to USD 10 million, with terms of 3–15 years.

OPIC also offers other specialized loan programs.

- *Hybrid loans* combine elements of corporate finance and project finance. They use cash flow and collateral from the domestic parent company and the project company to craft an acceptable loan structure. Hybrid finance structures can be more costly than corporate finance structures. However, in many cases, the domestic sponsor may already have pledged its assets to its existing bank. OPIC may see value in the cash flow and collateral overseas that is not seen by a local U.S. bank, being sufficiently comfortable to consider the transaction.

OPIC, along with the U.S. Export-Import Bank, co-financed the USD 1.3 billion Jorf Lasfar Energy Company power generating project to privatize and expand the state-owned Jorf Lasfar power plant near Casablanca, Morocco. Sponsored by CMS Generation Company of Michigan and its partner ABB Energy Ventures, OPIC committed USD 200 million in financing and USD 200 million in insurance to the venture, which is Africa's biggest independent power project and limited-recourse financing to date. The Jorf Lasfar facility not only provides Morocco with 1.32 gigawatts of electrical power, but also generates tax revenue, provides jobs, and creates many sales opportunities for local and U.S. companies. The project is expected to use USD 644 million in U.S. goods and services and create more than 1,600 U.S. jobs. Because of the economic benefits in the United States and Morocco and because of the electricity need this project will meet, *Project Finance* magazine gave Jorf Lasfar its project of the year award in 1996.

- *Franchise loans* require the franchise or project to be at least 25 percent U.S.-owned. The loans must also be financially sound, foster private initiative and competition in the host country, and promise significant benefits to the social and economic development of the host country. Also, personal guarantees from franchise owners are required for all loans. Loan amounts should not exceed USD 4 million, and loans over USD 1.5 million should result in an operation with at least five units. Maximum loan amount is USD 4 million; minimum loan amount is USD 100,000.

Insurance

Insurance is available for investments in new ventures, expansions of existing enterprises, privatizations, or acquisitions with positive developmental benefits. Coverage is available for capital market investors, equity investments, parent company and third-party loans and loan guaranties, technical assistance agreements, cross-border leases, consigned inventory or equipment, and other forms of investment. Coverage is also available for contractors' and exporters' exposures (including certain breaches of contractual dispute resolution mechanisms and wrongful calling of bid, performance, advance payment, and other guaranties posted in favor of foreign buyers) and other risks.

- *Political risk insurance* protects U.S. companies against the following: (1) currency inconvertibility—inability to convert profits, debt service, and other returns from local currency into U.S. dollars and to transfer those dollars out of the host country; (2) expropriation—loss of an investment due to expropriation, nationalization, or confiscation by a foreign government; and (3) political violence—loss of assets or income due to war, revolution, insurrection, or politically motivated civil strife, terrorism, or sabotage. OPIC provides political risk insurance to U.S. investors, contractors, exporters, and financial institutions involved in international transactions.

In 1988, a U.S. company made an investment in a Liberian subsidiary to operate a rubber plantation. During the Liberian civil war, the subsidiary's property was seized by rebels and then damaged and destroyed by general military activities. OPIC found the claim to be valid and compensated the investor.

- *Equity investment coverage* is available for equity investments in new ventures or expansions or modernizations of existing enterprises, parent company and third-party loans and loan guaranties, technical assistance agreements, cross-border leases, and other forms of investment exposure.
- *Small Business Center (SBC) political risk protection* offers protection for small business' overseas investment against political uncertainties. The SBC provides insurance against loss or damage resulting from political violence, such as terrorism or war, nationalization or expropriation by a foreign government, or the inability to convert local currency and repatriate profits. One value-added function of this product is that applications will be processed within a 60-day period. Interest rates are fixed and based upon the nature of the risk, and terms extend up to 20 years and generally offer up to USD 15 million in coverage. Any U.S. small business with annual revenues less than USD 35 million is eligible for coverage.

OPIC also provides special insurance programs for the following:

- Equity protection
- Financial institutions
- Oil and gas
- Natural resources (other than oil and gas)

- Technical assistance
- Contractor and exporters
- Capital markets

Funds Program

OPIC has supported the creation of privately owned, privately managed investment funds that make direct equity and equity-related investments in new, expanding, or privatizing companies. By providing long-term, patient growth capital and facilitating critically needed technology and management skills development, these funds act as a catalyst for private sector economic activity in the developing countries served.

These funds have invested in more than 300 business projects in over 40 countries around the world and play a critical role in providing capital, technical know-how, and management assistance in important emerging markets. The funds are structured, like all OPIC programs, to be self-sustaining. As of March 31, 2001, the Investment Funds Program supported 27 funds by committing USD 2.3 million in direct loans or loan guarantees. (This figure includes only OPIC loans and loan guarantees.) These funds have invested USD 2.1 billion in 370 businesses in 48 countries, with an average investment size of USD 5.7 million per company.

The direct equity investments of OPIC-supported funds complement OPIC's insurance and project finance activities. By supplementing the capital of funds that are privately financed and managed by experienced private investment professionals, OPIC can help profit-oriented enterprises in the emerging markets access risk capital, management guidance, and financial expertise.

III. ELIGIBILITY AND APPLICATION PROCESS

Financing

OPIC finances investment projects with substantial U.S. participation that are commercially and financially sound, that promise significant benefits to the social and economic development of the host country, and that foster private initiative and competition. OPIC does not support projects that result in the loss of U.S. jobs, that adversely affect the U.S. economy or the host country's development or environment, or that contribute to violations of internationally recognized worker rights.

All projects or transactions considered for OPIC financing must be commercially and financially sound. They must be within the demonstrated competence of the proposed management, which must have a proven record of success in the same or a closely related business, as well as a significant continuing financial risk in the enterprise. OPIC's criteria are the same whether it is making a direct loan or issuing a loan guaranty.

Potential project sponsors interested in obtaining financing should provide OPIC with the following:

- Form 115—Application for Financing
- Detailed business plan of the project
- Identity, background, and audited financial statements of the project's proposed principal owners and management
- Planned sources of supply, anticipated output and markets, distribution channels, competition, and the basis for projecting market share
- Summary of project costs and sources of procurement of capital goods and services
- Proposed financing plan, including the amount of proposed OPIC participation and financial projections
- Pro forma financial statements of the proposed project
- Brief statement of the contribution the business is expected to make to local economic and social development

Form 115 as well as a helpful supplemental guide, are available online through OPIC's web site. OPIC encourages applicants to fax or send the application via overnight mail to avoid unnecessary delays.

Insurance

OPIC insurance is available to citizens of the United States; corporations, partnerships, or other associations created under the laws of the United States, its states, or territories that are beneficially owned by U.S. citizens; foreign corporations at least 95 percent owned by investors eligible under the above criteria; and other foreign entities that are 100 percent U.S. owned.

To apply, investors must register projects with OPIC before the investment has been made or irrevocably committed. Registration is free of charge and, to the extent permitted by law, treated as confidential business information. To register, an investor must submit Form 50—Request for Registration for Political Risk Insurance. Upon receipt of Form 50, OPIC will send a confirmation letter and application forms. A registration is valid for two years and may be renewed in 1-year increments. Registration of a project is not binding and in no way constitutes a commitment to issue insurance, nor does it indicate that OPIC's eligibility criteria have been met. Finally, the appropriate insurance application form must be completed and submitted. All forms are available on OPIC's web site.

Funds Program

Each investment by a fund must meet OPIC's statutory and policy requirements, including respecting impacts on the U.S. economy and employment, the environment, and worker rights. Project sponsors seeking long-term growth capital for projects potentially of interest to an OPIC-supported fund should approach the appropriate fund directly.

OPIC's guarantee, backed by the full faith and credit of the United States, may be applied only to the debt portion of the fund's capital. OPIC-guaranteed debt must be held by "eligible investors" as defined in OPIC's governing statute. In general, eligible investors include: U.S. citizens; U.S. corporations, partnerships, and other organizations that are more than 50 percent beneficially owned by U.S. citizens; and foreign entities wholly owned by U.S. citizens. OPIC does not offer any guarantee of the fund's equity, and all equity investments in OPIC-supported funds are fully at risk and subordinate to any OPIC lending or guaranteed debt.

OPIC does not participate in investment decisions made by the fund. However, each proposed fund investment must be submitted to OPIC for review to determine whether such an investment is consistent with OPIC's statutory and policy criteria and the terms of the financing.

Those interested in this type of funding should contact the specific fund directly. A list of these funds is available on OPIC's web site.

IV. CONTACTS

Headquarters:
Overseas Private Investment Corporation
1100 New York Avenue, NW
Washington, DC 20527
Tel: (202) 336-8400
Fax: (202) 408-9859
Internet: www.opic.gov
Email: info@opic.gov

SOCIETA ITALIANA PER LE IMPRESE ALL'ESTERO (SIMEST)

I. INTRODUCTION

SIMEST was created by the Italian Ministry of Foreign Trade in 1991 to support Italian entrepreneurs in all aspects of international business. In 1998, SIMEST's services were broadened to provide financial resources to Italian companies operating in foreign markets. As a member of the EDFI, SIMEST has an extensive network of information and contacts to assist Italian businesses with international operations.

II. PRODUCTS AND SERVICES

In January 1999, SIMEST began administering financial support for exports and international projects. This consists of providing interest rate support for export credits and loans for direct investments in foreign firms, as well as granting supported loans for market penetration programs, participation in international tenders and pre-feasibility and feasibility studies, and technical assistance programs.

Financing

- *Loans* are granted to exporters of goods and services outside the EU. These programs may include the establishment of permanent branch offices abroad, of sales and customer services networks, and of specific promotions outlets (market research and advertising). The majority of these loans are granted to SMEs. The interest rate is equal to 40 percent of the reference export rate, and the amount can be up to 85 percent of the planned expenditure, not to exceed EUR 2 million. In 2001, 156 loans were granted for a total of EUR 175.2 million. Loan duration does not exceed a maximum duration of 7 years, including a pre-amortization period of no more than 2 years.
- *International tenders* support the participation of Italian companies in international tenders in non-EU countries. Total financing may not exceed EUR 1 million per company and EUR 2.6 million for each international tender and will vary according to the value of tenders. Financing has a maturity of up to 4 years, including a pre-amortization period of no more than 18 months.

- *Technical assistance financing* covers expenses related to technical assistance programs linked to Italian exports or investments in non-EU countries. Financing covers 100 percent of the outside estimate to a ceiling not higher than EUR 516,000. The maximum duration of the financing is up to 4 years, including a pre-amortization period of 1 year.
- *Pre-feasibility and feasibility study financing linked to BOT projects* finances the expenses linked to the award of a work order in non-EU countries for BOT projects. Financing covers up to 50 percent of the outside estimate to a ceiling not higher than EUR 361,000. The maximum duration of the financing is 3 1/2 years, including a pre-amortization period of 6 months.
- *Feasibility study of financing linked to Italian exports or investments abroad* covers 100 percent of the outside estimate to a ceiling not higher than EUR 361,000. The maximum duration of the financing is 3 1/2 years, including a pre-amortization period of 6 months.

Interest Rate Support

- *Foreign direct investment incentives* are designed to assist Italian companies in buying shares in SIMEST holdings in non-EU countries. Incentives take the form of an interest subsidy on loans. Support is equal to 50 percent of the reference rate for the industrial sector. Up to 90 percent of the equity capital required in foreign companies with an upper limit equal to 51 percent of the investee company's total capital is eligible. Loan duration does not exceed 8 years, including a pre-amortization period of no more than 3 years.
- *Export incentives* allow Italian businesses to supply foreign buyers with machinery, plants, and related services with deferred medium- or long-term payments on competitive terms in line with those offered by other EU and OECD exporters. Support is offered as an interest subsidy or stabilization for export credit loans and covers the difference between the market rate demanded by the lending bank and the subsidized rate (established by international agreements) charged to the foreign buyer.

Export Credit

SIMEST support is offered to firms producing capital goods and provides them access to instruments serving to neutralize the effects on the competitiveness of Italian exports of similar mechanisms employed by the ECAs of other countries.

- *Supplier credit* is intended to isolate foreign customers from the risk of interest rate movements by allowing them to obtain medium- or long-term financing at the fixed rates set by the OECD. Supplier credit is also intended to enable exporters to use a financial instrument, discounting without recourse or forfeiting, which allows them to hedge credit risks at a cost comparable to that of products typical of other ECAs.
- *Buyer credit* provides the stabilization of the interest rate on large syndicated loans (more than EUR 10 million) with an average repayment term of more than 7 years.

Equity Investment

SIMEST is willing to buy shares worth up to 25 percent of the capital stock of foreign countries whether Italian-controlled or joint ventures, assume quotas of foreign investments, and finance foreign shareholdings or form financing pools with merchant banks and/or multilateral finance institutions. SIMEST is also willing to buy shares in Italian or foreign companies that promote and develop commercial and industrial projects abroad and facilitate access to international and supranational financing and internationalization programs.

A venture capital fund has been endowed with EUR 10.3 million by the Ministry for Productive Activities to be used to support Italian SMEs that acquire equity interests in joint ventures that have been or are to be set up in the Federal Republic of Yugoslavia with the participation of SIMEST and/or FINEST. This fund acquires additional equity interests up to 25 percent of the capital of such ventures, with a limit of EUR 258,000 for each investment.

III. ELIGIBILITY AND APPLICATION PROCESS

Contact company headquarters for more information.

IV. CONTACTS

Headquarters:
SIMEST
Corso Vittorio Emanuele II, n. 323
00186 Rome
Italy
Tel: 3906 686351
Fax: 3906 68635220
Internet: www.simest.it
Email: info@simest.it

Business Relations
Tel: 3906 68635399/68635351
Fax: 3906 68635401

SWEDFUND INTERNATIONAL AB (SWEDFUND)

I. INTRODUCTION

Swedfund is an investment banking institution offering risk capital and assistance for investments through a variety of financial solutions. The fund's primary objective is to help create profitable companies to stimulate economic growth. Services are offered primarily to Swedish companies looking to invest in Africa, Asia, Latin America, and Central and Eastern Europe. Although Swedfund may be willing to invest in any developing country, its focus tends to be on countries with a per capita GNP of less than USD 3,000 per year. Investments are made in most industries, excluding companies manufacturing or distributing weapons, tobacco, or alcohol.

Swedfund has made over 150 investments in 50 countries. Typical investments range from SEK 1 million (approximately USD 118,000) to SEK 50 million depending on project size. Swedfund is willing to accept no more than the same level of risk as its Swedish partners, providing a maximum of 30 percent of the total investment capital required.

II. PRODUCTS

Loans and Guarantees

Swedfund has access to an important network of local and international financing bodies, thereby providing companies with access to potential co-financiers. Some of the products Swedfund offers include ordinary shares, preference shares, leasing, loan guarantees, participating loans, subordinating loans, and secured loans.

Investment Capital

Swedfund may become a shareholder in investment or venture capital funds in developing countries and in Eastern Europe. These funds are often co-owned with other international or local financial institutions and companies and have a specially appointed fund manager. They provide venture capital—generally in the form of equity—to local companies in one or several countries.

When an investee company has achieved a sustainable and profitable operation, Swedfund will sell its shares in the joint venture company. The rules for and timing of exits are established at the outset in the shareholders' agreement. Swedfund sees its financial commitment to a company in a long-term perspective, adopting an investment horizon of 5–10 years. Projects co-financed by Swedfund must meet the requirements of Swedfund's environmental policy, as well as the World Bank's environmental guidelines.

III. ELIGIBILITY AND APPLICATION PROCESS

To apply for assistance, interested companies must submit a preliminary investment proposal, which includes the following:

- Description of the Swedish and local partners, including experience, current activities, financial strength and proposed financial contribution, and exposure
- Description of the project to include background, products, market, technology, raw materials, organization, management, and so on
- Preliminary investment and financing plan, including preliminary profitability projections for the project

Once a proposal is submitted, Swedfund will review it and contact the interested party to discuss its decision.

IV. CONTACTS

Headquarters:
Swedfund International AB
Sveavägen 24-26
Stockholm, Sweden
Tel: 46 8 725 94 00
Fax: 46 8 20 30 93
Internet: www.swedfund.se
Email: info@swedfund.se

Olle Arefalk, Managing Director
Tel: 46 8 725 94 07
Email: olle.arefalk@swedfund.se

Kurt Karlsson, Director, Investment Operations
Tel: 46 8 725 94 11
Email: kurt.karlsson@swedfund.se

Elisabeth Mattisson, Director, Finance and Administration
Tel: 46 8 725 94 04
Email: elisabeth.mattisson@swedfund.se

UNITED STATES AGENCY FOR INTERNATIONAL DEVELOPMENT (USAID)

I. INTRODUCTION

USAID is an independent federal government agency. Its history dates back to the Marshall Plan for Europe after WWII and the Truman Administration's Point Four Program. In 1961, President John F. Kennedy signed the Foreign Assistance Act into law and created USAID by executive order. For almost half a century, USAID has been the principal U.S. agency extending assistance to countries recovering from disaster, trying to escape poverty, and engaging in democratic reforms. The agency receives foreign policy guidance from the Secretary of State. Its goals are to support long-term and equitable economic growth and advance U.S. foreign policy objectives by promoting economic growth, agriculture, and trade; global health; and democracy, conflict prevention, and humanitarian assistance.

USAID is recognized as a leading development agency, based in part on such strengths as technical expertise, extensive field presence, and strong working relationships with host country governments and local and international institutions.

Through a variety of contracts, USAID offers goods and services necessary for the agency's operation. The Federal Acquisition Regulations (FAR), the USAID Acquisition Regulations (AIDAR), and the USAID Automated Directive System (ADS) govern the acquisitions.

Certain programs are implemented under the objective of the Foreign Assistance Act to contribute to the public good, where a transfer of funds (or other valuables) from USAID to another party takes place. Only warranted contracting/agreement officers in Washington and overseas have the authority to sign procurement and assistance instruments.

USAID maintains close partnerships with private voluntary organizations, indigenous organizations, universities, U.S. businesses, international agencies, other governments, and other U.S. government agencies. Overall, USAID has working relationships with more than 3,500 U.S. companies and over 300 U.S.-based private voluntary organizations.

USAID focuses on the following four regions:

- Sub-Saharan Africa
- Asia and the Near East
- Latin America and the Caribbean
- Europe and Eurasia

II. PRODUCTS

USAID employs acquisition and assistance mechanisms. Contracts, grants, cooperative agreements, and purchase orders are some of the instruments provided.

Grants

Grants, in whole or in part, are allocated for the program of a non-governmental organization (NGO), university, or institution with a stated purpose of enhancing the public good. The beneficiaries acknowledge the responsibility for achieving program objectives.

The Office of American Schools and Hospitals Abroad (ASHA) establishes grants for selected private, nonprofit universities and secondary schools, libraries, and medical centers abroad. ASHA has a record of assisting about 194 institutions in over 60 countries and facilitating the development and sustainability of libraries, schools, and medical centers. Its office currently manages a worldwide portfolio of over 100 grants and continues to award approximately 25 new grants every year.

Cooperative Agreements

A cooperative agreement in many aspects is identical to the provision of a grant; however, it requires greater involvement by USAID. Essential prerequisites include approval of annual work plans, designation of key positions and approval of key personnel, and USAID approval of monitoring and evaluation plans.

Terms

While for-profit firms are eligible for grants and cooperative agreements, USAID's policy is not to pay a fee or profit under such assistance instruments.

Technical Assistance

The Office of Transition Initiatives (OTI) aims to foster peace and democracy by distributing information, knowledge, and technology. The U.S. government has benefited from creative tools for bringing peace-building ideas to life, which OTI has developed by working in over 20 countries.

In April 2001, the Office of U.S. Foreign Disaster Assistance (USAID/OFDA) sent a team to Afghanistan to assess a destructive 3-year famine and to work on response strategies. During fiscal year 2001, USD 12.6 million was distributed as relief assistance to Afghans living in Afghanistan as well as in Pakistan. By trying to aid villagers and people forced to move to camps, USAID/OFDA wanted to eliminate further displacement. Those efforts were supported by the 2001 U.S. government humanitarian program, which totaled USD 178.7 million.

III. ELIGIBILITY AND APPLICATION PROCESS

Eligibility for USAID programs is based on the following:

1. Integrated packages of assistance are extended to sustainable development countries. The strategy and other provisions of the package are tailored to the specifics of the contracting country.
2. Private sector enterprises are in countries with minimum USAID presence, but where funding is necessary to promote civic society's growth and help in financial hardship.
3. Transitional countries having undergone a national crisis, a political transition, or a natural disaster and/or have an urgent need for assistance.

Policy on Competition Requirements: Assistance requirements can be found in the Annual Program Statements (APS) or the Requests for Applications (RFA). Postings are made available on the Internet unless special circumstances apply. In such cases, notice is made available in local publications including Mission Bulletin Boards. Competition for grants and cooperative agreements is closed and decided upon after an impartial review and evaluation of all applications.

IV. CONTACTS

Headquarters:
U.S. Agency for International Development
Information Center
Ronald Reagan Building
Washington, DC 20523-1000
Tel: (202) 712-4810
Fax: (202) 216-3524
Internet: www.usaid.gov

USAID Office of Procurement
Ronald Reagan Building
Washington, DC 20523
Tel: (202) 712-5130
Fax: (202) 216-3395
Email: AandAOmbudsman@usaid.gov

USAID Office of the Inspector General
P.O. Box 657
Washington, DC 20044-0657
Tel: 800-230-6539
Tel: (202) 712-1023
Email: ig.hotline@usaid.gov

USAID Office of Press Relations
Ronald Reagan Building
Washington, DC 20523-0016
Tel: (202) 712-4320
Fax: (202) 216-3524

Regional DFIs—MDFIs Supporting Member Country Development

This chapter covers the subset of DFIs that are multilateral organizations whose mission it is to support development by participating in projects in member countries. Often the membership base of these particular DFIs includes a combination of developed capital-providing countries and developing recipient countries as well as other DFIs. Initial capital is often provided by membership institutions who sit on voting boards, with a goal toward maintaining high credit ratings (A+ and above) so future funding requirements can be met through global debt issuance. Increasingly, these DFIs are involved in providing capital to local financial institutions so their reach can be broader.

ASIAN DEVELOPMENT BANK (ADB)

I. INTRODUCTION

ADB is a multilateral development finance institution dedicated to the reduction of poverty in Asia and the Pacific. ADB was established in 1966 and now has 59 members, 43 of which are in the region. To achieve its objectives, ADB provides different types of financial assistance to its developing member countries (DMCs). ADB provides assistance in the form of loans, technical assistance, grants, guarantees, and equity investments. ADB is headquartered in Manila and has 22 other offices around the world.

ADB actively provides support to the public sector. Lending in this sector amounted to more than USD 5.3 billion for 57 projects. USD 3.9 billion was provided from ordinary capital resources (OCRs) and USD 1.4 billion was provided from the Asian Development Fund (ADF). OCR loans are granted to

DMCs with higher economic development, whereas ADF loans are granted to DMCs with low average per-capita incomes and limited ability for the repayment of debt.

ADB is also involved in the private sector. ADB believes that through sustained growth in the private sector, poverty is reduced through increased jobs, investment, and a tax base. Within the ADB, the Private Sector Operations Department (PSOD) is in charge of all private sector operations. Additionally, ADB set up a venture capital firm called the Asian Finance and Investment Corporation (AFIC) to finance private sector enterprises in the bank's DMCs. AFIC concentrates on medium-sized industrial projects across a wide range of DMCs.

II. PRODUCTS

Loans and Guarantees

ADB supports private enterprises and financial institutions through hard currency loans without government guarantees. Loans usually have a level amortization with a grace period of 2–3 years. Fees for ADB floating rate loans typically include a once-only front-end fee of 1 to 1.5 percent of the loan amount and a commitment fee of 0.5 to 0.75 percent per year on the undisbursed amount. The interest rate and other terms of nonsovereign ADB loans vary depending on the risk and needs of the specific project. Factoring in country and project risks, interest rates are in line with the market rate for the given country and sector.

ADB also utilizes funds from ECAs, commercial financial institutions, and official funding agencies for their co-financing operations. Commercial co-financing of the private sector is provided as follows:

- Uncovered parallel loans are usually provided through bilateral institutions and international commercial leaders.
- With complementary financing schemes (CFS), ADB is a direct participant in the project and acts as a "lender of accord."
- Guarantees are divided into two types. Partial credit guarantees cover political and commercial risks, usually for long-term funds. Political risk guarantees cover political risks that may include breach of contract, expropriation, nontransfer of currency, and political violence.
- Export credit agency financing is available through direct loans or from commercial bank loans insured/guaranteed by ECAs.

Projects in which ADB is a direct participant are eligible for CFS loans. ADB acts as a "lender of record" and provides the administration services. CFS loans differ from direct loans in that co-financiers cannot use ADB as a debt service. Direct and CFS loans enjoy the privileges and immunities of being exempt from withholding taxes and restrictions on payment. Additionally, both loans share ADB's preferred creditor status, including enhanced coverage against sovereign risk. Credit analysis and due diligence of a CFS loan are facilitated through access to ADB's project appraisal and loan documentation. CFS loans also enjoy the privilege of bank regulatory authorities in the co-financier's home country, reducing the provisioning requirements on "lender of record" loans in most cases.

Loans from ADB combined with a CFS loan may be covered under a single loan agreement. ADB believes that all senior lenders to a project, including co-financiers, deserve debt service on an equal basis. If a debt is in default due to nonpayment of principal or interest, co-financiers of a CFS loan are allowed to accelerate the loan. ADB reserves the right to accelerate its direct loan based on an optional cross-default clause.

In January 2003, ADB approved a USD 62 million loan for India's first public-private partnership in the power transmission sector. A joint venture company, Tala-Delhi Transmission Limited, will construct power transmission lines from Siliguri in West Bengal to Mandaula near the capital, Delhi. The transmission lines will convey power from the Tala Hydro Electric Power Project in neighboring Bhutan as well as surplus power from India's eastern to northern region, where industries and households suffer from chronic power shortages.

The total cost of the project is USD 249 million equivalent. Debt will make up 70 percent of the financing, with 25 percent from ADB and 45 percent from commercial lenders. ADB's funding is a long-term loan from its ordinary capital resources. The long-term local currency debt financing solution offered by ADB will enhance sustainability and affordability of the project.

Technical Assistance

Technical assistance is provided by ADB to the public sector in the categories of project preparation, implementation of an ADB-financed project, and preparation of regional studies and conducts. Assistance is usually financed through a grant or loan but may also include a combination of the two. In 2001, a total of 257 technical assistance activities, amounting to USD 146.4 million, were approved for preparing and executing projects and programs.

Although technical assistance is not provided in the private sector, there is an opportunity for the private sector to get involved. For example, in 1997 ADB provided USD 162.3 million for 298 technical assistance grants—providing another USD 353.6 million of technical assistance components in its loan-financed projects. During this time, 384 consultants and 169 teams from consulting firms were fielded through technical assistance to provide advice; help formulate policies, programs, and projects; carry out studies; and provide training.

Equity Investments

ADB has used equity investments since 1983 to directly support private enterprises, private equity funds, and financial institutions. Equity investment helps ADB in its primary goal of reducing poverty in the Asia-Pacific region. The equity component of ADB's portfolio has increased since 1994 as a result of the increased demand for risk capital. As a policy, ADB regularly disposes of its investments, preferring instead to recycle funds once an investment has fulfilled its development role so it can be quickly reinvested in other development projects. Comparatively smaller investments are used to spur larger investments and attract international capital to the region. ADB also oversees risk management and corporate governance to achieve results in line with its development goals.

In 2000, ADB approved equity investment of USD 25 million in the Liberty New World China Fund. The fund is co-sponsored by Liberty Mutual, a diversified multinational financial services group, and New World Development Company, one of Hong Kong's largest conglomerates. While USD 150 million had already been raised by the sponsors and ADB, the target size for the fund is USD 300 million to USD 400 million.

The fund invests in high-growth SMEs in China, which directly benefit from the increasing disposable income of the Chinese population as well as from China's access into the WTO. The fund concentrates on four core business sectors: health care, consumer products, building materials, and automotive midstream and downstream services.

Fund Types

The Private Sector Operations Department of the bank operates several different types of funds in its portfolio. Each fund varies according to its structure, the source of capital raised, and how that capital is invested. The five types of funds in the Private Sector Group (PSG) Portfolio are as follows:

- *International portfolio investment funds* are closed-end funds that open emerging markets to foreign capital. Funds buy securities listed on local stock exchanges using portfolio investors' capital. These funds are not intended to control a company's management.
- *Venture capital funds* are usually significant equity stakes in SMEs and may provide management input. The main objective of these funds is to gain capital through a fund ranging from USD 20 million to USD 30 million. The fund is usually high-risk and requires substantial gains from a few successful investments.
- *Private equity funds* buy minority stakes in established but unlisted companies. Unlike venture funds, investee companies are often large and funds can be up to several hundred million dollars in size.
- *Domestic mutual funds* raise money from investors within a country and typically buy securities listed on a local stock exchange. Funds are open-ended, allowing small investors to exit by selling their shares to other investors.
- *Debt funds* are senior and subordinated debt instruments in local and foreign currencies. The main objective of these funds is to provide regular income for investors while providing significantly lower risk than equity funds. Debt funds are also a useful source of long-term debt for capital-intensive projects in developing countries.

ADB typically chooses to invest equity in productive enterprises for financing specific projects, financial institutions, and other investment funds. ADB also requires the right to appoint a member to the board of directors of the company in which it is investing.

III. ELIGIBILITY AND APPLICATION PROCESS

Eligible investments must be in the private sector of a DMC and owned by local or foreign private sector entities. Enterprises owned jointly by private interests and the government of a DMC may be eligible for ADB assistance, provided the majority of its equity is privately owned and controlled by private investors. ADB's total support for the project is limited to 25 percent of the total cost of the project or USD 75 million, whichever is lower. ADB's policy is that an equity investment must be limited to 25 percent of the total share capital and that ADB cannot be the largest single investor in an enterprise.

Private Sector Funding

Although there is no formal application, the following is a general list of the required items for the application process:

- Executive summary
- Applicant's view of ADB's role, including a proposal for an equity, debt, or co-financing agreement
- Project background
- Feasibility study examining the viability of the project in technical, financial, economic, and environmental terms (must be prepared by a "reputable consultant")
- History of the sponsor to include organization's background, past experience in project development, and financial history and ownership structure
- Ownership of project
- Project description
- Implementation arrangements
- Project operation
- Description of the market and marketing arrangements
- Environmental aspects
- Estimated costs, including major costs and local/foreign currency costs
- Financing plan
- Expected performance (operational/financial)
- Evaluation (financial/economic)
- Analysis of risk
- Financial model (two copies: one hard copy and one copy on a 3 1/2-inch floppy disk)
- Permitting and licensing to include a comprehensive list of permits and clearances required for project implementation

IV. CONTACTS

Headquarters:
Asian Development Bank
6 ADB Avenue, Mandaluyong City
0401 Metro Manila, Philippines
Tel: 632 632 4444
Fax: 632 636 2444

Mailing Address:
P.O. Box 789
0980 Manila, Philippines
Internet: www.adb.org/privatesector
Email: information@adb.org
privatesector@adb.org

Private Sector Operations Department
Robert M. Bestani, Director General
Tel: 632 632 6315

Private Sector Operations Division
Alfredo E. Pascual, Director
Tel: 632 632 6452

Private Sector Infrastructure Finance Division
Vacant

Adiwarman Idris, Head
Project Finance
Tel: 632 632 6379

Risk Management Unit
Michael Chen, Head
Tel: 632 632 6456

Asian Finance and Investment Corporation Ltd.
31/F Citibank Tower, Citibank Plaza
8741 Paseo de Roxas
1226 Makati City
Metro Manila, Philippines
Tel: 011 63 (2) 817-3806
Fax: 011 63 (2) 816-3209

African Development Bank (AfDB)

I. INTRODUCTION

The AfDB exists to assist regional member countries (RMCs) in breaking the cycle of poverty. Working toward this end, the bank seeks to promote the flow of external and domestic resources and investment and to provide policy assistance and technical advice to RMCs.

AfDB serves every nation in Africa and has the support of non-African nations such as the United States, Canada, Western Europe, Japan, Korea, China, India, Brazil, Argentina, Kuwait, and Saudi Arabia. The bank is the major source of external public financing in Africa, extending approximately USD 3 billion per year in new loans and grants.

AfDB uses its own unit of account (UA), which is equal to one IMF special drawing right. Because most loans are denominated in UA, the bank is sensitive to exchange rate fluctuations and publishes the exchange rate monthly for the currencies of all involved countries.

II. PRODUCTS

In the private sector, AfDB offers assistance to private enterprise and financial institutions through term loans, equity participation, quasi-equity investments, guarantees, underwriting, and advisory services. Firms in the private sector looking to establish, expand, and diversify productive facilities in a variety of industries are eligible for AfDB services. Other requirements may include one or more of the following: generation of foreign exchange and savings, creation of employment, improvement in labor skills, transfer of technology and acquisition of appropriate scientific equipment, and forward and backward linkage effects. Priority is given to firms that are export oriented and that have access to raw materials.

Loans

AfDB interest rates for loans are set according to risk and market conditions. Loans usually range from 5 to 12 years, with grace periods added based on need and the firm's cash flow. A one percent front-end fee is charged along with a one percent commitment fee and any legal fees that are incurred.

Equity and Quasi Equity

AfDB equity instruments take a variety of forms and are usually in local currency. The bank assumes no responsibility for the management of the firms in which it invests, but monitors the firm's progress closely, divesting once the objective of the investment is realized.

African Development Fund (AfDF)

The AfDF provides development finance on concessional terms to projects that are unable to acquire funding at commercial terms. The purpose of these projects is to further the bank's goal of poverty reduction. The fund incorporates 24 non-African state participants as well as the board of governors of the AfDB. In addition to financing, the fund also provides technical assistance and studies for approved projects.

Underwriting

AfDB may act as an underwriter of a portion of a security issued by the private or public sector. The bank assumes responsibility for the shares not sold and for the amount to be underwritten.

AfDB disburses its funds in four methods: reimbursement to a borrower, advance payment to a borrower, direct payment to a supplier of goods and services, and reimbursement to commercial banks. AfDB's lending instruments are tied to one or more of these methods. Methods can be used individually or in any combination.

The bank's resources are distributed in accordance with successive 5-year plans, which dictate the amount allocated to each sector. The four factors considered when determining distribution within a 5-year period are the bank's past experience in the sector, the volume of resources available, the priorities of member countries, and the absorptive capacity of the borrowing country.

Reimbursement to a Borrower

The first method of disbursement used by AfDB is also the least used. Rarely available without a prior agreement, this method refunds a borrower who has already made payments out of its own funds. The payment may be a completed transaction, a down payment, or a series of payments to a supplier.

Mr. Alhaj Adbisalaam Issa Khatibu (MP), Deputy Minister for Finance, Ministry of Finance for the United Republic of Tanzania, and Mr. Theodore F. Nkodo, Vice President, Operations, North, East, and South regions of the AfDB, signed two agreements for a loan of UA 36.94 million (approximately USD 46.82 million) and UA 1.31 million (USD 1.66 million) to the Technical Assistance Fund (TAF) grant to the United Republic of Tanzania to finance the Dar-es-Salaam water supply and sanitation project.

The project, approved by the board of directors of the AfDB on December 17, 2001, helps alleviate the critical problem of water shortage in Dar-es-Salaam by promoting private sector participation. It will contribute to poverty reduction and improve the economic and social well-being of the people of Tanzania by providing them with better access to clean water, thereby reducing the incidence of water-borne diseases among the vulnerable groups.

AfDB operations in Tanzania started in 1972. To date, it has committed a total of about USD 950 million for 65 operations. Of this amount, about USD 603 million has been disbursed.

Advance Payment to a Borrower

AfDB funds are disbursed to a special account used specifically for a project, the primary method for financing. Instruments tied to this method include project loans, loans to financial intermediaries, and structural adjustment loans. Project loans are made directly to a company or a company's bank to allow payments to be made as the project progresses. Loans to financial intermediaries are granted for up to 10 percent of the line of credit issued by the bank. Structural Adjustment Loans are granted primarily under this method, and the funds disbursed are divided for use in each of the phases of the project.

Direct Payment to a Supplier of Goods and Services

Upon request of a borrower, the bank may make direct payments to suppliers for goods and services already delivered or to be delivered. These payments are considered a withdrawal from the special account set up for a project.

Reimbursement to Commercial Banks

Although AfDB does not issue lines of credit from its own account, it will guarantee a commercial bank's issued line of credit. Guarantees are requested by the borrower and are primarily offered for use in paying suppliers of goods (but generally not works or services).

Terms

The AfDB's three funds offer slightly different terms. The Nigerian Trust Fund, the smallest of the funds, offers capital for Nigeria at a 4 percent interest rate over as much as 25 years, with up to a 5-year grace period. The commitment charge is 0.75 percent of the undisbursed portion. The AfDF offers loans for terms up to 50 years, with a maximum 10-year grace period. A 0.5 percent commitment charge also applies. Finally, the AfDB offers terms from 12 to 20 years, with grace periods up to 9 years and variable interest rates. The commitment charge is 1 percent of the undisbursed portion.

Each lending instrument has its own requirements, but eligibility for financing services from AfDB is the same across all methods of disbursement and lending instruments. The bank finances projects and programs that stimulate development in RMCs, with priority going to projects that benefit two or more countries assisting inter-African cooperation and those that intend to utilize or mobilize local resources.

The bank is not the largest shareholder in any project, nor does its investment exceed 25 percent of the share capital of the enterprise. Financing rarely is smaller than USD 100,000 and generally can be up to USD 10 million.

III. ELIGIBILITY AND APPLICATION PROCESS

Eligibility for assistance requires that the applicant be located and incorporated in a regional member country and be privately owned and managed. Enterprises partially owned by the government may also be eligible for bank assistance provided private ownership exceeds 51 percent of the voting stock, they satisfy the criteria of operational autonomy and managerial freedom, and they are run on a commercial basis.

To apply for a loan, interested enterprises must submit a feasibility study, including the following information:

- Description of the project
- Sponsors, including financial and managerial backgrounds
- Cost estimates, including foreign exchange requirements
- Financing plan indicating the amount of ADB financing desired

- Market prospect, including proposed marketing arrangements
- Implementation plan, including the status of government approvals

Once the information has been reviewed, the bank informs the applicant enterprise of its preliminary views and may ask for additional information or documents. Application forms can be downloaded from the AfDB web site.

IV. CONTACTS

Headquarters:
African Development Bank
Rue Joseph Anoma
01 BP 1387 Abidjan 01
Côte d'Ivoire
Tel: (225) 20-20-44-44
Fax: (225) 20-20-49-59
Internet: www.afdb.org
Email: afdb@afdb.org

ARAB FUND FOR ECONOMIC AND SOCIAL DEVELOPMENT (AFESD)

I. INTRODUCTION

The AFESD began operations in 1974 as a result of a declaration signed by the League of Arab States. AFESD is now an autonomous regional Pan-Arab development finance organization consisting of all states who are members of the League of Arab States. The mission of AFESD is to assist member countries in eliminating development constraints, increasing absorptive capacity and achieving higher rates of growth and to foster economic integration and cooperation among member countries. In support and enhancement of the role of the private sector in developmental efforts of member countries, the AFESD has begun evaluating financing requests received from the private sector in its member states in the fields of industry, tourism, health services, insurance, and storage.

II. PRODUCTS AND SERVICES

AFESD assists economic and social development by providing financing for development projects, encouraging the investment of private and public funds in Arab projects, and providing technical assistance services for Arab economic and social development.

Technical Assistance

Technical assistance extended by AFESD addresses and enhances development objectives of Arab countries and their institutional support. The fund extended 28 technical assistance grants during the year 2001, totaling KD 5 million (approximately USD 16.5 million).

III. ELIGIBILITY AND APPLICATION PROCESS

Preference is given to projects enhancing overall Arab development and to joint Arab projects. For application information, contact AFESD headquarters.

IV. CONTACTS

Headquarters:
Arab Fund for Economic and Social Development
P.O. Box 21923 SAFAT
13080 Kuwait
State of Kuwait
Tel: (965) 48 44 500
Fax: (965) 48 15750/60/70
Internet: www.arabfund.org
Email: hq@arabfund.org
Mr. Abdulatif Yousef Al-Hamad
Director General / Chair of the Board of Directors

BANCO LATINOAMERICANO DE EXPORTACIONES (BLADEX)

I. INTRODUCTION

BLADEX grew out of ideas presented at the Meeting of Governors of Latin American Central Banks in 1975. BLADEX was finally established in 1977, with the mission of channeling funds for the development of Latin America and the Caribbean regions by providing integrated solutions for the exports in those regions. The bank's headquarters are in Panama, providing a central location, a U.S. dollar-based economy, and an offshore banking center free from capital controls. The bank receives funding through the deposits of the region's central and local banks, credit facilities from international banks, and capital markets.

II. PRODUCTS

Trade Finance

BLADEX offers multiple types of short- and medium-term trade finance to cover the import of raw materials and capital goods and pre- and post-export finance. BLADEX also offers services in working capital financing, structured finance, and capital expenditure finance. Commercial letters of credit include banker's acceptances, discount of bills of exchange, and bank-to-bank reimbursements. Other BLADEX services include stand-by letters of credit, bank guarantees, documentary collections, syndicated loans, and commercial risk guarantees.

Country Risk Guarantees

BLADEX's financial products allow clients to guarantee up to 100 percent of their schedule of payments against countries with financial risk. Country risk guarantees appeal to direct investors, exporters and importers who want to insure their schedule of payments against government actions that may threaten payment in 23 Latin American and Caribbean countries. Guarantees protect against currency inconvertibility and transferability as well as moratorium, confiscation, expropriation, nationalization, war, and civil disturbance. The benefits include mitigation of cross-border exposure, protection of balance sheets against unpredictable events, facilitation of access to financing, more competitive pricing, and increased sales.

International Factoring

International factoring is an alternative to traditional sources of trade finance for companies that export on an open-account basis, offer their clients payments terms of up to 120 days, and wish to increase their cash flow and sure payment of their export receivables. For the exporter, international factoring allows for a commitment by its local bank ensuring the payment of invoices prior to shipment and possible advances of up to 80 percent of the face value of the assigned invoices and assigns the administration and collection of its international invoices to a financial institution.

III. ELIGIBILITY AND APPLICATION PROCESS

Contact company headquarters for more information.

IV. CONTACTS

Headquarters
Banco Latinoamericano de Exportaciones, S.A.
Apdo. 6-1497, El Dorado
Panamá, República de Panamá
Tel: (507) 210 8500
Fax: (507) 269 6333
Telex: 2240, 2356
Internet: www.blx.com/eng.html
Email: webmaster@blx.com

BANQUE OUEST AFRICAINE DE DEVELOPPEMENT (BOAD)

I. INTRODUCTION

BOAD was established in 1973 by the West African Monetary Union (UEMOA) to promote regional economic development and integration within its eight member states. These members include the Republic of Benin, Burkina Faso, the Republic of Côte d'Ivoire, the Republic of Guinea-Bissau, the Republic of Mali, the Republic of Niger, the Republic of Senegal, and the Republic of Togo.

The policies and economic development strategies of BOAD are based on the belief that the private sector is the true source of growth and the best means by which to create employment opportunities. To this end, BOAD intervenes directly with loans to private companies or indirectly through refinancings in favor of the national financial institutions or financial organizations that provide financing to SMEs. BOAD support in the private sector typically favors projects dealing with the creation, extension, modernization, improvement, and rehabilitation of the means of production and distribution, as well as privatizations.

II. PRODUCTS

Loans and Guarantees

The bank guarantees and extends loans, as well as acts as a financial adviser. BOAD provides diverse services to assist member states, including lease lines, participative loans, and specialized total advances. Additionally, BOAD is willing to invest on the following bases:

- *Long- and medium-term loans* finance investment projects for the following:
  - Repurchasing of companies and transfer to the nationals of the UEMOA
  - Means of production and distribution of goods and services
  - Lines of refinancing at the National Financial Institutions (IFNs)
- *Loan reduction* is available in the form of a per interest rebate for projects concerned with priority sectors of development.
- *Credit limits* contribute to the financing of microprojects and the development of SMEs.

The participation of a local bank or a financial institution in the financing of a project in which BOAD invests is essential. BOAD requires that institutional investors must hold between 25 and 40 percent of the total investment, including working capital. For the projects under development, the minimum contribution is evaluated by taking into account the structure of debt in the company and the project risk. In addition, BOAD requires the participation of a technical partner when the project calls for a technology not controlled by the promoter.

When the bank invests in the financing of a project, loans must be covered by specific guarantees. The range of the usual guarantees taken includes personal guarantees, assets of the company, and controlled cash accruals in an acceptable bank.

Equity Investments

BOAD participates in the acquisition of stock or social shares in the capital of companies or national financial institutions.

Technical Assistance

BOAD also provides a variety of technical assistance services, including the financing of feasibility studies; assistance in the preparation, promotion, and implementation of projects; and the preparation of sectoral meetings.

The bank gave financial assistance in the amount of FCFA 5 million to the Higher Multinational School for Telecommunications of Dakar for the organization of a regional forum on the development of telecommunications and FCFA 4 million for the financing of the round table of the Authority of Integrated Development of Liptako-Gourma (ALG).

III. ELIGIBILITY AND APPLICATION PROCESS

To be eligible for assistance, applicants must be one of the following:

- A member state of the UEMOA or its communities or publicly owned companies
- A company or private individual contributing to the development or the integration of the economies of the member states
- A person or an entity arising from the UEMOA or ready to invest in the UEMOA in operations covered by BOAD

Projects must demonstrate the following:

- Satisfactory financial profitability
- Compatibility with the objectives of the development of the country
- Existence of an adequate market
- Comparative advantages of the project compared to competition
- Prospects for total growth of the sector
- Costs and origin of labor and the raw materials
- Reliability of the technology and the management of the project
- Company financial plan and financial resources of the company

To apply for assistance, interested parties must submit the following:

- Formal financing request indicating the amount and form of investment
- Detailed project study covering the market conditions, organization and management of the project, as well as technical, financial, and economic aspects
- Audited financial statements for the past 3 years
- Audit of accounts in cases of acquisition of a holding for a new issue of capital
- Technical references including financial records of technical, financial, or commercial partners if necessary
- Documentation of existing goods in the event of contribution in kind or project reports of the repurchase of existing companies
- Banking references, basic statutes, and proposed guarantees

IV. CONTACTS

Headquarters:
Banque Ouest Africaine de Developpement
68, Avenue of the Release
P.O. Box 1172
LOME ~ TOGO
Tel: (228) 221 59 06/221 42 44/221 01 13
Fax: (228) 221 52 67/221 72 69
Telex: 5289 BOAD TG/5336 BOAD TG
Internet: www.boad.org
Email: boadsiege@boad.org

BLACK SEA TRADE AND DEVELOPMENT BANK (BSTDB)

I. INTRODUCTION

BSTDB is a relatively new regional multilateral financial institution that 11 member states established in 1998 to foster development and promote business among and for its member countries through the support of regional trade and financing projects. BSTDB members include Albania, Armenia, Azerbaijan, Bulgaria, Georgia, Greece, Moldova, Romania, the Russian Federation, Turkey, and the Ukraine. The three largest shareholders are Greece, the Russian Federation, and Turkey—each with 16.5 percent. Bulgaria, Romania, and the Ukraine are the second-largest shareholding group with 13.5 percent each. The remaining five members—Albania, Armenia, Azerbaijan, Georgia, and Moldova—each own a 2 percent share of the BSTDB capital. The total capital is about USD 1.4 billion.

BSTDB is committed to sound banking, transparency, fairness, efficiency, and flexibility. Because the bank is relatively new, it borrows from international capital markets and aims to attract foreign investors to co-finance projects. BSTDB plans to concentrate on:

- Project finance, including economic infrastructure investments.
- Trade finance, with intent to increase regional demand for goods and services as well as to establish credit lines and equity investments.

- Development of the private enterprise sector with aid from financial intermediaries.

II. PRODUCTS

The bank accepts proposals from public, private, and nonprofit sector entities, including companies, financial institutions, and government and nongovernment agencies. Project finance doubled in 2001 relative to 2000 with 11 transactions amounting to USD 87 million approved by the board of directors. The main project finance tools are loans, equity investments, and guarantees.

Loans

BSTDB loans are flexible and offer short- and long-term loans denominated in hard or local currencies on fixed or variable interest rates. Loans can be used to expand, modernize, or create an operation. Borrowers may be either state-owned or private.

Equity Investments

Equity investments are also flexible. BSTDB may purchase shares of an enterprise in the privatization process, in a new venture, or in a newly issued share in a project company. It also makes quasi-equity investments with subordinated loans, debentures, and redeemable preferred shares. Legal documents specify how the proceeds are to be spent, and that the bank will not hold a controlling interest in the company concerned or directly manage the enterprise with the vested interest.

Guarantees

BSTDB may provide a full-risk financial guarantee or 1) a partial guarantee, where it provides all-inclusive cover for a portion of debt service or 2) a partial risk-specific guarantee, where it covers specific risk events for all or part of debt service. Guarantees are provided on a conditional or unconditional basis. Guarantee fee pricing depends on the guarantee's specific coverage and risks. In general, the bank faces the same processing and supervision costs on guarantees as on other credit instruments; therefore, the bank's policy is to price guarantee fees in line with the margins it would charge on comparable loans of equivalent risk.

On October 29, 2002, BSTDB supported small business development in Azerbaijan by participating with an equity investment of USD 1.75 million for a 35 percent share in the establishment of Azerbaijan Microfinance Bank. The other founding shareholders included the EBRD (25 percent), the IFC (35 percent), and LfS Financial System GmbH (5 percent). The Azerbaijan Microfinance Bank provides financial services to micro and small-sized enterprises in Azerbaijan. The project aims to develop institutional microfinance, encourage entrepreneurship, support the financial sector by sharing best practice, and enhance economic activity for small businesses in the private sector.

Trade Finance

BSTDB Trade Finance Products are now available in Azerbaijan, Bulgaria, Georgia, Romania, Russia, and Turkey. The total amount of trade finance operations approved by the board of directors reached USD 97.1 million as of year-end 2001. BSTDB offers a number of trade finance options that parallel the ECA's products and terms. It offers short- and medium-term structured trade finance because these products are filling a demand for trade finance that other international finance institutions are not filling. Many Black Sea countries such as Albania, Armenia, Azerbaijan, Bulgaria, Georgia, Greece, Moldova, Romania, Russia, Turkey, and the Ukraine do not have ECAs.

On May 28, 2002, BSTDB extended a revolving credit line in the amount of USD 1 million to Commercial Bank—Bulgaria Invest A.D (CBBI), which was selected as a financial intermediary for the BSTDB Trade Finance Program in Bulgaria. The Pre-Export Finance Facility was used by CBBI to advance subloans to Bulgarian exporters primarily in the small- and medium-size sector to finance production and exports to the BSTDB member countries of the Black Sea region and to other countries. It enabled the exporters to propose deferred payment terms to their counterparts under export contracts.

Special Programs

The bank acknowledges the importance of developing and introducing new services. For example, as of July 4, 2001, the

Technical Cooperation Special Fund began operations. The proposed uses of the fund's capital include the following:

- Preparation of feasibility studies
- Preparation of reformatting
- Preparation of financial accounts
- Collection and presentation of data

Co-Financing

BSTDB also tries to attract foreign investors and to aid in pipeline investing. Official and commercial sources are potential co-financing partners of the bank.

III. ELIGIBILITY AND APPLICATION PROCESS

To be found eligible for BSTDB assistance, applicants must provide general information about the project sponsors, make a list of principal officers, naming their responsibilities; illustrate ownership structure; write a short history on the special purpose company; and outline major product categories and production and export volume. Applicants must also provide financial statements from the previous 3 years, disclose current debt obligations and terms, and claim assets.

BSTDB also wants detailed information about the proposed project, a feasibility study if available, a *project skeleton*, the idea, the history, the location, sponsors, a timetable, management, fixed and financial and working capital costs, contractors, and a marketing study and plan.

The other major component of the information requested details the financial structure of the proposed project, equity contribution, financing product, external finance, securities, and potential third-party support. If there is any other relevant information, the bank requests that it be included.

After all of the requested information is provided, the project goes through a standard evaluation process. First, BSTDB evaluates whether the proposed project fits with BSTDB's objectives and meets eligibility requirements. If the project is deemed eligible, a range of consultants will evaluate the project's viability from their particular disciplines: economic, technical, environmental, and financial. The consultants work closely with BSTDB clients, help shape the project, and even provide assistance for enhancing project quality. The main terms and conditions are determined and negotiated, then approved and signed by all parties.

For trade finance projects, applicants must provide information to establish that they meet the following criteria:

- Have active standing in trade finance
- Are financially sound
- Have audited financial statements for the last 3 years prepared according to International Accounting Standards that were conducted by internationally recognized accounting companies
- Are compliant with current national regulatory practices of the host country
- Have acceptable policies and procedures regarding credit operations
- Have trained and qualified staff capable of handling the latest financing techniques, especially in trade finance

IV. CONTACTS

Headquarters:
Black Sea Trade & Development Bank
1 Komninon str.
54624 Thessaloniki
Greece
Tel: (30) 310-290-400
Fax: (30) 310-221-796, 286-590
Internet: www.bstdb.gr
Email: info@bstdb.org

Azerbaijan, Bulgaria, Georgia, Romania, and Turkey
Project Finance
Manufacturing, Tourism, Transportation, Financial Sector
Orhan Aytemiz
Tel: 30 (310) 29-0439

Infrastructure, Energy, Telecommunications, High Technology
Gueorgui Horozov
Tel: 30 (310) 29-0441

Trade Finance
Nejdet Sarisozen
Tel: 30 (310) 29-0427

Programs
Ghinea Arminio Iorga
Tel: 30 (310) 29-0452

Albania, Armenia, Greece, Moldova, Russia, and Ukraine
Project Finance
Manufacturing, Tourism, Transportation, Financial Sector
Umberto Del Panta
Tel: 30 (310) 29-0440

Infrastructure, Energy, Telecommunications, High Technology
Konstantin Limitovski
Tel: 30 (310) 29-0438

Trade Finance
Steven Beck
Tel: 30 (310) 29-0426

Programs
Panayotis Gavras
Tel: 30 (310) 29-0453

Co-financing
Nikolay Danev
Tel: 30 (310) 290 486
Fax: 30 (310) 290 432, 286 590
Email: Ndanev@bstdb.org

CENTRAL AMERICAN BANK FOR ECONOMIC INTEGRATION (CABEI)

I. INTRODUCTION

Established in 1961, CABEI is committed to improving social and economic development by providing credit resources and technical assistance to Central America. Its areas of focus include telecommunications, transportation, energy, and social development. The mission of CABEI is "to promote the progress and integration of the isthmus in order to form a bloc of highly productive nations that can position itself competitively in the ever more demanding new international arena of the twenty-first century." The founding countries include Guatemala, El Salvador, Honduras, Nicaragua, and Costa Rica. Mexico and the Republic of China have been extraregional partners of CABEI since 1992. In March of 1995, the Argentine Republic was incorporated; in 1997, Colombia.

In the early 1990s, CABEI made a special commitment to the private sector to help realize its goal of regional development. CABEI offers financing with its own resources, as well as resources from capital markets, loan capital, donations, and other monetary funds. Financing to the private sector is carried out mainly by means of an extensive network of intermediary financial institutions (IFIs) to complement the capital requirements of the private sector. Additionally, the bank participates as a partner in three international investment funds in very important economic sectors. It finances a wide range of sectors, including environmental conservation, tourism, agribusiness, urban development, and poverty eradication.

II. PRODUCTS

Not until the 1990s did CABEI institute trade finance facilities. These facilities are limited to short-term rediscounting of trade paper. CABEI provides financial and technological support to private sector projects in the Central American region to establish and expand exporting. Projects include irrigation, drainage and soil conservation, nontraditional exports, tourism development, industrial development, agribusiness, energy, transportation, telecommunications, and infrastructure. CABEI's services include direct and co-financed credit, intermediated loans, guarantees, and co-financing.

III. ELIGIBILITY AND APPLICATION PROCESS

To obtain intermediated and direct/co-financed credit, an interested party must appear at a commercial bank of his or her country of origin to solicit the information on the procedures for obtaining access to credit with CABEI funds. CABEI will supply the names of the commercial banks. Alternatively, the interested party can find information on the available resources at these banks at the CABEI office in his or her country. CABEI has also established norms that guide the allocation of resources. The details can be found under Credit Procedures in the Table of Contents on CABEI's web site.

CABEI can finance private sector projects directly to the user up to a percentage no higher than 50 percent of the project as long as one or more commercial banks or financial institutions acceptable to CABEI assume, endorse, or guarantee part of the financing required for the project in a percentage no lower than 25 percent of said financing. The owner of the project to be financed must provide the remaining 25 percent.

IV. CONTACTS

Headquarters:
Central American Bank for Economic Integration
Apartado Postal 772
Tegucigalpa, MDC
Honduras
Tel: (504) 228-2243
Fax: (504) 228-2185/2186/2187
Internet: www.bcie.org
Email: relex@bcie.org

Guatemala
16 Calle 7-44, Zona 9
Ciudad de Guatemala, Guatemala
Tel: (502) 331-1260, 65, 66
Fax: (502) 331-1457
Email: WebMail-gt@bcie.org

El Salvador
Edificio Torre Roble, 8 nivel
Metrocentro
San Salvador, El Salvador
Tel: (503) 260-2244 ext. 47
Fax: (503) 260-3276
Email: WebMail-sv@bcie.org

Honduras
Edificio Sede BCIE
Boulevard Suyapa
Tegucigalpa, Honduras
Tel: (504) 228-2182
Fax : (504) 228-2183
Email: WebMail-hn@bcie.org

Nicaragua
Plaza España
Managua, Nicaragua
Tel: (505) 266-4120 ext. 23
(505) 266-7088 ext. 92
Fax: (505) 266-4143
Email: WebMail-ni@bcie.org

Costa Rica
25 Metros al este de la Fuente de la Hispanidad
San Pedro Montes de Oca
San José, Costa Rica
Tel: (506) 253-9394
Fax: (506) 253-2161
Email: WebMail-cr@bcie.org

ANDEAN DEVELOPMENT BANK (CAF)

I. INTRODUCTION

CAF was established in June of 1970 in Caracas, Venezuela. It was based upon the *Declaration of Bogota* of 1966, which outlined a program of action to implement "economic integration measures and for policy coordination among participating countries in the areas of trade, industry, finance and technical cooperation services." CAF is composed of 16 countries in Latin America and the Caribbean. Its principal shareholders are the five Andean countries: Bolivia, Colombia, Ecuador, Peru, and Venezuela. Its wide customer base is comprised of public and private sector organizations, governments of shareholder countries, and financial institutions. It acts primarily as a liaison between industrialized countries and the international market while financing the development of productive infrastructure.

CAF maintains a permanent presence in the world's most demanding markets, and it has supported over USD 4 billion in projects. Within the context of a globalized economy, CAF has assigned maximum priority to establishing a physical infrastructure and cross-border integration plan that contributes to the sustainable economic, social, and environmental development of the region. To this end, the majority of its operations are geared toward financing roads, energy, and telecommunications projects and, more recently, to the development of the navigation potential and integration of Latin America's river systems.

CAF also seeks to strengthen the financial systems of its shareholder countries, as well as the private productive sectors, directly and indirectly through national development corporations and the local commercial banking systems. CAF provides significant support to the microfinancial sector of the region and to programs in low-income rural communities.

II. PRODUCTS

Loans

CAF offers short-, medium-, and long-term loans to be used in any stage of project development.

- *Limited recourse lending loans* are used primarily for the infrastructure sector and usually arise from governmentally awarded concession contracts, such as mining, oil, or gas projects. Typically, these loans are used for BOT and BOO projects.
- *A/B loans and co-financing* attract external resources to the shareholder countries by providing the "A" portion from their own funds and distributing the "B" portion to international banks or institutional investors. This loan becomes mutually beneficial to the shareholder countries and to the borrower.

Equity Investments

CAF's equity investments are developed with companies and investment funds in strategic sectors, usually based on several core characteristics. These include the amount of resources "mobilized," the development impact on the particular region, CAF's decision-making rights, profitability, and exit mechanisms.

Investment Alternatives

CAF participates in deposit and regional bond issues, in addition to its investment products. These options are obtained at interest rates comparably favorable to the international market and are denominated in U.S. dollars. The client base consists of institutional depositors and investors in shareholder countries.

- *Deposits* are short term (1 day, 1 year) and consist of a minimum amount of USD 1 million.
- *Regional bond issues* bond terms are 3 years in duration with semiannual interest payments and principal payable upon maturity. Minimum deposit is USD 50,000, and investments may be redeemed every 6 months on interest payment dates.

Investment Banking

CAF provides seven investment-banking products, including underwriting services, special purpose trusts, partial guarantees, corporate finance, interest-rate swaps and derivatives, financial advisory services, and political risk insurance.

Special Funds

CAF also provides special funds in three areas:

- *Technical cooperation fund* resources are used to complement technical capabilities in shareholder countries to advance innovative programs.
- *Human development funds (FONDESHU)* are used to finance community projects in needy areas by supporting the financial institutions that provide for these projects.
- *Management of poverty alleviation funds* act as a third party to supervise and possibly co-finance projects aimed at alleviating hunger and rural poverty in Andean and Latin American countries.

III. ELIGIBILITY AND APPLICATION PROCESS

Contact company headquarters for more information.

IV. CONTACTS

Head office:
Corporación Andina de Fomento (CAF)
P.O. Box Carmelitas 5086
Ave. Luis Roche, Torre CAF
Altamira, Caracas
Venezuela
Tel: (58212) 209-2111 (master)
Fax: (58212) 209-2382
Telex: 27418, 23504
Internet: www.caf.com
Email: infocaf@caf.com

Bolivia
Edf. Multicentro—Torre "B", Piso 9
P.O. Box No. 550
Calle Rosendo Gutiérrez, Esq. Ave. Arce
La Paz, Bolivia
Tel: (5912) 443333 (master)
Fax: (5912) 443049
Telex: 2287CAFBV

Colombia
Edf. Corporación Financiera de Caldas
P.O. Box 17826

Carrera 7a, No. 74-56, Piso 13
Bogotá, Colombia
Tel: (571) 3132311 (master)
Fax: (571) 3132787
Telex: 41207CAFCO

Ecuador
Edf. World Trade Center,
P.O. Box 17-01-259
Torre A, Piso 13
Ave. 12 de Octubre No. 214-562 y Cordero
Quito, Ecuador
Tel: (5932) 224080 (master)
Fax: (5932) 222107
Telex: 22402 CAF-ED

Peru
Ave. Enrique Canaval Moreyra No. 380 Edf.
P.O. Box 18-1020, Lima 18
Torre Siglo XXI, Piso 19
San Isidro, Lima 27
Perú
Tel: (511) 2213566
Fax: (511) 2210968
Telex: 21074 PE CAF PERU

CARIBBEAN DEVELOPMENT BANK (CDB)

I. INTRODUCTION

CDB was formed in 1969 after the nations and territories of the Caribbean requested the assistance of the United Nations Development Program in establishing a financial institution for regional development. CDB finances projects that benefit individual member countries as well as the Caribbean region as a whole. Approximately two-thirds of CDB financing is for government projects, primarily infrastructure. The remaining one-third is for private sector projects, either through lines of credit to national financial institutions or to larger projects directly.

CDB has 25 regional Caribbean members and 5 nonregional members including Italy, Germany, China, Canada, and the UK. Only regional members are allowed to borrow from CDB.

Country governments, agencies, and political subdivisions, as well as private entities operating within those regional member countries, may participate. Financing is used primarily for development projects, particularly in agriculture, tourism, transportation, power, water, infrastructure, environmental protection, manufacturing, mining, and export services. For small-scale private sector financing, CDB channels loans to local development banks that, in turn, disburse loans to private entities.

CDB lending activities fall into two categories: ordinary operations, which are financed from the OCRs, and special operations, which are financed from the special funds resources (SFRs). SFRs are used to make loans of higher development priority and longer loan maturities and repayment periods than OCRs. OCRs amounted to USD 710 million in 2001, and SFRs amounted to USD 518 million. OCRs are financed by the World Bank, EIB, IDB, market borrowings, and matured subscriptions, whereas SFRs are funded by contributions from member and nonmember countries.

CDB has made private sector participation in development a high priority to further economic growth in the Caribbean region. More resources will be directed to market research, human resources development, technology innovation, and the creation of a stable and economically viable environment with sound corporate governance to attract private investment flows. The private sector includes companies formed through joint ventures involved with regional member countries as well as offshore subsidiaries in these countries.

II. PRODUCTS

CDB funds up to 40 percent of the cost of a project. Only projects with a maximum debt to equity ratio of 1 are considered. The minimum amount of financing provided for projects is USD 750,000. For smaller projects, CDB uses other financial intermediaries to disburse loans.

Loans and Guarantees

Loans made to regional member countries are divided into four categories, with Group 1 (Barbados, the Cayman Islands, the Bahamas, Trinidad, and Tobago) and Group 2 being comprised of more-developed countries (Anguilla, Antigua, Barbuda, and the British Virgin Islands), and Group 3 (Belize, Dominica, Grenada, Jamaica, Montserrat, St. Kitts, Nevis, St. Lucia, St. Vincent and the Grenadines, and Turks and Caicos Islands) and

Group 4 (Guyana) being comprised of lesser-developed countries. Loans made from the OCR are repayable over varying periods but do not exceed 17 years for Groups 1 and 2 and 22 years for Groups 3 and 4. Grace and repayment periods are calculated based on the project's projected cash flow and the borrower's ability to repay. Interest rates charged are variable and are reviewed semiannually. Currently, the rate charged is 5.75 percent to public entities and 9.5 percent to the private sector. In addition, a 1 percent commitment fee is charged on the amount undisbursed; and for loans made directly to the private sector, a 1 percent front-end fee is charged, with half of the front-end fee payable as deposit and the remainder payable upon project approval.

CDB approved USD 4.5 million in 2002 to support St. Lucia's commercial banana industry. Funds will be used to provide managerial, agronomic, technical, and financial assistance to improve the productivity of this industry. Financing will also be provided to help banana growers capitalize on existing banana markets and take advantage of new markets.

Loans made from the SFR have a maximum maturity of 10 years for Group 1, 25 years for Group 2, and 30 years for Groups 3 and 4. Interest rates for Groups 1 and 2 are 5 percent and 4 percent, respectively; interest rates for Groups 3 and 4 are 2 percent. These loans also carry a 1 percent service charge. The currency of repayment is in U.S. dollars. Amortization schedules are determined on the basis of projected cash flows. Total direct loans amounted to USD 62.3 million from 1997–2000.

Indirect loans are also made to financial intermediaries with small-scale project costs. From 1997–2000, indirect lending amounted to USD 412 million and was primarily focused on agriculture, tourism, and manufacturing.

Technical Assistance

Technical assistance is provided by CDB to regional members to assist in the development of projects, particularly as it relates to the expansion of international and intraregional trade. Technical assistance can be in the form of investment surveys, identification of projects and preparation of project proposals, assistance with implementation of projects, and assistance with remedying project deficiencies arising during the course of operation. Regional governments, regional institutions, and private entities may request technical assistance from CDB in the following sectors: forestry, agriculture, marketing, export trading, manufacturing, mining, tourism, and transportation among others.

There are four main categories of funding for technical assistance: 1) grants, 2) contingently recoverable loans, 3) loans, and 4) combinations of grants and loans. Grants are used to cover general studies such as sector assessments, training, and short-term consulting services. Contingently recoverable loans are used for pre-investment activity with specific capital amounts for project design, technological assessments, and pre-investment and preparation of various phases of a project. Loans are used for project implementation. Combinations of financing are used to ensure the viability of a project. Recipients of technical assistance financing must agree to cover 15 percent of the costs in cash or in kind.

Equity Investments

CDB also makes direct or indirect equity investments. Direct investments (preferred shares or convertible debentures) are made only when considered necessary to supplement a loan or an investment activity of a regional development in an institution or a local development finance institution. CDB invests directly in enterprises with an equity stake not exceeding one-third of the total equity of the business. Investments in ordinary operations do not exceed USD 50,000. For special operations, investments can be as much as USD 100,000. Equity positions using SFR have been limited to government-owned companies. Equity investments have been very limited because many businesses in the Caribbean are family-owned enterprise that are reluctant to provide equity stakes to outsiders for fear of diluting control. The regional capital market is also underdeveloped and does not provide sufficient liquidity for an efficient exit strategy.

III. ELIGIBILITY AND APPLICATION PROCESS

The project cycle at CDB is similar to the project cycle at the World Bank. Prospective borrowers must first approach CDB with a viable concept, including engineering and design studies, projected costs, and environmental impact studies. The project then must go through an environmental impact assessment. Once completed, projects are submitted to the loan committee, where the financial feasibility of the project is assessed. Once approved at this stage, the project is presented for final approval in front of the board of directors. This whole cycle generally takes an average of 2 years, although some projects may be fast-tracked.

Prospective borrowers should initiate project proposals by submitting preliminary inquiries. Once inquiries are approved, a loan application is sent and the entire project cycle begins. Proposals should include the following information:

- History of the business—for private entities, information should include names of holdings or subsidiary companies along with their interest and ownership relationship to borrower; for public entities, information should include financial and legal relationship to government
- General description of the project
- Plan of operations to include type and amount of goods and services, type and source of raw materials, availability of transportation, manufacturing processes and equipment, procurement arrangements, and management plans
- Feasibility studies, pre-investment surveys, and other documentation lending credence to the economic feasibility of the project
- Estimated costs, including contingencies
- Loan amount requested with proposed repayment schedule and terms of financing needed
- Proof of financing sought from other sources
- Financial statements for the previous three years
- Projected cash flows, including projected income, expenditures, and profits anticipated in the next 3 years
- Projected estimates of sales volumes, including distribution arrangements, marketing arrangements, and long-term sales contracts

Private entities seeking financing must also show proof of adequate collateral, such as a legal mortgage on land or other acceptable forms of insurance approved by the CDB that can cover the amount of the loan.

IV. CONTACTS

Headquarters:
Caribbean Development Bank
P.O. Box 408
Wildey, St. Michael Barbados
Tel: 246 431-1600
Fax: 246 426-7269
Internet: www.caribank.org
Email: info@caribank.org

Office of the President
Dr. Compton Bourne, President
Email: boumec@caribank.org

Directors Office
Dr. Warren Smith, VP of Finance and Corporate Planning
Email: smithw@caribank.org

Deputy Directors Office
Dennis Smellie, Deputy Director of Finance
Email: smellid@caribank.org

EUROPEAN BANK FOR RECONSTRUCTION AND DEVELOPMENT (EBRD)

I. INTRODUCTION

EBRD is the largest single regional investor in Central and Eastern Europe. This multilateral financial institution was created in 1991 when communism crumbled in Central and Eastern Europe and ex-soviet countries needed support to nurture a new economic environment. Despite its public sector shareholders, it invests mainly in private enterprises, usually in conjunction with commercial partners.

EBRD uses investment tools to help build market economies in 27 countries in Central and Eastern Europe and Asia. Through providing financing for the region's banks, businesses, industries, and investments, EBRD helps restructure, bolster, and protect new market economies. EBRD is owned by 60 shareholders—58 countries, EIB, and the European Community—and operates with EUR 20 billion in capital. Countries of operations include Albania, Armenia, Azerbaijan, Belarus, Bosnia and Herzegovina, Bulgaria, Croatia, Czech Republic, Estonia, FYR Macedonia, Georgia, Hungary, Kazakhstan, Kyrgyzstan, Latvia, Lithuania, Moldova, Poland, Romania, the Russian Federation, the Slovak Republic, Slovenia, Tajikistan, Turkmenistan, Ukraine, and Uzbekistan.

II. PRODUCTS

Direct Financing

EBRD provides direct financing for private sector activities, restructurings, and privatizations as well as funding for the infrastructure that supports these activities. EBRD provides financing for export and project investments and is often used to build and strengthen existing institutions. The main forms of EBRD financing are loans and guarantees, with an investment range generally between USD 500,000 and USD 2.5 million.

- *Loans* are provided to selected banks in their country of operation. These loans are structured to fund trade-related advances to local companies exclusively for the purpose of pre-shipment finance, post-shipment finance, and other working capital necessary for the performance of foreign trade contracts.

Terms
Loans can be extended to projects that further the social and economic development of the EBRD regions by creating jobs, expanding capital ownership, generating net foreign currency income, facilitating the transfer of resources and technology, and utilizing local resources. The tenor, interest rates, and fees of a loan contract are determined on a case-by-case basis, with creditworthiness and countries involved as determining factors. An administration fee of USD 100 is levied for consideration of all loans.

Rosneft-Sakhalinmorneftgaz (R-SMNG) is a leading Russian oil and gas company engaged in exploration, production, and marketing of oil and gas deposits on Sakhalin Island in the Russian Far East. R-SMNG is majority-controlled by Rosneft, a vertically integrated oil and gas company owned by the Russian state. A EUR 96 million EBRD load supports R-SMNG's investment program, which aims to maintain stable production and enhance the company's financial position. In particular, the financing allows the company to continue production drilling at the Odoptu-More field and to implement an Environmental Action Plan, which includes provisions for improvements in equipment and training for oil spill response and emergency response. The loan serves its working capital needs and enhances the company's liquidity by restructuring short-term debt. EBRD has syndicated EUR 40 million of the loan to three commercial banks.

- *Bank guarantees* are available to international confirming banks. EBRD guarantees cover the commercial and political risk of nonpayment by issuing banks in the countries where EBRD operates. It does not assume any risk of the exporter or the importer, and a letter of credit is issued in favor of the confirming bank. EBRD guarantees can cover up to 100 percent of the face value of the underlying trade finance. The development bank guarantees cover a wide range of goods and services, including consumer goods, commodities, equipment, machinery, cross-border engineering, construction, shipbuilding, and technical and other services.

A guarantee program issued by EBRD supported the export of wheat from Kazakhstan to Madeira for USD 1 million. A regional loaning bank took 50 percent of a USD 2 million transactions risk, and EBRD provided its guarantee for USD 1 million. The transaction promoted the transition process by supporting a Kazakh export to a destination that had little experience in foreign trade, thereby helping to establish an export market.

Special Funds

EBRD administers some special regional investment funds provided by public institutions and government bodies. These provide both debt and equity financing under the same approval procedures as regular EBRD investment programs. As of December 31, 2001, the bank administered 11 special funds: 8 investment special funds and 3 technical cooperation special funds.

- *The Baltic Investment Special Fund* focuses on private sector development through SMEs in Estonia, Latvia, and Lithuania.
- *The Financial Intermediary Investment Special Fund* accommodates SMEs through financial intermediaries in the EBRD's countries of operation.
- *The Balkan Region Special Fund* concentrates on SMEs and microbusinesses operating in southeastern Europe.
- *The Baltic Technical Assistance Special Fund*
- *The Russia Small Business Investment Special Fund*
- *The Russia Small Business Technical Cooperation Special Fund*
- *The Moldova Micro Business Investment Special Fund*
- *The EBRD Technical Cooperation Special Fund*
- *The Italian Investment Special Fund*
- *The SME Finance Facility Special Fund*
- *The EBRD SME Special Fund*

Business Development Programs

The following programs are designed to improve business operations by training management, sharing knowledge, and improving local consulting services.

- *The Turnaround Management Programme (TAM)* provides advice on management know-how and assists chief executives in building their business skills.
- *The Business Advisory Services Programme (BAS)* upgrades the knowledge and expertise of local consultants. These individuals, in turn, supply SMEs with expert advice on business performance.
- *The MBA Loan Programme* offers student loans to graduates accepted to the IMC Graduate School of Business in Hungary or the IEDC Bled School of Management in Slovenia.
- *The Joint Vienna Institute* presents seminars for enterprise managers, entrepreneurs, and government officials.

III. ELIGIBILITY AND APPLICATION PROCESS

Large Projects

EBRD is willing to accept projects located in the countries of operation that have a profitable outlook. Sponsors are required to contribute part of the equity and the minimum size project is EUR 5–15 million. Additionally, projects must stand to benefit local economies and must satisfy the environmental standard of both EBRD and the host country.

Small Projects

Financial intermediaries such as local commercial banks, microbusiness banks, equity funds, and leasing facilities are supported by EBRD with a common goal to provide financing for smaller ventures. Investment criteria are consistent with EBRD policy, but financial intermediaries make independent decisions about which SMEs they fund. Sound and sensible projects involving private sector development are considered. Each bank or program has its own requirements and investment limits. The financial intermediary should be contacted directly.

Loans From Local Banks

Under EBRD's mandate, banks oversee that all proposals pay due regard to environmental issues. Funds obtained must be used in accordance with the requests stated in the original business plan and cannot be extended to majority state-owned companies or for government-guaranteed projects. Equity contributions, in operating or new business, of around 35 percent are often required.

The requirements are as follows:

- Sound business plans for establishing or expanding a company's business
- Management with a proven track record
- Competitive products in the marketplace
- Information on owners/partners
- Financial history
- Security in the form of pledges, mortgages, etc.

Financial and Operating Leases

EBRD-supported leasing facilities provide leases covering a range of goods, such as commercial vehicles, equipment, and machinery, to small businesses. Local leasing companies should be contacted for specific requirements.

Equity Finance

Equity can be requested from EBRD-supported private equity funds or donor-supported equity funds. General investments such as business start-ups, expansion, and acquisitions qualify, whereas some funds specialize in financing companies in distressed situations that are in need of restructuring or mezzanine capital for a later stage. Fund investments tend to have a higher prospective return and require longer-term risk capital than standard EBRD projects. Investment criteria are consistent with EBRD policy, but fund managers make the investment decisions.

Bank Guarantees

All international commercial banks with a well-known record of trade finance activities in EBRD's region of operation are qualified. Sixty-five issuing banks are listed within 21 EBRD countries and about 200 confirming banks throughout the world. Interest rates and contract time line are determined based on a country's specifics as well as the type of goods and services. For example, the maximum tenor for guarantee contracts in Albania is 180 days, while the maximum tenor for contracts in Latvia is 3 or more years. A USD 100 administration fee is imposed by EBRD for all contracts submitted, which are subject to other fees as well.

IV. CONTACTS

Headquarters:
European Bank for Reconstruction and Development
One Exchange Square
London EC2A 2JN United Kingdom
Tel: 442-073-386-372
Fax: 442-073-386-690
Internet: www.ebrd.com
Email: generalenquiries@ebrd.com

Rogers LeBaron,
Bank Lending Dept.
Tel: 442-073-386-554
Email: generalenquiries@ebrd.com

Ms. Yelena Tonna, TFP Administrator
Tel: 442-073-386-813
Email: TonnaY@ebrd.com

Holger Muent, SME Specialist
Tel: 442-073-387-413
Email: Muenth@ebrd.com

EUROPEAN INVESTMENT BANK (EIB)

I. INTRODUCTION

EIB is the EU's multilateral financing institution. It was founded in March 2000 as a result of the Lisbon European Council for the purpose of increasing assistance to SMEs. The SMEs that EIB markets to are within Europe, acceding countries, or partner countries. The EIB is also mandated to operate in Central and Eastern Europe; certain Mediterranean countries that have applied for EU membership; Euro-Mediterranean countries; the African, Caribbean, and Pacific states (ACP); South Africa (OCT); and Asia, Latin America, and the Western Balkans.

EIB is the primary shareholder of the European Investment Fund (EIF). EIB holds 60 percent of the share, the European Commission holds 30 percent, and various European banks hold 10 percent. EIB holds a powerful position from which it can increase the competitiveness of European industries. It offers

SMEs venture capital, medium- to long-term loans, and guarantees. The venture capital it extends is limited to SMEs within the EU, but the loans and guarantees offered are global.

In 2000, EIB was given the authority to support EUR 2 billion for venture capital operations for 5 years. In 2001, it signed 36,776 contracts, approved 31,573 loans, made 31,573 disbursements, and raised 32,172 community and noncommunity currencies.

II. PRODUCTS

Loans

EIB offers loans to both the private and public sectors, as well as to the financial institutions that provide lending to SMEs.

- *Global loans* are designed for commercial banks or financial institutions that lend to SMEs for small- to medium-sized investment projects. These are new capital investment projects with value limit of EUR 25 million. The project sponsors can be local authorities or an SME. EIB will open a line of credit for the institution lending to the project, and, in return, the lending institution will advance funds for the project the SME or local authority is developing.

Terms
An SME is defined as having approximately 500 employees and a maximum amount of fixed assets of EUR 75 million. EIB will cover up to EUR 12.5 million and up to 50 percent of the investment costs. The maturities are generally medium- to long-term (5–12 years). The maximum term is 15 years, but this is only extended in special cases. The security, rates, and disbursement arrangements are made on a case-by-case basis with the intermediary bank.

- *Direct (individual) loans* are designed for the private and public sectors, including banks.

Terms
The minimum amount of the loan is EUR 25 million, and the loan can cover up to 50 percent of the investment costs. The term for the loan in the industrial sector is 12 years, but infrastructure projects have a longer maximum term of 20 years. In exceptional cases, infrastructure projects can have a term even longer than 20 years. These loans are available in the currencies of EU member countries, U.S. dollars, Japanese yen, Swiss

francs, a Central or Eastern European currency, or South African rand, depending on the borrower's wishes. Loans can also be disbursed in more than one currency.

Structured Finance Facility (SFF)

EIB established the Structured Finance Facility (SFF) to match financing demands for high-risk, high-cost infrastructure projects. SFF programs complement financing from commercial banks and capital markets, as well as add value to high-priority projects primarily within the EU. SFF works from a capital of EUR 750 million that is allotted every 3 years. With the SFF's broad range of financing mechanisms, the EUR 250 million per year is expected to generate between EUR 1.5 billion and EUR 2.5 billion. The four modes for financing are as follows:

- Senior loans and guarantees insuring pre-completion and early operational risk
- Subordinated loans and guarantees
- Mezzanine finance, including SMEs making a transition to a larger scale or restructuring
- Project-related derivatives

In April of 2002, EIB provided EUR 150 million in lending to the Schiphol Airport in Amsterdam for its fifth runway, currently under construction, and associated taxiways. The runway (3.8 kilometers long and 60 meters wide) is planned to remain operable regardless of weather conditions and to allow aircraft operation on long-haul routes. Schiphol Airport is located near Amsterdam at the heart of the country's "Randstad," a metropolis of over 5 million people around the Utrecht, Hague, Rotterdam, and Amsterdam areas.

The airport and associated businesses are expected to generate employment for over 54,000 people. This project will enhance operations of this well-positioned European airport and play a vital role in supporting the Dutch economy. The residents of the area will benefit from dispersed noise once the flight area is enlarged.

Venture Capital

The venture capital facility aims to strengthen the equity base of high-technology SMEs and those with strong potential. This facility offers venture capital funds, security packages for the funds, and conditional and subordinated loans. In 2000, the EIB and EIF made an agreement to work in close cooperation on the venture capital facility. EIB transfers the management of the risk from capital investments to the EIF. The EIF then becomes the point of contact for the SME's venture capital and portfolio guarantee transactions.

III. ELIGIBILITY AND APPLICATION PROCESS

- Strengthen economic and social cohesion between EU members with business activity, especially with poorer or less-developed regions
- Improve infrastructure for health and education
- Develop transport, telecommunications, and energy networks
- Preserve natural and urban environment, especially with renewable energy
- Secure the energy supply base with rational use, use of resources, and import diversification
- Assist SME development with loans and venture capital support

Evaluation

EIB's consultants evaluate a project for practical viability on-site, for environmental considerations, for compliance to procurement rules, for project cost and financial plan, and for the creditworthiness of the project's promoters/sponsors.

Decision Making

After a project has passed eligibility requirements and evaluation, EIB seeks the opinion of the member state concerned and of the European Commission. The final examination and decision making is the duty of EIB's Management Committee and its board of directors.

Project Monitoring

The EIB monitors a project during construction and throughout the loan repayment period. It ensures that loans are paid on time and that the funds are being used for the agreed-upon purpose. At the end, EIB evaluates the final results and the overall project.

Projects can be submitted to the bank officially or informally by:

- Potential promoters (private or public companies).

- Commercial banks wishing to involve the EIB in their finance plans.
- Public authorities and international or national DFIs.

Applications may also be submitted specifically to each product group, whereas requests for credits financed in the framework of global loans should be addressed directly to one of the intermediary banks and financing institutions that operates on the national, regional, or local level.

IV. CONTACTS

Headquarters:
European Investment Bank
100, boulevard Konrad Adenauer
L - 2950 Luxembourg
Tel: 352 43 79 1
Fax: 352 43 77 04
Internet: www.eib.org
Email: info@eib.org

Greece
364, Kifissias Ave & 1, Delfon
GR - 15233 Halandri, Athens
Tel: 30 (01) 682-4517
Fax: 30 (01) 682-4520

Belgium
Rue de la Loi, 227
B - 1040 Brussels
Tel: 32 (2) 235-0070
Fax: 32 (2) 230-5827

Spain
Calle José Ortega y Gasset, 29
E - 28006 Madrid
Tel: 34 (91) 431-1340
Fax: 34 (91) 431-1383

Germany
Lennéstrasse, 17
D - 10785 Berlin
Tel: 49 (30) 5900-4790
Fax: 49 (30) 5900-4799
Email: berlinoffice@eib.org

Portugal
Regus Business Center
Avenida da Liberdade, 110 - 2
P - 1269-046 Lisbon
Tel: 351 (1) 342-8989
Fax: 351 (1) 347-04

INTER-AMERICAN DEVELOPMENT BANK (IADB)

I. INTRODUCTION

Established in 1959 and headquartered in Washington, DC, IADB is the oldest and largest regional multilateral development institution. It is comprised of 46 countries, 26 of which are borrowing countries in Latin America and the Caribbean. Currently the IADB is the dominant source of public finance for development projects in this region, contributing between USD 6 billion and USD 7 billion annually. Loans are targeted at all aspects related to economic and social development, including agricultural and industrial productive sectors; infrastructure projects relating to transportation and energy; and the social sectors of health, education, and urban development. Currently the bank's priorities are in poverty reduction and social equity, competitiveness, modernization of the state, regional integration, and the environment. Also, in an effort to spur development, in 1995 the bank began to lend up to 5 percent of its ordinary capital for use by the private sector. This is done through its Private Sector Department (PRI) and its subsidiaries: the Multilateral Investment Fund (MIF) and the Inter-American Investment Corporation (IIC).

IADB funding comes from its own capital, funds raised in financial markets, and other available resources. Almost 80 percent (USD 6 billion to USD 9 billion annually) of the funds for disbursements from IADB come from borrowings in world financial markets, mostly in the form of bond issues. IADB's debt is AAA rated by the three major rating services in the United States. The bank also administers 45 trust funds that provide financing for several of its activities. Through its history, the Bank has approved USD 110 billion for projects, representing a USD 273 billion total investment. Annual lending has increased significantly, from USD 294 million in 1961 to a record of USD 10 billion in 1998.

In 2001, IADB approved USD 7.9 billion in loans—USD 3 billion for projects in social sectors, USD 2.4 billion for modernization projects of the state and reform programs, USD 1.7 billion for productive sectors, and USD 695 million for infrastructure. As a percentage of lending, 68 percent went to what IADB classifies as Group I countries (those with a per capita GNP above USD 3,200) and 31 percent went to Group II countries (those with a per capita GNP below USD 3,200).

IADB approved a USD 240 million loan to help build the 3,146-kilometer natural gas pipeline that will promote the integration of the Brazilian and Bolivian energy sectors; diversify energy sources in Brazil; and bring related benefits in the areas of environmental protection, economic growth, and institutional reforms. When the entire project is completed, the pipeline will bring natural gas from Rio Grande in Bolivia to Porto Alegre in southern Brazil, with intermediate distribution points in Sao Paulo, Curitiba, Florianopolis, and other cities. The project will enable Brazil to achieve its strategic plan of diversifying energy sources to include the cleanest of fossil fuels, helping to meet the expanding needs of its industrial south and reducing the use of high-sulfur fuel oil. For Bolivia, the pipeline represents important new sources of national income and an impulse to economic growth.

The total cost of the project is USD 1.67 billion. The IADB loan for the pipeline will help cover costs for the Brazilian sector. The pipeline will be built by Transportada Brasileira Gasoducto Bolivia-Brasil (TBG), a subsidiary of Petroleo Brasileiro, S.A., the state petroleum company. Other sources of financing for the project include the World Bank, the Andean Development Corporation, the EIB, BancoNacional de Desenvolvimento Economico e Social, the Export-Import Bank of Japan, and project partners and suppliers. Furthermore, TBG will sell 49 percent of its shares in the project to private investors, thereby helping to consolidate recent reforms in Brazil, permitting greater private investment in the energy sector.

The pipeline will be 32 inches in diameter in its initial section and 16 inches in its final section. It will have a total carrying capacity of 30 million cubic meters per day, to be achieved in several stages through the addition of compressor stations. Its medium-term carrying capacity will be 18 million cubic meters a day.

Source: IDB Press Releases

II. PRODUCTS

In an effort to improve competitiveness and efficiency in Latin America, the bank created the PRI in 1995 to mobilize private financing for private sector investments in infrastructure and capital market development activity. Usually, the PSD handles large loans and guarantees (over USD 10 million), while smaller loans and equity investments are managed by the IIC. Since only 5 percent of IADB's outstanding loans can be used for the private sector, the PRI works in partnership with commercial banks, institutional investors, and other co-lenders to help private sector companies finance their projects.

IADB provides financing from 50 percent (for more economically developed countries) to 80 percent (for less-developed countries) of a project. For the least-developed member countries, IADB may use its concessional resources to finance up to 90 percent of a project. Remaining project costs must be financed by the borrower with local resources.

Structured and Corporate Finance Lending

The PRI can help finance infrastructure and capital market-related projects on a corporate finance or project finance basis. Corporate finance loans are normally used for expansions and modernizations of existing productive capacities and are typically utilized for privatized public utility companies. The project finance basis is useful for new or greenfield operations that use a special-purpose company as the borrower of the loan and for the construction, ownership, and operation of the project.

The loans provided by PRI are usually structured in an A/B loan arrangement. The loan is a single agreement between the IADB and the borrower, yet other financial institutions are also involved. The IADB, through the PRI, provides the A loan from its own resources and from its own account and also acts as the lead lender, lender of record, and administrative agent for the entire loan facility. The bank then attracts banks and institutional investors to participate on a co-financing basis through the B loan. The one or two financial institutions acting as the B loan arrangers are involved in analyzing, structuring, negotiating, and syndicating the B loan. The financial institutions involved in an A/B loan arrangement benefit from it because they are conferred immunity from withholding taxation (due to IADB's relationship with borrowing countries) and the arrangement reduces or eliminates country risk reserve requirements for some institutions.

Terms

The terms can vary depending on the specifications of each project. IADB limits its participation in loans to 25 percent of the project costs with a USD 75 million limit. In some countries, specifically smaller countries with limited market access, this participation can be increased to 40 percent, but the limit still applies. Usually, the term length ranges from 8 to 15 years, but up to 20-year tenors are possible. Interest rates can be fixed or floating, and are set based on many considerations, including loan term, sponsor, project financial strength, financial market conditions, and specifications of the project. Applicable fees depend on each project, but usually include a project evaluation fee, a commitment fee, a one-time front-end fee, a structuring fee, and annual administration fees.

Guarantees

IADB offers partial-risk guarantees and partial-credit guarantees. Partial-risk guarantees require a government counterguarantee and may cover up to 100 percent of a loan for specific political risks such as sovereign contractual obligations and transferability. Partial-credit guarantees cover a portion of the private sector financing involved. These guarantees turn medium-term finance into a longer-term arrangement by issuing guarantees for longer maturities, by issuing liquidity guarantees in the form of put options and take-out financing, and by rolling guarantees that cover a fixed number of scheduled payments. This type of guarantee covers up to 50 percent of a loan and does not require a government counterguarantee.

- *Political risk and credit guarantee coverage* is given to private sector lenders seeking coverage for their loans to projects in IADB-borrowing countries. Coverage can be for all or selected maturities of a given loan and can be tailored to the specific needs of each project relating to noncommercial factors.
  - *Breach of contract guarantees* protect debt financing from the risks of selected contractual and/or fiscal undertakings by host country governments with private sector investors.
  - *Currency convertibility and transferability guarantees* protect against the specific risk of nonpayment arising from the inability of the borrower to convert local currency into foreign exchange and/or affect its remittance outside the host country (does not cover loss due to devaluation).

- Guarantees for other political risks, such as expropriation of physical assets and arbitrary confiscation by the government, are available.

Terms

Political risk guarantees cover up to 50 percent of project costs or USD 150 million, whichever is the lesser amount. Certain fees are applicable depending on the nature of the fee, including annual guarantee fees, commitment fees on undisbursed balances, and up-front fees.

- *Credit guarantees*—Several kinds of all-risk credit guarantees are available. These cover all risks for selected terms of a loan made by a commercial lender. Guarantees are tailored to the specifications of each project and client.

Terms

The limits that apply to credit guarantees are the same as those that apply to loans. Annual guarantee fees for credit guarantees are charged on a similar basis as the approximate spreads charged for long-term loans. The rates applied are based on specifications such as the term length of the underlying loan, corporate market benchmarks, and the overall risk involved in the project. Other fees are applicable, including project evaluation fees, commitment fees, a one-time front-end fee payable on the IADB guarantee, a structuring fee, and an administration fee.

Capital Markets Initiatives

The bank supports capital market initiatives that help develop long-term financing in the local currency and increase the liquidity of capital markets in IADB borrowing countries. To help develop the region's capital markets, IADB can provide financing for projects such as:

- Debt financing and/or guarantees to regional or national investment funds to mobilize venture capital equity resources and/or debt capital that is otherwise not commonly available to private sector projects or other long-term capital investments.
- Debt financing and/or guarantees for funds, leasing companies, or other financial intermediaries.
- Start-up debt financing and/or guarantees for local companies that guarantee locally issued private sector debt.

- Guarantees for local institutions, such as investment banks, commercial banks, and leasing companies, to allow them to securitize assets and to develop a medium-term corporate debenture market that will facilitate the channeling of long-term local currency financing.
- Co-lending arrangements with local financial institutions and institutional investors that have a developmental impact on the domestic capital market's long-term financing capabilities.

Terms

IADB can cover 25 to 40 percent of the proposed project costs for loans and up to 50 percent of project costs for transactions supported by a guarantee, not exceeding USD 75 million to USD 150 million per project. IADB does not participate in the equity of investment funds or individual companies.

IADB approved USD 21 million in financing for the construction and operation of the new river port facility of M'Bopicua in Uruguay. This private sector project, approved by the board of directors, consisted of a USD 10.5 million loan from IADB's ordinary capital and a syndicated loan of the same amount. The new port facility will provide the area with efficient and affordable alternative forms of transportation for the region's agricultural products.

III. ELIGIBILITY AND APPLICATION PROCESS

Public and private entities in the Latin American member countries, including national and regional authorities, are eligible to borrow from IADB. However, IADB does not finance projects if the host government objects to such financing.

To be eligible for PRI loans and guarantees, projects must:

- Be located in an IADB-borrowing-member country
- Ensure that individuals and/or companies established in any of the bank's member countries maintain majority control of the project's capital. (This includes the nonborrowing member countries.)
- Have the borrower of the loan or beneficiary of the guarantee be a private sector company
- Target the development of infrastructure and/or capital markets in Latin America and the Caribbean
- Benefit the economy of the host country
- Demonstrate technical and financial viability
- Comply with IADB environmental and social requirements

Interested firms must submit bids for evaluation under an international competitive-award process coordinated between the host government and IADB. Many bids for technical assistance projects are announced in international publications produced by organizations such as the United Nations. Interested parties should contact the PRI to discuss the details of the project. Prospective borrowers are expected to provide the following information:

- Description of the project, including history, scope, and time line for completion
- Description of the bidding process
- Ownership structure of the project company, including record of past performance and financial information on project sponsors
- Overview of participants and description of arrangements made with all relevant parties
- Outline of proposed financial structure, including project costs by major category of expenditure and expected sources and terms of equity and debt financing
- Overall business plan, including completion time line and description of management team
- Feasibility studies, market studies, and financial projections
- Expected security arrangements that can be provided to lenders
- Details of the concession agreement, if applicable
- Description of the regulatory and legal regime applicable to the sector and the project
- Review of the positive developmental impact of the project
- Information on environmental, social, and health and safety aspects, including regulatory compliance, project/site conditions, potential impacts and proposed mitigation and monitoring measures, and other applicable plans and procedures

After an initial analysis of the project and in-depth discussions with the project sponsors, the project is presented to the bank's review committee for confirmation of eligibility. For projects that are deemed eligible, IADB and the client enter into a mandate to seek the best financing alternatives for the project. IADB then reviews the project in more detail during a comprehensive due diligence process.

Firms may pre-qualify by filing their experience and capabilities with IADB in advance. IADB also uses the Data on Consultants (DACON) roster to maintain up-to-date information on eligible consulting firms.

IV. CONTACTS

Headquarters:
Inter-American Development Bank
1300 New York Avenue, NW
Washington, DC 20577
Tel: (202) 623-1383
Internet: www.iadb.org
Email: webmaster@iadb.com

Mr. Hiroshi Toyoda, Manager
Bernardo Frydman, Deputy Manager
Tel: (202) 623-1779

Michael Ratliff, Head of Group I
Transportation: Argentina, Brazil, Mexico, and Venezuela
All other sectors: Caribbean, Guyana, Paraguay, Suriname, and
Uruguay
Tel: (202) 623-3319

Roberto Vellutini, Head of Group II
Energy: Argentina, Brazil, Mexico, and Venezuela
All other sectors: Dominican Republic, Haiti, and Central
America
Tel: (202) 623-3837

Michael Ratliff, Head of Group III
Water & Sanitation: Argentina, Brazil, Mexico, and Venezuela
All other sectors: Bolivia, Chile, Colombia, Ecuador, and Peru
Tel: (202) 623-3885

Jack McDonald, Credit Risk Unit Head
Tel: (202) 623-1979

Robert Montgomery, Environmental & Social Unit Head
Tel: (202) 623-2384

Ellis J. Juan, Capital Markets Unit Head
Tel: (202) 623-3063

INDUSTRIAL DEVELOPMENT CORPORATION (IDC)

INTRODUCTION

IDC was established in 1940 by an act of South African parliament. Over the last 60 years, it has focused on bringing economic growth, industrial development, and economic empowerment to the region. With its years of experience and success at the national and regional level, IDC was the first South African developmental financial institution to have its mandate extended to the entire continent. The IDC supports its vision of industrial development by promoting entrepreneurship, supporting human capital projects, encouraging global involvement in the African economy, and building competitive industries and enterprises based on sound business principles.

II. PRODUCTS

IDC offers a variety of financing options depending on the sector and type of business, but assistance is most often given in the form of loan finance. Available finance methods include equity, quasi equity, commercial loans, wholesale finance, share warehousing, export/import finance, short-term finance, and guarantees.

- *Bridging finance and guarantees*—Entrepreneurs that have secured firm contracts are eligible for bridging guarantees and financing. This type of financing is short-term with an 18-month limit and competitive interest rates are based on the prime bank overdraft rate.
- *Financing for empowerment*—Financing for empowerment is geared toward emerging industrialists and entrepreneurs wishing to acquire a stake in formal businesses. Financing is done on a medium-term basis in the form of loans, equity, and quasi equity. This type of financing is available for management buy-ins/buy-outs, leveraged buy-outs, and strategic equity partnerships.
- *Financing for small and medium-sized beneficiation*—This facility is designed to meet the needs of small- to medium-sized mining beneficiation activities and jewelry manufacturers. Medium-term financing is available for the establishment or expansion of mining houses, the acquisition of mining assets, contract

mining, and the establishment or expansion of manufacturing capabilities.

- *Financing for the development of the techno-industry*—Entrepreneurs in the information technology, telecommunication, and electronics industries or new technological ventures with local or foreign technology partners are eligible for this financing. To be selected for equity, equity-related, or loan financing, candidates must submit a viable business plan to IDC.

- *Financing for the development of agro-industries*—Entrepreneurs in the agricultural, food, beverage, and marine sectors looking to expand their business are eligible. Financing is available in the form of loans, suspensive sales, equity, and quasi equity for all qualifying projects.

- *Financing for the expansion of the manufacturing sector*—This product is available to entrepreneurs wishing to develop or expand their manufacturing operations. Candidates must have a viable business plan and, if selected, are eligible for financing in the form of loans, suspensive sales, equity, and quasi equity.

- *Wholesale finance*—Wholesale financing is designed for intermediaries looking for wholesale funding to lend to individual entrepreneurs. Medium-term loans with a maximum of 6 years are available to candidates with a good record of business development, strong financial position and training and mentorship programs.

- *Financing for the export of capital goods*—Manufacturers and providers of exported capital goods and services are eligible for this type of financing. Through this facility, IDC hopes to provide competitive U.S. dollar and rand financing to prospective buyers of equipment.

- *Import credit facilities*—These facilities are available to local importers of capital goods requiring medium- to long-term credit. Credit guarantees are available in U.S. dollars and other currencies for medium- and long-term repayments of capital goods.

- *Short-term trade finance facilities*—Working capital is available through the IDC to help with the facilitation of orders. Revolving credit facilities are offered for 6 months pre-shipment or 6 months post-shipment.

- *Project finance*—Large projects in the metals, petro-chemical, manufacturing, agriculture, mining, and energy markets are eligible for IDC project finance. Financing can be in project finance (including equity and quasi equity) or debt finance (including balance sheet, project finance, and export and import).

- *Support Programme for Industrial Innovation*—Entrepreneurs and industrialists looking to develop South African–based products that have a significant technological advantage over existing technologies are eligible. Candidates for the program are assessed on management's ability in product or process development, financial ability to complete development, and ability to manufacture and market products. If selected, projects are eligible for a grant of 50 percent of actual costs incurred during development.

III. ELIGIBILITY AND APPLICATION PROCESS

In general, IDC finance is available for projects within South Africa, the South African Development Community (SADC) region and the rest of Africa. Financial and technical assistance are provided for the development of sizeable African projects exhibiting significant economic merit. These may be greenfield, expansion, or rehabilitation projects in a variety of sectors: manufacturing in its broadest sense, agriculture and agro-processing, mining and mineral beneficiation, energy and gas, tourism, information technology and telecommunications, industrial infrastructure, and selective franchising.

Candidates must have a feasible business plan, a good record of business development, and a strong financial position. Training and mentorship programs are preferred.

IV. CONTACTS

Headquarters:
Industrial Development Corporation
19 Fredman Drive
Sandown
2196
South Africa
Tel: 27 (0) 11 269-3000
Fax: 27 (0) 11 269-3116
Internet: www.idc.co.za
Email: callcentre@idc.co.za

Mailing Address:
P.O. Box 784055
Sandton
2146
South Africa

INTER-AMERICAN INVESTMENT CORPORATION (IIC)

I. INTRODUCTION

Established in 1996, the IIC is a multilateral financial institution that is part of the IADB Group. Within the IADB Group, IIC works to provide financing and consulting services to private Latin American and Caribbean enterprises. It primarily concentrates on the needs of SMEs whose expanded or established business would help its member countries.

In 2001, IIC received 63 funding requests: 19 were considered and approved; 16 of these were approved for a loan. IIC disbursed USD 98 million dollars in loans in 2001. The other three projects were approved for equity investments totaling USD 30 million. Three of the loans were co-financed and aided in mobilizing an additional USD 55 million in funds. In addition, IIC acquired an equity participation in two investment funds that will further leverage IIC and its clients' capabilities. The total cost of projects financed by IIC in 2001 was USD 673 million.

There are 37 members of IIC. They consist of Latin American, Central American, and Caribbean countries as well as Mexico, the United States, and many European countries.

II. PRODUCTS

Loans

The IIC's developmental financing program targets SMEs in Latin America and the Caribbean. SMEs targeted are those having an especially difficult time obtaining access to long-term financing.

ALE Combustiveis S.A., a fuel distribution company in Minas Gerais, Brazil, received an IIC USD 6 million loan to expand its fuel distribution network. The ALE network is a compilation of small- to medium-sized companies that operate gas stations. The expansion plan includes acquiring or building 310 environmentally safe gas stations throughout Brazil. The project should take two years to complete, generating 2,000 new jobs in the process.

Terms

Loans are denominated in U.S. dollars. IIC contributes 33 percent to a new project or 50 percent to the costs of an expansion project. Most loans are variable in rate and based on LIBOR, but IIC may offer convertible, subordinated, or participated loans.

Equity Investments

IIC will make equity investments that cover 33 percent of the invested company's capital. At maturity, IIC will sell its shareholding to a local stock market, interested third parties, or the project proponents under a pre-agreed share purchase arrangement.

Co-financing

Part of IIC's mission is to mobilize funds for companies and ventures that have no other financing options. One of the ways IIC accomplishes this mission is by co-financing. With this instrument, IIC can make more funds available to a project by combining its direct lending resources with a commercial lending institution. Having IIC, a multilateral status organization, take part in the funding of a project makes financial institutions more likely to take a risk on the SME project. It also lowers the risk and loan amount for an outside financial institution.

Under co-financing, IIC acts as the administrator of the loan. IIC loan cannot be subordinated to the participating lender's portion. On the other hand, IIC often arranges longer maturities than commercial lending institutions, thereby mitigating the financial stress to the SME.

III. ELIGIBILITY AND APPLICATION PROCEDURES

Eligible Companies

Companies with sales ranging from USD 5 million to USD 35 million make up IIC's target market, but on a case-by-case basis, IIC does work with companies having excess of USD 35 million in sales. Generally, the companies are majority owned by IIC member-country citizens, but IIC will finance joint venture companies that are not majority owned by IIC member-country citizens in special circumstances. The profitability and long-term financial viability of the company is also taken into consideration. Other considerations fall under one main category—the company's impact on economic development; for example, job creation, foreign currency savings, privatization, economic integration between Latin America and the Caribbean, and improvement of domestic management skills.

Eligible Financial Institutions and Equity Funds

IIC is discerning of the viability of institutions and funds, but is flexible in the various types of institutions and funding it will cooperate with in fulfilling its aforementioned mission. For example, IIC generally cooperates with the leading institutions in their regions that are in the top quartile in terms of profitability, capital adequacy, asset quality, or other measures of financial soundness. On the other hand, it accepts financial institutions of all kinds, such as commercial banks, leasing institutions, finance companies, and specialized financial services companies.

IIC invests in sector, country, and regional equity funds. The minimum criteria for equity funds are as follows:

- Focuses on Latin American and Caribbean companies
- Focuses on companies with USD 35 million or less
- Has an experienced investment and capital-raising staff
- Presents a developed investment strategy with defined parameters
- Has definite legal structures, investment return parameters, and expenses consistent with market prices

Application Procedure

Interested companies must send their business plan and company description to the IIC Corporate Finance Division Chief in Washington, DC, or to the regional office in their area. Interested financial institutions that want to on lend to SMEs or establish an agency line need to send their most recent audited financial statements and a brief proposal for the funds to the Financial Services Division Chief in Washington, DC. If the project meets the basic eligibility requirements, IIC will request more detailed information.

IIC may, after reviewing the information, request an on-site project appraisal and meeting with the project sponsors and IIC senior management. In this case, IIC charges a project appraisal fee as well as other applicable fees.

When the appraisal goes well, IIC writes a preliminary terms proposal. When the transaction is approved, IIC finalizes the terms. Disbursement occurs in agreement with the outlined loan/equity agreement. The company must submit quarterly reports detailing project progress, company operations, audited financial statements, and pertinent information. IIC requires its clients to stay in constant contact so it can monitor the loan and investment portfolio.

IV. CONTACTS

Headquarters:
Inter-American Investment Corporation
1300 New York Avenue, NW
Washington, DC 20577
Tel: (202) 623-3900
Fax: (202) 623-3815
Internet: www.iadb.org/iic
Email: iicmail@iadb.org

Colombia, Ecuador, Peru, Venezuela
Andean Regional Office
Avda. 40 A No. 13-09, Piso 7
Edificio UGI
Apartado Aéreo 12037
Bogotá, Colombia
Tel: (571) 288-2006, 288-7244, or 323-9180 ext. 233
Fax: (571) 288-0357

Central America Regional Office
Belize, Costa Rica, El Salvador, Guatemala,
Honduras, Nicaragua, Panama
Edificio Centro Colón, Piso 12
Paseo Colón, entre calles 38 y 40
Apartado postal 1142-1007
San José, Costa Rica
Tel: (506) 233-2543, 221-7387, or 233-7043
Fax: (506) 257-0083

Southern Cone Regional Office
Argentina, Bolivia, Brazil, Chile, Paraguay, Uruguay
Andes 1365, Piso 13
11.100 Montevideo, Uruguay
Tel: (598-2) 901-6063
Fax: (598-2) 900-8899

Bahamas, Barbados, Dominican Republic, Guyana, Haiti, Jamaica, Mexico, Suriname, and Trinidad and Tobago, contact IIC headquarters in Washington, DC
Roldan Trujillo , Financial Services Division Chief
Tel: (202) 623-3922
Fax: (202) 623-2036

Steven Reed, Corporate Finance Division Chief
Tel: (202) 623-3981
Fax: (202) 623-3802

NORTH AMERICAN DEVELOPMENT BANK (NADB)

I. INTRODUCTION

NADB began in the wake of the North American Free Trade Agreement (NAFTA). NADB is bilaterally funded with equal participation between the United States and Mexico. The bank operates under the mission of being a binational partner in an effort to facilitate economic and social development through the development of environmentally sound infrastructure. The NADB works toward this goal by supporting development projects in the border region.

II. PRODUCTS

Loans and Guarantees

NADB loans provide direct financing for infrastructure projects when private sector funding is unavailable. Loans include direct loans, interim financing, participation in municipal bond issue, or a partial loan guarantee. Maturities on loans range from 10 to 25 years and must be paid back in their original currency.

Institutional Development Cooperation Program (IDP)

The IDP is a grant program dedicated to helping public utilities fortify their institutional capacity and develop a stronger financial foundation. Funding for the program is made possible through bank earnings. With these grants, communities are able to carry out projects to better the management and development of their utilities.

153

Solid Waste Development Program

The purpose of the program is to help public solid waste utilities in border communities. Private sector firms are eligible, but they must agree to reimburse the funds within the time frame provided by the bank. Grants are awarded for amounts up to USD 200,000 per project. The amount may be increased to USD 300,00 for regional projects where two or more communities benefit. Up to half of the cost of development can be covered by a grant, with the ultimate percentage being determined by the NADB on a per project basis.

III. ELIGIBILITY AND APPLICATION PROCESS

To be eligible for a loan or guarantee, projects must meet the following criteria:

- The project must be located within 100 kilometers (62 miles) of the international border between the U.S. and Mexico
- The project must be certified by the Border Environment Cooperation Commission
- The project must be an environmental infrastructure project involving potable water, water pollution, waste treatment, or municipal solid waste, and so on

For application information, contact the NADB office directly.

IV. CONTACTS

Headquarters:
North American Development Bank
203 South St. Mary's, Suite 300
San Antonio, TX 78205
United States
Tel: (210) 231-8000
Fax: (210) 231-6232
Internet: www.nadb.org
Email: webmaster@nadb.org

EASTERN AND SOUTHERN AFRICAN TRADE AND DEVELOPMENT BANK (PTA BANK)

I. INTRODUCTION

The PTA Bank was created in 1985 after the establishment of the Preferential Trade Area (PTA). The trade area is now known as the Common Market for Eastern and Southern African States (COMESA). COMESA is a regional trading group consisting of 21 African states dedicated to promoting the economic prosperity of its members through regional integration. PTA Bank was set up as the financial wing of COMESA, charged with promoting economic cooperation among member states. The formation of COMESA has led to relaxation of tariff and nontariff barriers among member countries, facilitated cross-border production, established trade and research linkages between states, and improved communication systems within the region. PTA Bank's goals are to increase trade among its members, support international financial institutions in financing regional projects, and act as a catalyst to attract foreign direct investment to the region.

The two main activities of the bank are project finance and trade finance. The bank supports only project finance activities that are sponsored by private enterprises promoting the development and employment of the COMESA region. In terms of trade finance activities, PTA Bank supports COMESA region companies that wish to export and international companies that wish to import raw materials into the COMESA region. PTA Bank assistance in the trade finance area is available for both the private and public sector.

PTA Bank's financial activities are recorded in Units of Account for the Preferential Trading Area (UAPTAs). UAPTAs are pegged to the IMF's SDR (special drawing rights), which is an international reserve asset calculated according to a basket of currencies including the U.S. dollar, Japanese yen, the euro, and pound sterling. As of January 2003, 1 SDR is equal to USD 1.37. In 2001, total approvals for project and trade finance activities were UAPTA 86.9 million, with 26.9 million for project finance and 60 million for trade finance.

II. PRODUCTS

Loans and Guarantees

In the project finance area, PTA Bank offers direct loans to specific projects, co-financing with other lending parties, lines of credit to development agencies, and loan guarantees. Project finance lending is available only for corporations registered in one of the bank's member states. Loans with high priority generally adhere to the following criteria: high regional economic impact, utilization of PTA materials and production, promotion of intra- and extra-PTA trade, development of member states' technology and skills, promotion of majority ownership by PTA nationals, promotion of development of women, environmental soundness, and expansion of employment opportunities. PTA financing focuses on projects that are regionally based, utilizes local resources, and has an export-oriented component.

Loan amounts range from a minimum of UAPTA 150,000 per project to a maximum of UAPTA 5 million. Lines of credit range from UAPTA 5 million to UAPTA 10 million. Interest rates vary depending on the risk of the project, but currently they average 12 percent p.a. for loans and 10 percent p.a. for lines of credit. Facility fees of 1 percent must be paid up front, and commitment fees are applicable on the remaining undisbursed portion of the loan after 60 days. The maximum maturity is 7 years with a 2-year grace period. Repayments are done on a quarterly basis. Lines of credit and loans to the quasi-public sector are secured through government guarantees, whereas loans to the private sector are secured through the first legal charge on fixed assets.

In 2001, a UAPTA 4.6 million loan was granted to Africell, a private company owned by Mauritius Telecommunications and private entrepreneurs in Burundi, to finance the extension of a GSM telecom network across the country. The loan was be used to purchase telecommunications equipment, including a prepaid billing system and an international switching system. Africell was only the second cellular GSM operator in Burundi. GSM's systems include mobile radio communications, public pay phone services, and other telecommunications services.

The bank's priority sectors for lending are the following: manufacturing, agriculture and agribusiness, tourism, infrastructure, mining, and banking and finance. The bank also considers SME lending a high priority and has extended lines of credit to DFIs to lend to this sector.

Trade finance loans are available for pre-shipment activities (working capital) as well as post-shipment activities (providing export liquidity for companies receiving deferred payments). PTA Bank also arranges loan syndication for large-scale projects and provides lines of credit for suppliers and buyers in the export sector. Interest rates for trade finance loans are based on LIBOR plus a spread based on the risk profile of the individual applicant. Trade finance facilities are short-term in nature and range from 90 to 180 days with an average of 1 year. The minimum disbursement amount is USD 250,000. In 2001, the total pre-shipment finance disbursements were UAPTA 33 million. Import disbursements in the form of lines of credit amounted to 17 million.

Technical Assistance

Technical assistance is provided by PTA Bank to its member states to identify, prepare, finance, and implement projects related to the bank's priorities. Gender issues are seen as a priority, and the bank is in the process of setting up special funds to provide technical assistance to identify and promote projects that ensure greater economic opportunities for women. Capital market development is also a high priority, and a special fund to provide technical assistance to member countries is now under consideration. The bank plans to introduce its own securities to be publicly traded by member states, and it will provide technical assistance to realize this project.

Equity Investments

The bank will consider making up to a 15 percent equity investment in any enterprise involved in a bank-approved project. PTA Bank does not assume a controlling interest and only makes equity investments to catalyze a project and ensure its success.

III. ELIGIBILITY AND APPLICATION PROCESS

Project finance loan applications may be found online at PTA's web site. Applicants must be private companies from one of the member countries and must submit a project that is aligned with the bank's goals of promoting regional economic development and trade with an export orientation. The initial application requests the following information: country, company name, sector, list of project shareholders, description of project, cost, financing requested of PTA and other sources of financing, and contact information. The application must be submitted with a feasibility study that includes the following components:

- *Introduction*—relevant industry and investment prospects of country of proposed project
- *Project description*—project/company background and description
- *Marketing analysis*—supply and demand, marketing and distribution, competitive environment, and product pricing
- *Technical analysis*—location, utilities, plant, machinery, and process

- *Raw materials and other input supplies*—material availability, reliability, and pricing
- *Legal aspects*—board and management structure and contractual agreements
- *Project financing*—cost estimates and financing and investment schedule
- *Financial analysis*—projected income, balance and cash flows, and break-even analysis
- *Economic analysis*—value added tax, foreign exchange, employment, and investment evaluation
- *Loan security proposal*—first legal charge on assets
- *Special features and risks*—based on individual project

Upon review of the application and feasibility study, the bank prepares an analysis highlighting strengths and weaknesses of the project in reference to the concept, commercial viability, and technical feasibility. At this point, further information may be requested from the applicant. Once the application package is complete, it is sent to the Credit Committee, then to the board of directors for final approval. Before loan disbursement, the bank requires proof from the applicant of adequate security to ensure the loan.

For trade financing, the initial application should include the same information as required for project financing. However, additional information is requested, including the following:

- *Borrower background information*—contact information, company background, and legal status
- *Required facility*—type and intended use of credit
- *Key industry information*—competition, buyers and suppliers, risks, and description of trade cycle
- *Management*—background information on key personnel
- *Management information system*—planning and control and monitoring systems
- *Financials*—3 years of audited financial statements and aged analysis of creditors and debtors
- *Security*—list of properties to be pledged as security and approximate value
- *Present banking*—types of facilities, terms, and outstanding payments

Proof of security must be provided before disbursement. Security can be in the form of first charge on assets (fixed assets or stocks of commodities, raw materials, or equipment), assignment of receivables, bank guarantee, or cash collateral.

IV. CONTACTS

Headquarters:
Eastern and Southern African Trade and Development Bank
22nd and 23rd Floors, NSSF Building, Bishops Road
Nairobi
Kenya
Tel: 254 2 2712250
Fax: 254 2 2711510

Mailing Address:
Eastern and Southern African Trade and Development Bank
P.O. Box 48596
Nairobi
Kenya
Internet: www.ptabank.org
Email: official@ptabank.org

Business Development
Yitaferu Kissaye, Principal Officer
Tel: 254 2 2712250

Credit Facilities and Business Development
Dr. Lindani B A Ndlovu, Director
Tel: 254 2 2712250

Administration and Corporate Services
Yotam Longwe, Director
Tel: 254 2 2712250

5

Selected National DFIs—
Supporting Projects in
Sponsor Country

This chapter covers national developmental financial institutions (NDFIs), which are government-owned, government-funded, and government-supported development institutions created to lend to or invest in developmental projects only within their national boundaries. Almost every developing country has a NDFI, so depending on the location of a project, the resources available from the relevant NDFI should be explored. Although some of these institutions like KDB also provide financing outside of their countries, or to foreign investors, their primary purpose is to serve as the national development financial institution. This chapter provides detailed information on the NDFIs in 10 of the largest emerging markets: Brazil, China, India, Indonesia, Korea, Mexico, Poland, Russia, South Africa, and Turkey. In some instances, several institutions provide assistance. Mexico has two; India has four; Argentina, on the other hand, relies on the programs of IADB and has not established a developmental agency of its own. Appendix B provides information about other NDFIs around the globe.

BRAZILIAN ECONOMIC AND SOCIAL DEVELOPMENT BANK (BNDES)

I. INTRODUCTION

BNDES was established in 1952 and currently disburses nearly USD 11 billion annually. BNDES is the primary source of long-term funding for Brazilian development projects in the private sector, including foreign companies in Brazil. It also provides limited financing in the public sector for certain social/infrastructure projects. The bank defines seven priority areas on which it focuses: modernization of productive industries, infrastructure, support for exports, social development, MSMEs, reduction of regional inequalities, and privatization.

II. PRODUCTS

Loans and Guarantees

Automatic BNDES loans provide for private company operations of up to R 10 million (approximately USD 2.8 million) per company per year. The terms are determined based on payment capabilities, and guarantees are negotiated on a case-by-case basis with the financial institution.

The FINAME credit line is disbursed to finance the acquisition of machinery and equipment manufactured in the domestic market. Additionally, it covers the leasing of domestic equipment. Terms for this credit line are up to 60 months for financing up to R 7 million (approximately USD 1.9 million); for amounts over that, the term is decided according to the repayment capacity of the enterprise.

Credit Insurance

BNDES provides credit insurance much like that provided by ECAs. BNDES offers insurance against certain commercial and political risks for the export of goods and services. Also, through BNDES-exim, the bank provides pre-export financing, which covers the production of goods and services, as well as post-export financing, which covers the skill of goods and services abroad on the basis of supplier and buyer credits.

Technical Assistance

BNDES also provides technical assistance, which is available upon request for state privatization purposes.

III. ELIGIBILITY AND APPLICATION PROCESS

Private companies that are legally incorporated and that have established operations in Brazil are eligible for financing through BNDES. To apply, potential customers must submit a preliminary application, downloadable from the BNDES web site. However, if the financing request is for an amount less than R 10 million, the customer should contact a BNDES-accredited financial institution.

IV. CONTACTS

Headquarters:
Brazilian Economic and Social Development Bank
Av. República do Chile 100/180 andar
20139-900
Rio de Janeiro—RJ
Brazil
Tel: (5521) 2277-7200/7210
Fax: (5521) 2220-8244
Internet: www.bndes.gov.br/english
Email: contact@bndes.gov.br

President
Tel: (21) 2277-7001/7002 and 3088-7001/7002
Fax: (21) 2533-1538

Office of the President
Tel: (21) 2277-7021/7003 and 3088-7021/7003
Fax: (21) 2533-1665

Modernization of Productive Sectors
Tel: (21) 2277-7231/7232 and 3088-7231/7232
Fax: (21) 2533-1572

Infrastructure
Tel: (21) 2277-8238/8288 and 3088-8238/8288
Fax: (21) 2262-8123

Urban and Social Development
Tel: (21) 2277-6748/6749 and 3088-6748/6749
Fax: (21) 2240-3749

Privatization
Tel: (21) 2277-8061/8062 and 3088-8061/8062
Fax: (21) 2240-3890

Micro, Small, and Medium Enterprises and Regional
Development
Tel: (21) 2277-7220/7230 and 3088-8231/8232
Fax: (21) 2220-7909

Exportation
Tel: (21) 2277-8231/8232 and 3088-8231/8232
Fax: (21) 2220-6425

CHINA DEVELOPMENT BANK (CDB)

I. INTRODUCTION

CDB was established in 1994 as a wholly government-owned policy bank with a registered capital of approximately USD 6 billion. Its mission is to support the nation's regional development policy by fostering the construction of infrastructure and industry through financing instruments. Industry support is focused on the following: power, railway, highway, petroleum and petrochemical, telecommunications, and urban infrastructure. Moreover, CDB is committed to help narrow the gap of economic development between China's coast region and its central and western regions and to direct and rationalize the size and structure of the nation's fixed investments. CDB has also been designated as an onlending agent for loans made or guaranteed by the World Bank and the ADB to the central government.

II. PRODUCTS AND SERVICES

Loans and Guarantees

CDB offers a variety of financial instruments to aid in the development of industry within its region. The majority of loans are targeted at projects in central and western China. Domestic loans are targeted toward the energy and transportation sectors.

Advisory Services

In 1999, CDB introduced investment banking advisory services to further serve the country's economic development interests. These services target companies and industries where opportunities for capital raising and business improvement exist.

Underwriting Services

In 2000, CDB began underwriting corporate bonds. The following year they participated in four deals and ranked first among competitors in terms of number of deals and market share.

III. ELIGIBILITY AND APPLICATION PROCESS

CDB uses the following criteria when determining eligibility for a project:

- The proposed project must comply with the state's macroeconomic policies, industrial policies, and regional development policies
- The borrower must achieve a BBB (inclusive) CDB customer credit rating
- The equity of the proposed project must meet government standards
- The proposed project must have significant market prospects and repayment ability
- A sound credit structure must be in place

For more information on how to submit an application, contact CDB headquarters.

IV. CONTACTS

Headquarters:
China Development Bank
29 Fuchengmenwai Street, Xicheng District
Beijing, 100037
China
Tel: (86-10) 6830-6688/6830-6561/6830-6568
Fax: (86-10) 6830-6521
Internet: www.cdb.com.cn

Hong Kong Office
Rm. 3307-08, One International Finance Ctr.
1 Harbour View St. Central
Hong Kong
Tel: (852) 2801 6218
Fax: (852) 2530 4083

INDUSTRIAL DEVELOPMENT BANK OF INDIA (IDBI)

I. INTRODUCTION

IDBI was initially established in 1964 as a wholly owned subsidiary of the Reserve Bank of India. In 1976, ownership was transferred to the Indian government in order to engage in financing, promoting, and developing industry and in assisting in the development of such institutions. In 1994, IDBI was allowed to extend its ownership to the public (up to 49 percent), and it is now primarily concerned with the long- and medium-term financing of industry. Private sector financial instruments are provided through IDBI Bank, a subsidiary. IDBI provides financial assistance in rupee and in foreign currency for green-field projects, expansion, modernization, and diversification purposes.

II. PRODUCTS AND SERVICES

Loans and Guarantees

To cater to the diverse needs of corporate clients, IDBI offers various products and services such as equipment finance, asset credit, corporate loans, direct discounting, and working capital loans to finance acquisition of capital assets or equipment and to meet capital expenditure and/or incremental long-term working capital requirements.

- *Project finance* provides long-term finance for new projects and expansion, diversification, and modernization of existing products in the form of term loans, underwriting, direct subscription to equity capital, and deferred payment guarantees. An up-front fee of 1 percent is required, and 25 percent of the project cost must be financed by the client.
- *Equipment finance* is provided to corporations for the purpose of acquiring specific machinery or equipment. Companies must be financially sound and have been in operation for a minimum of 5 years. Certain exclusions apply. Contact IDBI headquarters for more information.
- *Equipment asset credit* is provided to corporations seeking to acquire new machinery or equipment. The line of credit is valid for up to 1 year and may cover up to 85 percent of the cost of equipment. A 1 percent fee is required up front, and repayment is expected within 6 years.
- *Working capital loans* provide a loan component of working capital finance to companies already assisted by IDBI. IDBI is willing to finance up to 80 percent of the working capital gap. Repayment is typically expected within 12–18 months.
- *Corporate loans* provide finance for capital expenditure and long-term working capital. IDBI covers up to 70 percent of the cost of capital goods or raw materials, components, and so on to be purchased or imported.

- *The Venture Capital Fund* was established to encourage commercial applications of indigenous technologies or adaptation of imported technologies and development of innovative products and services holding substantial potential for growth and bankable ventures involving higher risk, including those in the information technology sector. IDBI targets investments with high-growth prospects and a potential for capital appreciation and clear-cut exit within a time frame of 3–5 years. Funding is available through equity, term loans, or convertible debts up to 80 percent of the project cost. Repayment is expected within 5 years, with a moratorium of 1–1.5 years.

IDBI also provides indirect financial assistance through refinancing of loans extended by primary financial institutions and by way of rediscounting of bills of exchange arising from the sale of equipment on deferred payment terms.

Technical Assistance

IDBI provides merchant banking and a wide array of corporate advisory services as part of its fee-based activities. These include professional advice and services for issue management, private placement of equity/debt instruments, project evaluation, credit syndication, share valuation, corporate restructuring (including mergers and acquisitions), and divestment of equity. IDBI also offers other services on a commission basis, including opening letters of credit and remitting foreign currency on behalf of its assisted companies for import of goods and services.

IDBI also offers other various services, including film financing, direct discounting of bills, equipment leasing, bill rediscounting, and rehabilitation finance.

III. ELIGIBILITY AND APPLICATION PROCESS

Typically, an up-front fee of 1 percent is charged, and lending is usually available to companies that have been in operation for more than 5 years. Project proposals and written documentation of financial viability must be provided.

IV. CONTACTS

Headquarters:
Industrial Development Bank of India
IDBI Tower
WTC Complex
Cuffe Parade

Colaba, Mumbai-400005
India
Tel: (91 22) 218-9111
Fax: (91 22) 218-1294
Internet: www.idbi.com

INDUSTRIAL INVESTMENT
BANK OF INDIA (IIBI)

I. INTRODUCTION

Established in 1956 as the Industrial Reconstruction Bank of India, the Industrial Investment Bank (IIBI) changed its name in 1997. It remains fully owned by the government of India. The name change signified a change in focus from looking at repairing weak industries to assisting greenfield projects.

II. PRODUCTS AND SERVICES

Project Finance

IIBI provides financial assistance in the form of short-, medium-, and long-term loans; demand loans; working capital facilities; equity participation; asset credit; and equipment finance. The bank also provides guarantees. It is also willing to invest in capital market instruments such as shares, debentures, bonds, and money market instruments.

Technical Assistance

IIBI is experienced in providing consulting and advisory services throughout the project life cycle. Some of these services include engaging in leasing, hiring, and purchasing finance; acting as a trustee of any deed securing any instrument; and providing consultancy and merchant banking, warehousing, factoring, depository, and custodial services. It is also experienced in setting up subsidiaries in the form of investment companies to deal in capital and money market instruments and may operate as an authorized dealer in foreign exchange.

III. ELIGIBILITY AND APPLICATION INFORMATION

Contact IIBI headquarters for more information.

IV. CONTACTS

Headquarters:
Industrial Investment Bank of India
19, Netaji Subhas Road
Calcutta 700001
India
Tel: 220-9911, 220-0435/220-0561
Fax: (033) 220-8049
Telex: 21-7197 IRBI IN
Internet: www.iibiltd.com
Email: iibiho@vsnl.com / iibi@vsnl.com

Eastern Zonal Office
AG Towers (4th Floor)
125/1, Park Street
Calcutta 700017
Tel: 229-2895
Fax: (033) 245-7460
Email: iibiezo@vsnl.com

Northern Zonal Office
Jeevan Prakash (10th Floor)
25, Kasturba Gandhi Marg
New Delhi 110001
Tel: 331-2819
Fax: (011) 335-7526
Email: iibinzo@vsnl.com

Southern Zonal Office
Spencer Plaza (7th Floor)
769, Anna Salai Chennai 600002
Tel: 331-2819
Fax: (044) 852-4905
Email: iibism@vsnl.com

Western Zonal Office
Earnest House (11th Floor)
194, Nariman Point
Mumbai 400021

Tel: 204-0489
Fax: (022) 245-7460
Email: iibiwzo@vsnl.com

Ahmedabad Branch Office
Nature View (5th Floor)
Ashram Road
Ahmedabad 380009
Tel: 658-0501
Fax: (079) 658-0421
Email: iibiabo@adl.vsnl.net.in

Bangalore Branch Office
N-603, (6th Floor) Manipal Centre
47, Dickenson Road
Bangalore 560042
Tel: 559-7352
Fax: (080) 558-9836
Email: iibiblbo@vsnl.com

Guwahati Branch Office
Arun Prakash Mansion (2nd Floor)
G. S. Road, Bhangagarh
Guwahati 781005
Tel: 56-2073
Fax: (0361) 54-5211

Hyderabad Branch Office
United India Insurance Co. Building
Basheer Bagh (7th Floor)
Hyderabad 500029
Tel: 323-2892
Fax: (040) 323-3192
Email: iibihbo@hd2.dot.net.in

Lucknow Branch Office
94, M.G. Marg (lst Floor)
Lucknow 226001
Tel: 23-8397
Fax: (0522) 23-8401

SMALL INDUSTRIES DEVELOPMENT BANK OF INDIA (SIDBI)

I. INTRODUCTION

SIDBI was established in 1990 for promoting, financing, and developing of industries in the small sector. SIDBI also works closely with similar institutions to coordinate efforts that benefit this sector. SIDBI assistance flows to export, industrial manufacturing, transportation, health care, and tourism sectors and to professional and self-employed individuals setting up small-sized professional ventures.

The authorized capital of the bank increased from approximately USD 95 million to USD 220 million. The Industrial Development Bank of India (IDBI) is the largest shareholder of SIDBI, although a recent amendment to its charter provides for divesting of 51 percent of the equity share capital subscribed and held by IDBI in favor of Life Insurance Corporation of India, General Insurance Corporation of India, public sector banks, and other institutions owned or controlled by the government of India.

II. PRODUCTS AND SERVICES

Loans and Guarantees

SIDBI provides an array of financial products. including direct finance, bills finance, refinance and line of credit, international finance, marketing finance, microcredit, fixed deposits/bonds, venture financing, equity assistance, and promotional and developmental assistance.

- *Project finance* assists companies setting up new small sector industries (SSIs), with preference being given to units in export, import, and high technology and those promoted by entrepreneurs with a good track record. Term loans may not be less than Rs 15 million (approximately USD 314,000), although the limits for states in the Eastern Region, Northeastern Region, Jammu and Kashmir, and Himachal Pradesh may be Rs 7.5 million (approximately USD 157,000).
- *Working capital term loans* help SSI units starting commercial production while minimizing difficulty during the upscaling of operations. It is expected that working capital arrangements will be turned over to commercial banks within 3–5 years.

Assistance may be provided to new or existing SSIs as well as to units graduating to medium scale.

- *Development of industrial infrastructure financing* is available for the setting up of industrial estates and the development of industrial areas. Project costs may not exceed Rs 100 million (approximately USD 2 million). Repayment is expected within 10 years, with a moratorium up to 3 years.
- *Foreign Currency Term Loans (FCTLs)* are available for the setting up of new projects, as well as for expansion, diversification, technology upgradation, and modernization of existing units with a good track record. FCTLs are extended in USD, DEM and euro currencies at an interest rate equal to 3 percent over 6-month LIBOR for USD and 2.5 percent over 6-month LIBOR for euro and DEM currencies. Repayment is expected within 5 years, with a moratorium of up to 1 year.

Microfinance

SIDBI has launched a major project christened "SIDBI Foundation for Micro Credit" (SFMC) as a proactive step to facilitate accelerated and orderly growth of the microfinance sector in India. SFMC is envisaged to emerge as the apex wholesaler for microfinance in India, providing a complete range of financial and nonfinancial services such as loan funds, grant support, equity, and institution-building support to the retailing microfinance institutions (MFIs) so as to facilitate their development into financially sustainable entities, in addition to developing a network of service providers for the sector.

Technical Assistance

Aside from providing financing, SIDBI also provides developmental and support services to SSIs under its Promotional and Developmental (P&D) schemes. This assistance is designed to ensure enterprise promotion, human resource development, technology upgrades, environmental and quality management, information dissemination, and market promotion. P&D initiatives are oriented to serving rural entrepreneurs and youth, particularly women, through programs that empower and motivate them to undertake entrepreneurial ventures.

III. ELIGIBILITY AND APPLICATION PROCESS

Generally, all forms of organizations, proprietaries, partnership firms, and limited companies can receive various types of assistance from SIDB as long as they fall into the SSI classification.

IV. CONTACTS

Headquarters:
Small Industries Development Bank of India
SIDBI Tower
15, Ashok Marg.
Lucknow 226001
India
Tel: 288547-50
Fax: 0522-2208637
Internet: www.sidbi.com

BANK MANDIRI

I. INTRODUCTION

Bank Mandiri was established in 1998 in response to the Asian financial crisis of 1997 through the merger of four state-owned banks including Bapindo, the Indonesian Development Bank. Bank Mandiri now provides comprehensive financial services to more than 6 million corporate and individual customers as well as SMEs in Indonesia. Bank Mandiri is well diversified and is particularly active in the mining, retail, cement, power, oil and gas, and aviation sectors. The bank has been making significant progress in growing its SME customers. As of March 31, 2002, loans to retail customers (including SMEs) reached approximately USD 1 billion, an increase of 16.8 percent from same period in 2001.

II. PRODUCTS AND SERVICES

Project Finance

Bank Mandiri project finance combines loan structures with effective solutions in financial engineering. Project financing is ideal for financing large-scale projects that could be achieved through contractual arrangements such as BOT, BOO, or Build Lease and Transfer (BLT) that require longer terms for completion. Like many private finance lenders, Bank Mandiri bases its credit decisions primarily on the cash flow generating capacity of the borrower, which is typically a SPV, but will also take a security interest in all the project assets.

Structured Finance

Structured finance instruments such as pre and post-export financing, import financing, and import guarantees serve the bank's goal of enabling Indonesia to become a leader in the Asian economic community. Instruments are focused on minimizing commercial risks, protecting customers from uncertainties, and repairing companies' financial structures. The Structure Finance Division provides a variety of solutions in financial engineering, professional analysis, and other business efforts to improve the Indonesian international trade businesses.

Trade Finance Services

Bank Mandiri's trade finance services are designed to mitigate the risks of export/import trade by providing the financial resources necessary for success in this industry. Lines of credit can be accepted around the world, offering competitive rates and optimal solutions.

III. ELIGIBILITY AND APPLICATION PROCESS

Project Finance

Customers can apply for project financing through one of the bank's credit instruments or in combination with one of the credit instruments available, such as working capital loans, investment credit, bonds, floating rate notes, medium-term notes, convertible bonds, and others.

For more information on the eligibility and application process, contact Bank Mandiri's headquarters.

IV. CONTACTS

Headquarters:
Bank Mandiri
Plaza Mandiri, 22nd Floor
Jl. Jend. Gatot Subroto Kav. 36-38
Jakarta 12190
Tel: (62-21) 524-5577
Fax: (62-21) 526-3581
Internet: www.bankmandiri.com

Hong Kong Branch
7th Floor, Far East Finance Centre
16 Harcourt Road, Hong Kong

Tel: 852-2527-6611
Fax: 852-2529-8131

Singapore Branch
16 Collyer Quay #28-00
Hitachi Tower
Singapore 049318
Tel: 65-532-0200
Fax: 65-532-0206

Cayman Island Branch
Grand Cayman, One Cayman House
North Church Street, 2nd Floor
Cayman Island, BWI
Tel: 1-1345-9458894
Fax: 1-1345-9458892

KOREA DEVELOPMENT BANK (KDB)

I. INTRODUCTION

KDB is the bilateral development bank of Korea. The vision of KDB is to lead the Korean financial industry in globalization, to utilize a universal banking system, to support the "strategic industries of the 21st century," to act as a leader in international finance, and to develop as well as support investments relating to North Korea.

II. PRODUCTS

Structured Finance

KDB offers three types of structured financing:

- *Ship/aircraft financing* supports the airline industry through tax-saving structures with ECAs and investment banks. It also supports ship leasing.
- *Project finance* primarily benefits air terminals, power plants, and tollroads. However, it is also used for the benefit of the Korean banking industry.
- *Asset-backed securitization* refers to financial products such as collateralized loan obligations used in aiding corporate restructuring, typically for financial institutions.

Infrastructure Finance

KDB's infrastructure finance offers a full range of project finance services, including advisory services. Its financial advisory service assists in the creation of project proposals for bidding purposes, participation in the negotiation processes, development of financial models to adequately analyze and evaluate a project, and effective project management.

Trade Finance

KDB offers the following types of trade finance:

- *Export trade finance* includes advising on documentary credit, negotiation, and collection of a bill of exchange; forfeiting; and renegotiating.
- *Import trade finance* includes the issuance of documentary credit for import of general goods and agricultural goods under the U.S. Government's GSM 102 program and under the Coface guarantee program.
- *Banker's acceptance* accepts bills of exchange issued by exporters overseas under documentary credit issued by Korean banks.

Merger and Acquisition Advising

KDB also provides advisory services for mergers and acquisitions. Included in these services are commentaries on targeted companies, opinions on fairness and pricing, negotiation of acquisitions, as well as divestitures, integration of merging concerns, and leveraged buyouts.

Venture Capital

KDB uses its venture capital facilities to support small- to medium-sized unlisted Korean companies. Typically, this support is facilitated through direct equity investments. Usually, the types of firms financed are high-technology companies with high growth potential. KDB also provides assistance to client companies looking to raise future amounts of equity. Between its establishment in 1998 and the end of fiscal year 2000, KDB's venture capital made 214 investments totaling USD 170 million. On average, the investment size was USD 816,793.

III. ELIGIBILITY AND APPLICATION PROCESS

Contact KDB headquarters or the nearest regional office for more information.

IV. CONTACTS

Headquarters:
Korea Development Bank
16-3, Youido-dong, Yongdeungpo-ku
Seoul 150-973
Korea

International Finance Department
Tel: 82-2-787-7407/7408/7409
Fax: 82-2-787-7491/7497
Internet: www.kdb.co.kr

Tokyo
Room 305, Fuji Bldg.
2-3 Marunouchi 3-chome
Chiyoda-ku, Tokyo 100, Japan
Tel: (81-3) 3214-4541
Fax: (81-3) 3214-6933
Email: tokyo@kdb.co.kr

Shanghai
Pos-plaza, 480 Pudian Road Pudong
New Area
Shanghai, 200122, China
Tel: (86-21) 6875-1234
Fax: (86-21) 6875-1177
Email: shanghai@kdb.co.kr

Singapore
8 Shenton Way
#07-01/02 Temasek Tower
Singapore 068811
Tel: (65) 6224-8188
Fax: (65) 6225-6540
Email: singapore@kdb.co.kr

London
99 Bishopsgate (16th Floor)
London EC2M 3XD, U.K.
Tel: (44-20) 7426-3550
Fax: (44-20) 7426-3567
Email: london@kdb.co.kr

New York
32nd Floor, Mutual of America Life Insurance Bldg.
320 Park Avenue
New York, NY 10022
Tel: (212) 688-7686
Fax: (212) 421-5028
Email: newyork@kdb.co.kr

Ireland Ltd.
KDB Ireland Ltd.
Ground Floor, Russell House Stokes Place
St. Stephen's Green
Dublin 2
Ireland
Tel: (353-1) 4753-644
Fax: (353-1) 4753-658
Email: kdbireland@kdb.co.kr

Asia Ltd.
KDB Asia Ltd.
Suite 2101-2103, Two Exchange Square
8 Connaught Place
Central Hong Kong
Tel: (852) 2524-7011
Fax: (852) 2810-4447
Email: kdbasia@kdb.co.kr

Frankfurt Representative
KDB (Deutschland) GmbH
Rahmhofstrasse 2-4, Postfach 60313
Frankfurt am Main, Germany
Tel: (49-69) 920713-0
Fax: (49-69) 920713-99
Email: frankfurt@kdb.co.kr

Beijing Representative
1601 China World Tower No. 1
Jian Guo Men Wai Ave.
Beijing 100004, China
Tel: (86-10) 6505-4901
Fax: (86-10) 6505-4903
Email: beijing@kdb.co.kr

BANCOMEXT

I. INTRODUCTION

Bancomext, Mexico's export development bank, has been in operation for 65 years and has 35 offices in Mexico and 42 offices worldwide. The mission of the bank is to promote the international competitiveness of Mexican businesses, as well as attract foreign investment and joint ventures. Currently the most important export-related sectors include automotive, electronics, food and beverage, textiles, and tourism. Bancomext primarily serves SMEs because they typically require more assistance than large corporations in the areas of financing, training, business skills, technical assistance, and information about and access to foreign markets. Bancomext operates on the belief that increasing the strength and number of SMEs will decrease Mexico's dependence on imports, foster job growth, and strengthen the economy.

In 2002, the bank's goal was to finance up to USD 6 billion. In the first half of 2002, Bancomext provided assistance to 828 Mexican companies to launch international operations with foreign buyers and to attend international business events. Over 200 training courses were provided, and almost 500 requests for distribution channel research, exportable supply promotion, and market research services were filled. Besides the 35 official Bancomext offices, the bank also operates 96 foreign trade service centers throughout Mexico to provide export information, publications, and guidance. The United States is the destination of 89 percent of Mexico's exports, with the remaining 11 percent comprised of Japan, Canada, the EU, other Central American countries, and China. Therefore, Bancomext's services are geared toward exporting to these countries.

II. PRODUCTS

Investment Financing

Bancomext offers treasury services, letters of credit, fiduciary services, investment banking services, and guarantees. Investment banking services are offered to companies involved in the export of Mexican goods and services, including those participating in international tenders. Services include structured financing for national and international companies involved in infrastructure projects, as well as corporate finance support for Mexican companies. Bancomext also assists exporters seeking international growth by finding sources of capital from national and foreign investment funds.

Direct Financing

In 2001, Bancomext disbursed USD 4.8 billion in loans. Credit is granted primarily to exporters directly, but it is also granted to export suppliers. SMEs make up 95 percent of the recipients of credit.

- *PYME Digital 250 Program* provides financing through lines of credit for SMEs seeking loans of USD 250,000 or less for working capital or for capital goods financing.
- *PYME Digital 50 Program* is available to small exporters seeking to finance the production and commercialization of their goods and services abroad. The maximum amount available under this program is USD 50,000.

Companies seeking financing in excess of USD 250,000 must apply under different criteria and meet certain eligibility requirements.

To pay off its debts and to construct and launch a new satellite, Satmex, a Mexican-based satellite operator, secured USD 300 million in loans from Bancomext; the U.S. Ex-Im Bank; and Coface, a French export credit agency. U.S.-based Loral Space and Communications, a NYSE-listed company, controls Satmex with a 70 percent interest. The Mexican government owns 25 percent, and a local telecommunications group owns the remaining 5 percent. Loral Communications is the world's largest provider of fixed satellite services, including leasing for corporate data networks, broadband data transmission, and Internet connectivity.

Guarantees

Guarantees for pre- and post-shipment are provided to the exporting community and national banks against occurrences of nonpayment during the production cycle or commercialization of a good or service due to unforeseen political or business risks in the country of destination. In 2001, Bancomext offered USD 673 million in guarantees. To qualify, applying banks must pay a commission and value added tax to Bancomext for the amount of the guarantee. Once approved by Bancomext, guarantees cover a maximum of USD 8 million for individual exporting companies and USD 80 million for groups (such as professional associations).

Specific guarantees are provided for the modernization or extension of production plants in Mexico that are involved in exporting. This involves the guarantee of credit used for the purchase of equipment and for projects aimed at increasing the production of exportable goods. These guarantees carry a maximum term of 7 years, covering 50–70 percent of the amount of credit based on individual strengths of the company, with a maximum of USD 5 million.

Technical Assistance

Bancomext offers specialized financial advising services. It also offers a professional training and development program for exporting entrepreneurs. For beginning exporters, courses are offered providing basic knowledge and information on how to begin exporting, including information on marketing, information technology, and rules and regulations; the accessing of letters of credit; exportation to North America; distribution and logistics; international pricing; legal issues in exporting; and so on. Bancomext also offers training for established exporters wishing to expand their business. For such exporters, courses are offered in negotiating and forming strategic international alliances, buying and selling internationally via the Internet, participating in international consumer fairs, and so on.

Technical support is also provided to Mexican companies wishing to improve their production processes, obtain ISO 9000 certificates, carry out promotional campaigns, and conduct international market studies. In the first half of 2002, 245 training courses were offered and 2,564 companies were given technical assistance and support.

Bancomext also operates an online service, Exportanet, which provides trade intelligence to exporters. The web site includes a directory of importers, commercial opportunities, the ability to search for foreign partners, information assistance to small businesses looking to begin exporting, and information on exporters seeking a Mexican consumer base abroad. In 2001, there were 1,700 subscribers.

Foreign investors wishing to invest in Mexico are also offered detailed information on labor force rules, tax structures, government incentives for foreign investors, and other basic information on starting new enterprises in Mexico. Particular attention is paid to the manufacturing sector and to companies wishing to operate in one of Mexico's industrial parks. Detailed export and import amounts in USD are provided by product categories. Cost information related to production and general information on Mexico's investment climate are also provided.

Equity

Bancomext offers venture capital funds to viable businesses through SINCAS, through Capital Investment Societies, and through its venture capital investment funds. Bancomext is involved in the following funds: Sinca Agrosid, Multinational Industrial Fund, Fomede, ZN Mexico Trust II, and Monterrey Capital Partners.

III. ELIGIBILITY AND APPLICATION PROCESS

Financing

Mexican companies seeking financing under PYME 50 must use these funds for the export of goods and services in Mexico's targeted sectors (automotive, tourism, electronics, manufacturing, and so on) and must show documentation of exporting business. The funds must be used to buy raw material, enhance production, or acquire services that directly affect the cost of production or must be used another way that is directly related to improving the exporting competitiveness of the business. The business also must have registered at least two exports in the prior 12 months, and for services, the business must have been in operation for the 12 months prior to the application for credit. The business must also not have any outstanding debts with Bancomext, be in good credit standing, and be fully insured for the amount requested with insurance that is approved by Bancomext. Bancomext's web site has a basic eight-question survey with the aforementioned components that allows companies to see if they qualify for financing. To be eligible for PYME 250, companies must also fill out the same basic questionnaire and present it and the required documents to a local Bancomext office, which will submit the information to a credit bureau for verification.

To apply for financing of USD 250,000 and up, companies must meet the same basic requirements: show proof of exporting, have insurance that covers the amount of credit sought, and have a financing structure in place that allows proceeds from export sales to flow into a designated Bancomext account to cover the line of credit. Interest rates are set according to TIIE/LIBOR. In addition, the company must prove the venture is viable. Documents that may be requested include marketing videos, pamphlets, proof of a market niche, proof of production capacity, proof of technological capabilities, and detailed explanations of the factors of the particular company that will lead to its exporting success. Companies must also provide requested information about past credit as well as legal papers pertaining to official registration of the business.

To be eligible for investment banking or other financial services, the company must be economically viable, promote the acquisition of Mexican goods and services, show proof of the ability to generate positive cash flows, and have assets or cash flows that can cover the amount of credit sought.

Guarantees

Eligibility for guarantees for the modernization or extension of a plant include financial projections showing positive cash flows, satisfactory credit history, maximum indebtedness of 60 percent for companies with more than 1 year of operation and a maximum indebtedness of 50 percent for companies in operation less than 1 year, and proof of no suspension of payments or no losses in operations in the previous or present fiscal period.

IV. CONTACTS

Headquarters:
Bancomext
Camino a Santa Teresa 1679
Jardines del Pedregal
Delegación Alvaro Obregón
01900 México, D.F.
Tel: 525-481-6042
Fax: 525-481-6157
Internet: www.bancomext.com
Email: bancomext@bancomext.gob.mx
privatesector@adb.org

Investment Banking
Ing. Luis Alfonso Acosta Cobos, Director
Email: lacosta@bancomext.gob.mx

PYME
Cecilia Che, Promoter
Tel: 5449-9415

Laura Hernandez, Promoter
Tel: 5449-9228

Financial Advising
Javier Lozano Dubenard, Executive
Tel: 5481-6057

Bancomext Centers of Training, Advising, and Information
Jose Roberto Rivera
Tel: 5449-9259

NACIONAL FINANCIERA (NAFIN)

I. INTRODUCTION

NAFIN, Mexico's largest development bank, is dedicated to the modernization and economic development of Mexico through policies that strengthen and support business owners, economic sectors, private companies, the development of financial markets, and the growth of underdeveloped regions. Its primary objective is the development of MSMEs in Mexico's private sector. NAFIN also contributes equity to joint ventures. NAFIN is financed by the issuance of short- and long-term bankers' acceptances, such as bonds issued directly or through specific trust funds in the Mexican market. NAFIN has also received debt capital from the World Bank and IADB and remains one of the oldest borrowers of these multilateral organizations.

NAFIN was established in 1934. Since its inception, it has been controlled by the government of Mexico. A wide variety of financial products are offered, including loans, credit lines, foreign exchange and investment banking services, and training and technical assistance. NAFIN offers specialized services for international investors seeking joint ventures or strategic alliances in Mexico. NAFIN has also signed agreements with OPIC to work toward improving risk mitigation and management, especially as it relates to promoting international joint ventures.

One of NAFIN's goals for 2002 was to increase credit to the private sector by 16 percent through its role as a second-tier bank, complementing the services of commercial banks. NAFIN has also been actively involved in promoting the development of supplier networks and production chains through the increased use of technology. Increased electronic support has been fostered in financing, credit processing, business development, and the financial markets.

Wal-Mart, which operates over 500 stores in Mexico, and is now the dominant retailer in Mexico, signed an agreement with NAFIN to assist its more than 4,000 small- and medium-sized suppliers throughout Mexico in collecting on accounts in a more efficient and less costly manner. Suppliers can now access accounts and billing information online.

II. PRODUCTS

Loans and Guarantees

NAFIN offers fixed-rate loans to small- and medium-sized businesses in Mexico for investment in working capital, fixed assets, technological development, environmental improvement, and liability restructuring. The maximum loan amounts are the equivalent of USD 10 million in Mexican pesos, with a term of 10 years, disbursed through NAFIN's network intermediaries of commercial banks, credit unions, leasing companies, and other approved entities. NAFIN arranges short-, medium-, and long-term credit operations at floating rates, as well as second-tier credit operations for the expansion and modernization of companies at an interest rate based on LIBOR plus a spread, with a maximum term of up to 20 years.

NAFIN also provides financing for Mexican companies generating net foreign currency or whose products are priced in international currency at up to 100 percent of the loan in U.S. dollars at the rate of interest set by banks based on the 3-month LIBOR plus a spread with terms of 1–10 years.

Guarantees are provided to Mexican companies to invest in fixed assets and working capital, particularly in areas of high priority, such as environmental improvement projects and technological innovation. NAFIN assumes a risk of up to 50 percent for working capital and 70 percent for fixed assets and up to 80 percent for environmental improvement projects at a maximum of USD 3.3 million.

Projects that generate imports of capital goods into Mexico or that foster exports of goods to Mexico's trading partners are eligible for loans. NAFIN also issues letters of credit to international suppliers. Dollar-denominated loans are at an interest rate at a spread over LIBOR.

Equity Investments

NAFIN provides direct equity investments to companies for specific projects, becoming a shareholder of up to 20 percent for up to 5 years. NAFIN provides working capital for the modernization of facilities, machinery and equipment, and other purposes. NAFIN also has a program for indirect equity investments aimed at attracting direct, long-term overseas investments in certain sectors. Investors are offered long-term borrowing at preferential rates where they are participating in a portfolio of multiple firms, thereby assuming only portfolio risk. NAFIN will set up a specialized private investment fund, called a SINCA (Sociedades de Inversiones de Capitales), where NAFIN is a minority institutional shareholder. These are closed funds with a 10–12 year life. Most SINCA funds are fully invested, but funds are still available to support the following types of projects:

- *Agro-industrial sector funds* are available to new or recently created projects for nontraditional products focused on exports with high profitability that require capital resources of between USD 300,000 and USD 900,000 and whose assets do not exceed USD 3 million.
- *Chiapas project funds* are available for aquaculture, tourism, and agro-industrial projects located in Chiapas that are profitable and viable and that require capital resources between 5 and 10 million pesos.
- *Veracruz project funds* are available to trade, industrial, and service industry projects that are viable and profitable, are located in Veracruz, and require capital investment between 3 and 5 million pesos.
- *Tabasco project funds* are available to small business projects located in Tabasco that are viable and profitable and require capital resources between 2 and 5 million pesos.

Technical Assistance

Through an agreement with the European Investment Partners Program, NAFIN has agreed to assist Mexican and European companies in developing strategic alliances and joint ventures. For European companies interested in direct foreign investment, NAFIN offers technical assistance in the form of an analysis of the business environment and pre-feasibility studies that include potential customers, regulations, tariff advantages, incentives, production costs, legal issues, potential suppliers, and so on. NAFIN can also arrange field trips for the purpose of gathering more detailed information on land and construction, infrastructure issues, logistics and transportation, labor issues, as well as other areas of interest. For companies interested in joint ventures, NAFIN can identify and help negotiate and structure joint ventures, licensing agreements, subcontracting, alliances between manufacturers, and mergers and acquisitions. NAFIN can organize forums where potential business partners meet to discuss issues of mutual concern. Once an alliance is agreed upon, NAFIN offers start-up equity resources to the company, long-term financing to develop the project, and assistance in obtaining international or venture capital funds.

NAFIN also provides assistance to improve supplier networks within Mexico and to raise the quality of production through consulting services and quality assurance certification programs such as the ISO 9000. NAFIN finances technical assistance programs at a maximum of 2 years at the TIIE rate at a maximum of USD 30,000. NAFIN also promotes Mexico's infrastructure through the development of industrial parks by providing financing for feasibility studies; park creation, operation, and promotional expenses; and strengthening and expansion of existing parks. Terms of credit are up to 20 years depending on the project's cash flow, with interest at TIIE or 3-month LIBOR.

III. ELIGIBILITY AND APPLICATION PROCESS

Equity Participation

To be eligible for equity participation, a company must submit a project proposal summary of three to four pages explaining the viability of the project. For more information, contact NAFIN headquarters.

IV. CONTACTS

Headquarters:
Nacional Financiera, S.N.C.
Av. Insurgentes Sur 1971
Col. Guadelupe Inn
01020, Mexico, D.F.
Tel: 01 55 53 25 64 00
Fax: 53 25 60 41
Internet:www.nafin.com
Email: info@nafin.gob.mx

C.P. Mario Laborin Gomez, General Director, Mexico
Tel: 525 325 6000
Equity Investment Programs
Florina Hernández
Tel: 525 325-6632/33

EUROCENTER
Beatriz Montellano
Tel: 525 325-6810

London Branch
19th Floor, 1 Angel Court
London EC2R 7HJ, U.K.
Tel: (44 207) 417 0016
Fax: (44 207) 417 5115

Washington Representative Office
1615 L Street, NW, Suite 310
Washington, DC 20036
Tel: (202) 338-9010/11
Fax: (202) 338-9244

Tokyo Representative Office
811 Kokusai Building
3-1-1 Marunouchi
Chiyoda-Ku, Tokyo 100-000 5
Japan
Tel: (813) 32 84 03 31/32
Fax: (813) 32 84 03 30

New York Representative Office
Nafinsa Securities, Inc.
21 East 63rd Street
New York, NY 10021
Tel: (212) 821-0300/25
Fax: (212) 821-0330

BRE BANK

I. INTRODUCTION

Founded in 1986, the initial purpose of the BRE Bank was to offer foreign exchange credits to Polish exporters for investment and technology financing. Since that time, the bank has widened its activity, especially in foreign trade transaction services. In 1989, IFC and the World Bank gave BRE credit lines for the private and cooperative sectors to develop export and consumable industry. In 1998, BRE Bank merged with Polski Bank Rozwoju, the Polish Development Bank, to increase profit as well as its activity to include commercial and investment banking. Now the primary activity of the bank is to provide services to SMEs.

II. PRODUCTS AND SERVICES

BRE Bank offers a diverse range of products and services, including maintenance of bank accounts, acceptance of savings and term deposit accounts, performance of financial settlement services, granting and drawing of loans, bills of exchange and check operations, acceptance and placement bank deposits, guarantees, dealings in foreign currencies, servicing of state loans, issuing and trading of securities, custodial services, provision of future and forward financial transactions, and factoring. Other activities include provision of economic and financial advice; administration of funds, including pension funds; share brokerage; establishment and participation in banks and companies at home and abroad; provision of electronic banking services; and related financial services.

Loans and Guarantees

- *Short-term financing* bridges the gap in the working capital of clients. The form of financing depends on the overall cash cycle, the transaction being financed, or the one-off extraordinary need for cash. The most widely used short-term financing products include a variety of bank loans. Other products improve liquidity when the company has outstanding receivables under invoices or bills of exchange. Companies with a strong financial standing can apply for an exposure limit assigned by the bank to provide a special package of liquidity-improving products under simplified procedures. The largest corporations active in Poland can receive special financing for several weeks at an interest rate linked to the current situation on the money market. Companies with attractive fixed assets are offered lease back opportunities.

- *Long-term financing* provides large corporations with capital to finance mid- and long-term investments. Products include investment and mortgage loans and the issuance of debt or equity. If the scale of necessary financing exceeds the capacity of a single bank, BRE Bank arranges and leads syndicated loans.

- *Trade finance* provides funding to suppliers. Solutions may include credit financing of the production of goods to be exported (pre-shipment finance) or the discounting of receivables under a letter of credit, a bill of exchange, or an invoice (post-shipment finance). Export factoring ensures uninterrupted current financing combined with the assignment of all confirmed export receivables and the maintenance of settlement accounts. Backed on the cooperation between BRE Bank and the Export Credit Insurance Corporation (KUKE), the bank's clients can insure their export receivables against commercial and other risks, including any change in the value of their receivables or payables in foreign currencies.

- *Trade guarantees* play an essential role in securing mutual obligations of trade partners in domestic as well as foreign sales. BRE Bank guarantees are available to domestic economic units (companies, enterprises, and so on) conducting exchange of goods and services, investors of modernizing and developing projects, city councils and local governments, as well as domestic and foreign banks and financial institutions.

Asset Management

BRE Bank offers a variety of asset management services ranging from issuing bonds and other securities to risk management products.

- *Investment of excess cash* offers fixed-rate terms, treasury bills and bonds, debt securities issued by municipalities and corporations, and mortgage bonds issued by mortgage banks. This asset management service is an increasingly popular form of investment for institutional clients.

- *Capital market investment* enables the bank to become an intermediary in the trading of various instruments on both domestic and foreign markets. BRE Bank offers a custody service for all securities.

- *Financial risk management* protects companies against the risk of the volatility of fixed rates, interest rates, and stock prices.

Instruments offered by BRE Bank hedge the value of receivables and payables in foreign currencies as well as interest receivables and payables under executed or scheduled deposits or loans. The main benefit to the client is the hedged risk of losses and the capacity to project accurately the company's financial results. Financial risk management products offered by the bank are also an attractive form of speculative investment to those companies that accept higher risks.

III. ELIGIBILITY AND APPLICATION PROCESS

Contact BRE Bank headquarters for more information.

IV. CONTACTS

Headquarters:
BRE Bank
Ul. Senatorska 18
00-950 Warszawa
Poland
Tel: (0 22) 829 00 00
Fax: (0 22) 829 00 33
Internet: www.brebank.com.pl
Email: redakcjaportalu@brebank.com.pl

Investor Relations
investor.relations@brebank.com.pl

Private Banking Department
Ul. Królewska 14
00-950 Warszawa
Tel: (0 22) 829 07 69, 829 02 67
Fax: (0 22) 829 14 40

RUSSIAN REGIONAL DEVELOPMENT BANK (RRDB)

I. INTRODUCTION

The RRDB was established in 1996. It has since grown to have a presence in all segments of the financial market, with various foreign currency instruments, while maintaining extremely conservative risk-management principles. Authorized capital stock has risen to 575 million rubles (approximately USD 18 million), meaning RRDB has become one of the largest Russian banks in terms of capital.

II. PRODUCTS AND SERVICES

Loans and Guarantees

RRDB offers a variety of short- and long-term credits in rubles and other foreign currency:

- Short- and medium-term credits for replenishing working capital and the acquisition of inventory holdings
- Overdraft facilities
- Structured credit
- Letters of credit
- Syndicated credits
- Leasing operations

The bank also provides revocable and irrevocable guarantees, securing the clients' financial obligations. The bank's specialists help to choose the most suitable form of guarantee and consult the client on devising a guarantee scheme for business expansion.

Anticipating the investment boom on the pension fund market, RRDB acquired the Portfolio Investments Management Company for the specific purpose of working with nonstate pension funds within existing legislation. RRDB successfully operates on the market, managing assets of several nonstate pension funds.

Technical Assistance

The bank is prepared to give expert support or take the resolution of problems upon itself in restructuring enterprises; reorganizing financial flow; optimizing taxes; analyzing and devising strategic development, including investment strategies; and increasing the investment appeal of enterprises. RRDB participates in the development and coordination of financial schemes, allowing for the implementation of complex intersettlements and the restructuring and liquidation of current and accumulated debts. The bank also offers services for the development and performance of complex long-term projects in the sphere of corporate finance. This includes measures to promote and manage the circulation of a client's securities.

III. ELIGIBILITY AND APPLICATION PROCESS

Contact RRDB headquarters for more information.

IV. CONTACTS

Headquarters:
Russian Regional Development Bank
129594 Moscow, Sushchevsky Val, 65
Russia
Tel: (095) 933-03-43
Fax: (095) 933-03-44
Telex: 414294 RRDB RU
Internet: www.vbrr.ru
Email: bank@vbrr.ru

DEVELOPMENT BANK OF SOUTHERN AFRICA (DBSA)

I. INTRODUCTION

The DBSA was established in 1983, but transformed in 1996 to meet the needs of the new South Africa and the SADC region. The mission of DBSA is to improve the socioeconomic conditions and quality of life for the people of southern Africa. Specifically, DBSA invests in infrastructure and facilitates the provision of infrastructure development finance, finances sustainable development, responds to development demands, and acts as a catalyst for investment. Investment activities are directed toward the areas of water and sanitation, energy, transportation, telecommunications, and information technology.

II. PRODUCTS AND SERVICES

Project Finance

The Private Sector Investments Business Unit develops private sector projects in southern Africa. Primary activities include the identification, appraisal, and financing of projects involving private provision of infrastructure (PPI). Such projects include service agreements, delegated management and leasing arrangements, BOT and other concessions, and privatization. DBSA also provides technical assistance to clients in connection with PPI. This unit offers a variety of financial instruments, including:

- Loan finance
- Equity investments
- Guarantees
- Refinancing commitments

Technical Assistance

Technical assistance is provided to cover the provision of information, advice, and professional services with respect to the structuring of PPI projects and all facets of the processes leading to project implementation. DBSA's role in this regard is not intended to be all-inclusive, and where private sector organizations are better placed to provide these services, the Unit will assist clients in securing appropriate support. Fees are normally charged for professional services rendered.

III. ELIGIBILITY AND APPLICATION PROCESS

Contact DBSA headquarters for more information.

IV. CONTACTS

Headquarters:
Development Bank of Southern Africa
1258 Lever Road
Headway Hill
Midrand
South Africa
Tel: 011-313-3911
Fax: 011-313-3086
Internet: www.dbsa.org
Email: webmaster@dbsa.org

Private Sector
Tel: 011-313-3004
Fax: 011-313-3627
Email: johnb@dbsa.org

Executive Manager of Operations
JH deV Botha
Tel: 011-313-3377
Fax: 011-313-3720
Email: divb@dbsa.org

DEVELOPMENT BANK OF TURKEY (DBT)

I. INTRODUCTION

DBT was originally founded in 1975 under the name of the State Industry and Laborer Investment Bank. In 1988, the name was changed, as well as the bank's ability to provide funding support for sectors other than industry. The mission of DBT is to provide funding and operational support to enterprises incorporated as joint stock companies based on criteria such as profitability and efficiency through lending and acquiring interest; channeling local and international savings into investments aimed at achieving economic development; contributing to development of the local capital market; financing local, international and international joint investments; and performing all development and investment banking operations.

Since 1990, DBT has obtained over USD 118 million in revenues, and since its inception, it has acquired an interest in almost 100 companies. Although it is classified as a state-owned bank, due to its shareholding structure, the bank considers that its primary reason for existence is to lend financial support for investment and entrepreneurship potential of the Turkish private sector, particularly industry and tourism sectors.

II. PRODUCTS AND SERVICES

Loans and Guarantees

DBT provides short-, medium-. and long-term cash and non-cash loans denominated in Turkish lira or any other currency and carries out lending transactions based on leasing or sharing profits. It is willing to acquire and sell all types of securities and issue guarantees for bonds, as well as extend loans to companies and acquire interests in local and international companies and carry out rehabilitation, bonification, and consolidation where deemed necessary. DBT may also found a company under the bank's leadership and acquire and sell shares issued by associated undertakings. Guarantees may be issued, and DBT may act as an intermediary for any Turkish or foreign person or entity after receiving appropriate collateral security. Specifically, DBT is also willing to provide project-based lending, financial leasing, and financing through the acquisition of an interest in capital.

Technical Assistance

DBT carries out or procures performance of research, project development, and training projects and provides technical assistance. DBT may take any action to ensure that companies with which it maintains financing relations operate efficiently.

DBT may also carry out all kinds of foreign exchange transactions, including but not limited to imports, exports, invisible transactions, and hold currency positions.

III. ELIGIBILITY AND APPLICATION PROCESS

To be eligible for the borrowing of loans in connection with any investment project, an investor must provide proof that it is a joint stock company. Other requirements are as follows:

- Applicant must have an Investment Incentive Certificate from the Undersecretariat of Treasury in connection with the proposed investment.
- If a loan from a specific fund is being requested, it must meet the requirements set out in the decree and communiqué governing that fund's functions.
- An investigation about the applicant and technical, economic, and financial assessments regarding the project must produce satisfactory results.

DBT is authorized to acquire interests in local and international companies in any place, sector, or branch of business that it deems appropriate and that is in line with its mission, provided the amount and conditions of the acquisition is determined by the bank itself.

IV. CONTACTS

Headquarters:
Development Bank of Turkey
Izmir Caddesi No. 35
06 440 Kizilay
Ankara
Turkey
Tel: (90-312) 417 9200
Fax: (90-312) 418 3967
Internet: www.tkb.com.tr
Email: tkbhaberlesme@tkb.com.tr

TÜRKIYE SINAI KALKINMA BANKASI (TSKB)

I. INTRODUCTION

TSKB was established in 1950—with the support of the World Bank and the cooperation of the government of the Republic of Turkey, the Central Bank of Turkey, and the leading commercial banks of Turkey—as the first investment and development bank of Turkey. Its mission is to provide assistance to the private sector, primarily in the industrial sector; to encourage and assist the participation of private and foreign capital incorporations in establishing in Turkey; and to assist in the development of the capital market in Turkey.

Since its inception, the bank has provided support for more than 3,500 investment projects and has participated in the share capital of more than 100 companies. Further, through the offering of equity shares of such companies to the public, TSKB has been a significant milestone in this field and thus assumed a prominent and vital role in fostering the development of capital markets.

II. PRODUCTS AND SERVICES

Loans and Guarantees

The loans provided by TSKB as an investment and development bank have been concentrated on medium- and long-term projects, particularly for the purpose of investment. However, TSKB also extends short-term working capital loans to meet financing requirements in the operating period. The bank also provides a full range of banking services in relation to foreign trade financing. The following are the loan products offered:

- Investment loans
  - Foreign currency loans
  - Foreign currency indexed TL loans
  - TL loans
- Working capital loans
  - Medium-term loans
  - Short-term loans
- Special type of credits
- Leasing facilities

Equity

TSKB has been participating in equity in Turkey since the 1960s, contributing to the establishment of industrial enterprises. TSKB continues to contribute to Turkey's success with a diversified range of activities in investment banking activities. It boasts an extensive relationship network of private equity funds, investment banks, and venture capital funds worldwide as well as a highly experienced team of experts.

Technical Assistance

TSKB offers an extensive range of products designed to assist companies through all phases of project development.

- *Valuation consultancy*—TSKB may prepare feasibility and appraisal reports and conduct valuation projects for privatization administrations as well as other private and public sector companies.
- *Mergers/acquisitions*—TSKB may act as an adviser and intermediary to assist in finding financial partners for companies in order to help finance additional working capital requirements or planned investments. It also provides services to enhance the effectiveness of the competitive strategies of clients.
- *Research activities*—TSKB's Research Department team looks at economic, market, industry, and company data to enhance the performance of clients' portfolios and to help companies and individuals accurately set their strategic direction. Research analysts use a variety of sector periodicals, conferences, workshops, and meet with company executives to provide clients with accurate recommendations.

Treasury Services

The Treasury Department of TSKB performs a variety of transactions and operations in the domestic and international money markets, including managing bank and cash positions; providing treasury bills and government bonds; and making repo and reverse transactions, foreign exchange transactions, and foreign exchange securities transactions.

III. ELIGIBILITY AND APPLICATION PROCESS

Loans are made available according to the eligibility of projects, and they are evaluated from economic, technical, financial, and administrative standpoints by a competent project appraisal staff composed of engineers, economists, and financial analysts.

IV. CONTACTS

Headquarters:
Türkiye Sınai Kalkınma Bankası
Meclisi Mebusan Caddesi, No. 161
80040 Fındıklı Istanbul
Turkey
Tel: (212) 334 50 50
Fax: (212) 243 29 75
Internet: www.tskb.com.tr
Email: info@tskb.com.tr

Corporate Finance
Tel: 90 212 334 53 40

Technical Services
Tel: 90 212 334 50 07

Region-to-Region DFIs

This chapter covers region-to-region DFIs. These DFIs are a relatively new phenomenon. BADEA and ISDB were the first to be established in 1975, and the others were created subsequently as a particular regional group of countries identified a need to support projects that (for environmental, fiscal, or national security reasons, among others) foster improved social and economic stability.

ARAB BANK FOR ECONOMIC DEVELOPMENT IN AFRICA (BADEA)

I. INTRODUCTION

BADEA began operations in Khartoum, Sudan, in 1975. Though funded by the governments of the member states of the League of Arab States, BADEA is an independent international institution enjoying full international legal status and complete autonomy in administrative and financial matters. The purpose of the bank is to strengthen economic, financial, and technical cooperation between Arab and African countries by financing economic development in non-Arab African countries, stimulating the contribution of Arab capital to African development, and providing technical assistance required for the development of Africa.

BADEA directs its financing efforts toward improving living conditions, particularly to projects related to rural development and the rural environment, such as rural water supply and sewerage, and projects aimed at reducing implications of drought and desertification. Since its inception, BADEA has financed 303 development projects, 258 technical assistance operations, 24 loans for the private sector, and 14 special operations in the context of the Urgency Aide Program benefiting several African countries affected by drought and desertification, in addition to 59 loans extended through the Special Arab Aid Fund for Africa.

In September 2002, a loan agreement in the amount of USD 3.8 million was signed between the Republic of Senegal and BADEA. This loan financed the "Reclamation of Irrigated Areas in the Province of Bakel" project, which sought to increase agricultural production, reduce mural migration and poverty, and create seasonal and permanent job opportunities. Additionally, the project offered support to increase the participation of women in agriculture, as well as to improve transportation, support agricultural research, and conserve the environment. With this new loan, total commitments of BADEA to the Republic of Senegal will amount to U.S. 139 million. The loan will be repaid in 28 years, including a grace period of 6 years, at an annual interest rate of 2 percent.

II. PRODUCTS AND SERVICES

Loans and Guarantees

Loans and sureties are granted to development financing institutions of a local, mixed, or regional nature that participate in the financing of major economic projects, especially in industrial and agricultural fields, to make up any deficit from external sources of financing. BADEA's contribution to the financing of any given project cannot exceed 50 percent of the total cost of the said project, and the amount of financing for the said project cannot exceed USD 15 million. However, for small projects with a total cost not exceeding USD 10 million, financing may be increased to 80 percent of the total cost of the project. BADEA also provides technical assistance in the form of unrepayable grants.

Technical Assistance

Technical assistance is provided to aid companies in acquiring modern production techniques and knowledge. Technical and financial assistance is aimed at identifying opportunities conducive to economic development, preparing related programs and projects, drawing up financing schedules, and ensuring the schedules are implemented, especially as this affects Arab-African joint ventures.

III. ELIGIBILITY AND APPLICATION

To be considered eligible for assistance, organizations must be one of the following:

- A government of an African country, including any province, agency, or organization thereof
- A public or private company, organization, or project carrying out its business in African countries and whose capital the governments or citizens of those countries hold a majority
- A mixed African or Arab-African company whose purpose is economic development

Development operations financed by BADEA follow a procedure cycle that is almost identical for all kinds of projects whose technical, economic, and financial feasibility has been established. Projects must have a reasonable economic rate of return and should promote development in the beneficiary country. The application process is as follows:

- Identification of project to include a detailed request or proposal
- Desk review and determination of the project's scope to include local and foreign costs, financing plan, other financing sources, economic situation, and development policy
- Preliminary approval
- Project appraisal and submission to board of directors
- Consultation with other co-financiers
- Negotiation and signature of loan agreement
- Declaration effectiveness of loan agreement
- Project implementation
- Supervision and follow-up

IV. CONTACTS

Headquarters:
Arab Bank for Economic Development in Africa
P.O. Box 2640
Khartoum
Sudan
Tel: 249-11-773646 /773709
Fax: 249-11-770600/770498
Telex: 23098/22739/22248 SD
Internet: www.badea.org
Email: badea@badea.org

ISLAMIC DEVELOPMENT BANK (ISDB)

I. INTRODUCTION

The ISDB was established in 1975 with the purpose of developing member countries economically and socially in accordance with Islamic law. The functions of the bank include participating in equity, granting loans, and operating special funds for assistance to Muslim communities in nonmember countries. Additionally, the bank is responsible for promoting foreign trade, providing technical assistance, and aiding personnel engaged in development activities in Muslim countries to conform to the Shari'ah.

II. PRODUCTS

Loans and Guarantees

ISDB offers lines of financing to national development financial institutions (NDFIs)/Islamic banks as an indirect method of project finance. The goal is to help these financial institutions and banks finance installment sales and leasing operations. With this option available, the hope is to increase small- and medium-sized industries in member countries. Typically, the line of financing is denominated in Islamic dinar, but it may be repaid in any convertible currency. The usual amount of a line ranges between approximately USD 720,000 and USD 7.2 million.

Additionally, the ISDB offers three types of trade financing:

- *Import Trade Financing Operations (ITFOs)* are designed for the finance of imports to be used for developmental reasons.
- *Export Financing Schemes (EFSs)* finance "nontraditional export sectors."
- *Islamic Bank's Portfolio* is designed to aid importers/exporters in the private sector.

Technical Assistance

Private sector assistance is given to the least-developed member countries, even though all member countries are eligible. Technical assistance for the private sector is usually provided in the form of loans, grants, or a combination of the two. Furthermore, when this technical assistance comes in addition to project financing, it is usually provided in the same form as the financing for the project. For example, when a project is funded through loans, the technical assistance will comes through loans as well. Additionally, ISDB provides technical assistance to banks and institutions already receiving financing from the ISDB. The purpose of this line is to improve the way by which the financing by NDFIs/investment banks are utilized. This is accomplished using a "pipeline of eligible project proposals selected through feasibility studies" by private sector sponsors and the company doing the project.

III. ELIGIBILITY AND APPLICATION PROCESS

The ISDB requires the following criteria for a project to be eligible for assistance:

- The project must be in a member country in the private sector. However, a project that is jointly owned by the private sector and public enterprise may be eligible as well.
- The project must improve the "operating environment for the development of the private sector."
- The project must be compatible with ISDB objectives, and there must be a rationale for its medium-term strategic agenda (MTSA). Additionally, the project should be justified economically.
- The project must be feasible in technical, institutional, and managerial terms.
- The project must generate a reasonable cash flow to cover the financial liabilities and to provide a significant return to its investors.

For ISDB assistance, most applicants are required to apply through the ISDB governor's office. After clearance has been received, the application is processed. The first step in the application process is to submit an outline of the project. The outline must contain the following information:

- Description
- Names of the sponsors
- Cost estimates
- Financing plan (must give an idea about the amount of financing requested)
- Market prospects
- Memorandum and articles of association of the company/project (in some cases)
- Audited accounts and financial statements (for established companies or projects whose financing will be used for expansion purposes)

IV. CONTACTS

Headquarters:
Islamic Development Bank
P.O. Box 5925
Jeddah 21432
Kingdom of Saudi Arabia
Tel: (9662) 6361400
Fax: (9662) 6366871
Telex: 601 137 ISDB SJ
Internet: www.isdb.org
Email: idbarchives@isdb.org.sa

NORDIC ENVIRONMENT
FINANCE CORPORATION (NEFCO)

I. INTRODUCTION

NEFCO was established in 1990 by the five Nordic countries of Denmark, Finland, Iceland, Norway, and Sweden as a multilateral venture capital institution. Its mission is to facilitate the implementation of environmentally beneficial projects in neighboring Central and Eastern Europe, with effects that benefit the Nordic region. NEFCO finances projects that modernize industrial and energy production processes; projects that produce equipment to improve environmental conditions or that invest in such enterprises; and that offer environmental services such as waste management, recycling, and water and wastewater treatment.

II. PRODUCTS AND SERVICES

NEFCO participates as a risk-capital investor providing loan financing and/or equity investments in projects that usually involve participation by one or more cooperating partners from the Nordic region. NEFCO offers a variety of services including loans, guarantees, equity investments, and more.

Loans and Guarantees

NEFCO's participation in a project is generally in the range of 25 to 35 percent of the total financing. Loan amounts typically range from EUR 125,000 to EUR 3 million. As NEFCO regularly co-finances projects with other financial institutions, it prefers to focus its investments on the environmental aspects of the project.

NEFCO participates in the financing of a project through

- Loans on market terms
- Loans with equity features
- Subordinated loans or mezzanine financing
- Guarantees

Medium- and long-term loans and guarantees are usually provided on market terms. In some cases, subordinated loans and loans with equity features may be provided. Often the loans are extended in addition to NEFCO's equity participation in the project.

Since 1996, NEFCO has administered a special Nordic facility for concessional financing of selected environmental projects within the neighboring region. Through this facility, projects can be supported by grants.

Equity Investment

NEFCO aims at participating as an active investor, typically through subscriptions of equity and shares, facilitating mobilization of the necessary equity base for a project. NEFCO then participates as a partner in the project. NEFCO requests the right to nominate a representative to the board of project companies, at least in the early phase of a project. Participation in a project does not need to follow pre-set time limits and participation in a project can be for as long as necessary. However, since NEFCO operates as a revolving fund, the nature of its participation is that over time, it prefers to terminate holdings through acceptable exit mechanisms. NEFCO does not accept a majority ownership or a dominating position for itself.

III. ELIGIBILITY AND APPLICATION PROCESS

In general, to be eligible for NEFCO assistance, projects should be financially viable and based on cooperation between local and Nordic enterprises. The main criteria for NEFCO's participation in projects include the following:

- The project is located in one of NEFCO's countries of operation.
- The project has a relevant environmental effect.
- The project is based on long-term cooperation through investments in enterprises, primarily through the formation of joint-venture companies or corporate acquisitions.

- The project has a Nordic company or institution as business partner.
- The project is economically, financially, institutionally, and technically viable.

All financing decisions are made by the board of NEFCO, which is made up of one representative from each member country. Presentation of new project proposals to the board is preceded by a comprehensive appraisal of the project to examine the project's environmental, technical, economical, financial, and institutional feasibility. Among other factors, the technology in question is examined for its suitability to obtain desirable environmental effects. An important base for the project evaluation is an adequate feasibility study. NEFCO usually assumes that the other partners will prepare or will have prepared a study, which is then submitted to NEFCO.

NEFCO has no application guide but expects a brief project description in which the following items are included:

- Nordic partner(s)
- Project country
- Local partner(s)
- Project category, e.g., energy efficiency, water
- Environmental benefits
- Size of the financing
- Other financiers
- Possible feasibility studies

IV. CONTACTS

Headquarters:
Nordic Environment Finance Corporation
Fabianinkatu 34
P.O. Box 249
FIN-00171 Helsinki
Finland
Tel: 358 9 18001/1800344
Fax: 358 9 630 976
Internet: www.nefco.org
Email: info@nefco.fi

Harro Pitkanen, Managing Director
Harro.pitkanen@nefco.fi

Torben Vindelov, Senior Investment Manager
Torben.vindelov@nefco.fi

Nordic Southern African Development Fund (NORSAD)

I. INTRODUCTION

NORSAD began operations in 1991 as a joint initiative between the Nordic countries of Denmark, Finland, Norway, and Sweden and the SADC to support economic and industrial development by promoting and financing sound business cooperation between private sector enterprises. The agency is the manager of the NORSAD fund, with capital of approximately EUR 50 million, donated by the four Nordic governments. NORSAD also works closely with Nordic Development Finance Institutions (NDFIs) to provide loan financing when an NDFI provides equity to a project company.

NORSAD provides loans and matchmaking services for projects and recommends commercially viable equity-based joint venture proposals from SADC promoters to interested partners in the Nordic countries. Under certain circumstances, Nonequity partnerships involving technology transfer are also eligible for NORSAD financing.

II. PRODUCTS AND SERVICES

Loans and Guarantees

NORSAD finances all types of private sector activities with the exception of pure trade activities. Loans and guarantees may be used for working capital as well as capital investments.

Terms

NORSAD prefers not to be the only lender in larger projects, and financing normally does not exceed 50 percent of the total project cost or EUR 2 million. Loans are provided in any of the Nordic currencies and in euro. Maximum repayment periods for loans are 7 years, including a grace period of not more than 2 years. Repayment is normally done in quarterly installments. Interest rates are fixed and generally range from 7 to 10 percent per annum. A commitment fee of 1 percent of the approved loan is payable upon acceptance of the NORSAD loan offer. A smaller fee is charged for each loan disbursement.

Guarantees in foreign currency to other financial institutions for loans and credit can be granted for a maximum period of 7 years. An annual guarantee fee of 2 to 5 percent is charged on the outstanding balance.

NORSAD loans and guarantees must be covered by collateral, which may be extended by the project company or by a third party and must cover the commercial risk on the project company. There are no fixed rules for the type of collateral acceptable to NORSAD. Any security offered is assessed on its own value with regard to factors such as ability to honor NORSAD's debt in case of default by the project company, stability of the local currency, hard currency generation, and ability to sell the assets.

III. ELIGIBILITY AND APPLICATION PROCESS

NORSAD is willing to finance any commercially viable business venture in the SADC region provided the project and NORSAD's financing has a positive development impact on the host country. Projects must also meet the following criteria:

- A Nordic partner must make a direct equity investment in the project company, or a long-term technical agreement is established between the project company and a Nordic company. An investment by an NDFI, or a local financial institution if funded by an NDFI, must also fulfill this criteria.
- The project is technically feasible and economically viable without subsidies and undue protection.
- At least 40 percent of the project cost must be covered by equity or quasi-equity instruments provided by the project promoters and other investors.
- The project must have a positive impact on the host country.
- The project must meet international environmental standards.

To apply, contact the nearest NORSAD office.

IV. CONTACTS

Headquarters:
NORSAD
Anglo American Building, 6th Floor
74 Independence Avenue
P.O. Box 35577
10101 Lusaka
Zambia
Tel: 260 1 255663/4, 255773/4
Fax: 260 1 255432
Internet: www.norsad.org
Email: norsad@norsad.org

Angola
Emilio Grioñ
Tel: 244 2 343 392
Email: em.grion@ebonet.net

Botswana
Niels Schultz
Tel: 267 39 59 474/316 4714
Email: Schultz@botsnet.bw

Denmark
Steen Donner
Tel: 45 33 77 33 77
Email: di@di.dk

Finland
Hans Östermark
Tel: 358 6 312 9495
Email: hans.ostermark@pp.nic.fi

Malawi
Arthur Stevens
Tel: 265 622 029
Email: pirimiti@malawi.net

Mozambique
Paulo Negrão
Tel: 258 1 82 317 555
Email: aam@tropical.co.mz

Namibia
Klaus Endresen
Tel: 264 61 230 526
Email: klendre.bridge@iwwn.com.na

Norway
Mr. Kim D. Kristmoen
Tel: 47 66 91 84 19
Email: kim@puku.net

Swaziland
Fritof Jensen
Tel: 268 42 20765/40 442 50
Email: helbo@africaonline.co.sz

Sweden
Mats Nilsson
Tel: 46 8 520 146 43
Email: interconsult@swipnet.se

Tanzania
Sudipto Das and Noli Mantheakis
Tel: 255 222 113119
Email: tanruss@raha.com

Zimbabwe
Anthony Golding
Tel: 263 4 494 357
Email: goldfish@pc2000.co.zw

Selected Quasi DFIs

This chapter provides an overview of a few important DFIs that now have a significant amount of private sector ownership. Most of them started out as traditional national DFIs, but that over time acquired or merged with other commercial or investment banking groups, so that today they have a much broader product offering and only minority stakes owned by a government. These organizations are referred to as quasi DFIs.

DEVELOPMENT BANK OF SINGAPORE (DBS)

I. INTRODUCTION

DBS was established with government funding and a social mandate like any other development bank, but today it is fully diversified and operates much like a standard corporate commercial bank. Though DBS still adheres to its original mandate as a development bank in providing long-term project financing, it has also developed its commercial banking, retail banking, investment banking, asset management, and insurance divisions. In 1961 the government of Singapore created the Economic Development Board to modernize and industrialize Singapore after it was freed from British rule. In 1968, DBS grew out of the Economic Development Board to provide financing to the industrial sector.

DBS is listed on the Singapore and Malaysia stock exchanges. At DBS's inception, the government was the majority shareholder, with banks, insurance companies, and corporations holding the remaining shares. DBS's full-scale commercial banking capacity developed in the 1970s with the growth of Singapore's financial sector. Though DBS originally started with assistance from the World Bank and ADB, today DBS's growth is based on its ability to mobilize commercial banking deposits, which have become 80 percent of DBS's lendable resources.

Among corporate customers, after housing loans, loans to the building and construction sector represented the highest concentration of loans in 2001 (14 percent) with manufacturing (9.0 percent) and transportation (8.6 percent) representing the next two highest concentrations. Total corporate lending was SGD 70.6 million (approximately USD 40.6 million). Today the DBS group is Singapore's largest bank and consists of the DBS bank, DBS asset management, and DBS Vickers Securities. DBS has also acquired banking subsidiaries abroad in Korea, Hong Kong, Indonesia, and Thailand. Total assets in 2001 were USD 7.3 billion, making it one of the largest banks in Southeast Asia. DBS has over 100 branches in Singapore and has a network of 1,300 correspondent banks.

DBS is the regional market leader in treasury services, custodial services, and corporate lending. Though it is Singapore's main source of medium- and long-term financing, it is also actively involved in short-term banking services. DBS has also made strategic alliances with TD Waterhouse to strengthen its brokerage capacity and financial advisory services and with CGNU, Britain's largest insurer, to enhance its insurance division.

II. PRODUCTS

Loans and Guarantees

Project financing is available for companies interested in power, telecommunications, oil and gas, and infrastructure projects. Long-term loans are available in foreign as well as local currencies. DBS also has the capacity to issue bonds and arrange syndicated loans or a combination of instruments. Import and export financing facilities for corporate customers include such services as letters of credit, shipping and airway guarantees, trust receipts, and discounting of receivables. Medium-term financing in local and foreign currencies is also available. Bank guarantees on imports are available at a rate of 1/8 percent for collection of import bills with additional flat fees and shipping guarantees at 1/4 percent with additional flat fees. For export guarantees, the rate is 1/8 percent for negotiation and confirmation of documentary credits and a commission of 1/8 percent for collection of outward bills.

In addition to its retail bank, which services individuals in Singapore and Hong Kong, DBS has an international banking presence with branches all over Asia, including China. DBS is involved in capital markets activities, raises funds in the equity and debt markets, as well as provides mergers and acquisitions, and offers financial advisory services. DBS has initiated initial public offerings (IPOs) over the Internet and has also issued bond IPOs and asset-backed securities. DBS has a strong position in the debt capital markets, being involved in deals such as the Singapore telecommunications deal of SGD 1 billion (approximately USD 575 million) in bonds. DBS is also a leading bank in Asia in the area of interest rate swaps and options.

Equity Investments

DBS Asset Management is actively involved in portfolio management. It manages accounts of individuals, investment companies, pension funds, corporations, and unit trusts. DBS is also involved in venture capital through the Transtech Venture Capital Fund, the largest of its kind in Singapore. DBS Capital Investments Limited is in charge of managing venture capital activities. In 2001, DBS screened over 300 companies and conducted due diligence on 40 of them. DBS and other venture capital firms invested jointly in these new enterprises.

III. ELIGIBILITY AND APPLICATION PROCESS

Private companies wishing to utilize any DBS services are encouraged to contact DBS directly through email or phone. Because DBS no longer operates as a traditional development bank, its rates are commercially competitive and dependent upon the individual project and parties involved.

IV. CONTACTS

Headquarters:
Development Bank of Singapore
6 Shenton Way, DBS Building Tower One
Singapore 068809
Tel: 65 6327 2265
Fax: 65 6227 6811
Internet: www.dbs.com
Email: corpbank@dbs.com

Tuan Lam, DBS Equity
Tel: 852 2913 5607

Stephen Finch, DBS Debt Markets
Tel: 65 6878 5812

Kan Shik Lum, DBS Capital Markets
Tel: 65 6878 6382

DBS Asset Management Ltd
8 Cross Street
#27-01 & 06
PWC Building
Singapore 048424
Tel: 65 6878 7801
Fax: 65 6221 7018

DBS Trading Ltd.
8 Cross Street
PWC Building #02-01
Singapore 048424
Tel: 65 6533 9688

SOCIÉTÉ IINTERNATIONALE FINANCIÈRE POUR LES INVESTISSEMENTS ET LE DÉVELOPPEMENT EN AFRIQUE (SIFIDA)

I. INTRODUCTION

SIFIDA was founded in 1970 by 120 prime banks and industrial groups, including the African Development Bank and the IFC, as a private international investment company for Africa. Following a restructuring in 1996, SIFIDA's main shareholders are now the BNP PARIBAS Group and its six banking affiliates in West and Central Africa. Minority shareholders include the AfD and the DEG. For over 30 years, SIFIDA has been actively contributing to the development of the African private sector, providing assistance through structured trade finance, equity participations, and financial engineering.

II. PRODUCTS AND SERVICES

Trade Finance

SIFIDA provides African exporters with short-term lines of credit to allow them to pre-finance their production cycles or their supply of primary commodities. Pre-financing arrangements have a maximum duration of 1 year, possibly renewable, and allow African exporters to increase significantly their export volume, particularly to Europe and other African countries.

SIFIDA may also rely on its contacts in the banking community to syndicate pre-financing facilities with other banks that have confidence in its experience in the field of structured trade finance and in its knowledge of African export networks.

SIFIDA can also handle all documentary operations for its African exporting clients—in particular, the collection and negotiation of documentary credits. It can organize bridge financing on behalf of African companies by means of documentary credits in favor of suppliers of goods or services, with the guarantee of development institutions, which granted them investment credits. SIFIDA pays the suppliers in advance of disbursement of these institutions, which usually are not familiar with the documentary aspects of the suppliers.

Equity Investment

SIFIDA invests in listed companies mainly following IPOs, taking equity participations in well-managed, profitable companies active in the productive sectors of the economy (industry, agribusiness, tourism, and so on). SIFIDA generally gives priority to export-oriented companies that are in a better position to face monetary depreciation risks. SIFIDA is also able to take equity participations in the financial sector, such as commercial banks, merchant banks, and leasing and insurance companies—in such cases, in close cooperation with the BNP PARIBAS Group.

Subject to acceptable forecast profitability, SIFIDA is able to invest in any profitable and well-managed company requiring share capital, conditional upon an exit possibility being defined in advance (listing on a stock market within 2–3 years or repurchase agreement with the main shareholders), as SIFIDA's objective remains to achieve a reasonable rotation of invested funds.

Financial Engineering

SIFIDA has aided in the structuring of long-term financing for more than 100 projects in approximately 40 African countries. SIFIDA has close links with commercial banks interested in African projects as well as with major international development finance institutions (IFC, ADB, Proparco, DEG, AFREXIMBANK, to name a few), and is familiar with the criteria and procedures applied by these institutions and guarantee mechanisms that can be sought for various types of financing. Furthermore, thanks to its vast network of contacts and its practical experience of Africa,

SIFIDA can offer to investors and project sponsors in Africa a wide range of advisory services for project financing to include the following:

- Development of financing plans and approach strategies for potential lenders
- Project finance structuring and mobilization of medium- or long- term credits: identification of potential investors, negotiation and assistance during the preparation of the financing agreements, research on guarantees and political risk insurance, assistance in the setting up of repayment mechanisms, and so on
- Assistance in mobilizing shareholders funds: private placements, debt equity conversions, and investment funds
- Financial restructuring: privatizations, rehabilitations, mergers and acquisitions, and divestitures

SIFIDA also has extensive experience with debt conversion. Through this mechanism, an investor can convert the claim he or she owns (or which he or she can acquire) on a state into, for example, a participation in the shareholding of a local company. In the Franc Zone, this mechanism is particularly appropriate for privatizations. SIFIDA has concluded several operations of this type, for its own account and on behalf of third parties, in several African countries. SIFIDA can also act as financial adviser to governments or investors for specific transactions.

III. ELIGIBILITY AND APPLICATION PROCESS

Trade Finance

To be eligible for financing through this mechanism, applicants must adhere to the following requirements:

- Experienced exporter with a sound financial record
- Availability of a sales contract for the pre-financed goods between the exporter and reliable buyers acceptable to SIFIDA
- Delegation of export sales proceeds in favor of SIFIDA
- Pledge of goods stored in warehouses, guarantee of an acceptable local bank, or other acceptable guarantee

Requests for financing should include the following information:

- Information on the exporting company: history, shareholders, board of directors, organization and management, activity reports, and recent accounts
- Banking references
- Description of the procedure for the acquisition of goods and/or the manufacturing process
- Transportation and storage facilities
- Detailed information on the sales contracts and buyers

When pre-financing is linked to an investment project, a project feasibility study should be included in the financing request.

Equity Investment

SIFIDA equity investments are mainly in companies listed on the stock markets of countries such as Botswana, Côte d'Ivoire (BRVM), Ghana, Kenya, Malawi, and Morocco. Apart from the usual investment criteria (positive analysis of the company's structure and of its trading prospects, favorable socioeconomic environment, satisfactory financial prospects, and so on), criteria for equity investment should include the following:

- Strong profitability prospects resulting in payment of appreciable dividends
- An African stock exchange listing or a prospective listing within 2–3 years or an exit mechanism guarantee by acceptable parties

IV. CONTACTS

Headquarters:
Société Internationale Financière pour les Investissements et le Développement en Afrique (SIFIDA)
22 rue François-Perréard, POB 310
1225 Chêne-Bourg / Geneva
Switzerland
Tel: (41) 22 869 20 00
Fax: (41) 22 869 20 01
Internet: www.sifida.com
Email: headoffice@sifida.com

Mr. Philippe Séchaud, Managing Director

NATIONAL DEVELOPMENT BANK OF SRI LANKA (NDB)

I. INTRODUCTION

The NDB is the largest project lender in Sri Lanka and offers a wide variety of financial products including commercial banking, investment banking, insurance, stock brokering, leasing project financing, environmental consulting, and housing finance. Formed in 1979 by the Sri Lankan government, NDB has since transformed from a government-owned development financial institution to a profitable privatized group of companies. NDB lists shares in the Colombo Stock Exchange although the government still owns approximately 12 percent of its shares. NDB has 13 branch offices and is headquartered in the capital of Colombo, Sri Lanka. In 2001, NDB acquired ABN Amro's Sri Lankan operations, which have allowed NDB to expand its product offerings and offer more advanced and competitive services particularly in commercial banking. NDB has also entered into strategic alliances with Citibank, Commonwealth Development Corporation UK, and the IFCO.

NDB's goal of achieving long-term economic growth for Sri Lanka is focused on developing private capital from local and international markets. Sri Lanka still relies on multilateral agencies and foreign governments to assist in financing infrastructure projects and other basic development needs. However, NDB states that in order to achieve long-term, sustainable growth for Sri Lanka, the bank must attract private capital and channel it to profitable use. Although NDB offers a diverse array of financial products to corporate and retail customers, its core competency is project lending to corporate customers. NDB funds project lending through expanded capital market operations and raising deposits from corporate and retail customers. NDB also plans to continue lending to SMEs.

In addition to the acquisition of the former ABN Amro Sri Lanka operations, the NDB group is comprised of the Eagle Insurance Company, which is a member of the Zurich Financial Services Group; Ayojana Fund Management, which manages private equity investments and venture funds; Citi-National Investment Bank, which handles corporate restructuring, mergers, acquisitions, infrastructure development, and privatization; and NDB Housing Bank, which in conjunction with the International Finance Corporation, provides private sector housing financing.

II. PRODUCTS

Loans and Guarantees

Project financing is NDB's core product, accounting for 67 percent of the value of approved direct facilities in 2001. Leasing, guarantees, and import loan and commercial papers account for the remaining 33 percent of approvals. Due to a lack of concessionary credit lines and a solid deposit base, NDB's interest rates were not as competitive as those in the market of commercial banks. The average size of a facility approved by headquarters was Rs 14 million, and the average size approved by a branch was Rs 2 million. Lending to the service sector dominates NDB's portfolio, which includes activities such as transportation, construction, telecommunications, energy, health care, and information technology. Metals and chemicals, including the manufacturing of plastics, electrical appliances, activated carbon, and petroleum products, were the second-highest category of lending. The garment sector, which accounts for over 40 percent of Sri Lanka's industrial production, continues to receive special attention from NDB because of the global factors affecting the industry and its national importance.

- *SMILE II*—NDB headquarters has a specialized Small and Medium Industries (SMI) Direct Lending Unit that focuses on SMEs. Loans of up to Rs 7 million may be approved, with an interest rate between 12.3 and 14 percent. Technology transfer loans are available to cover 75 percent of the cost of a project at a rate of 3 percent, with the remaining 25 percent provided in the form of a grant. The repayment term of technology loans is 7 years with a 2-year grace period; all other loan repayment terms are at 10 years with a 2-year grace period.
- *SMAP (Small & Medium Enterprises Assistance Project)*—Funded by ADB and facilitated by NDB, SMAP provides loans to SMEs with a fixed-asset maximum of Rs 20 million. The terms under SMAP are similar to those of SMILE II but are currently being renegotiated.
- *KFW (Kreditanstalt fur Wiederaufbau)*—This German development bank provided NDB a loan facility for the support of microenterprises targeted specifically at women-owned businesses and for businesses generating employment opportunities. Loan maximum is Rs 350,000 per project with a 14 percent interest rate and a repayment period of 6 years with a 2-year grace period.
- *E-Friends*—Environmental lending is also a priority of NDB through a program called E-Friends. Companies are eligible to

receive interest-free loans for technical assistance as well as soft loans at an interest rate of 8.5 percent with a maximum of Rs 600,000 for implementation of pollution control projects. The NDB works with the CEA (Central Environmental Authority) to determine projects that meet the standards of the local environmental regulations and also with ERM (Environmental Resources Management) Lanka, a consulting firm, to bring new technologies to projects. Vehicle service stations as well as food, rubber, and textile plants are the main recipients.

NDB and IFC have arranged for equity and debt financing for Suntel, a joint-venture company comprised of the global telecommunications giant Telia AB of Sweden, the Asian Infrastructure Telecommunication Fund of Hong Kong, and the Metropolitan Group of Companies, which provides solutions that include basic telephony and total telecommunications solutions. In 2001, Suntel, Sri Lanka's largest private telecommunications operator, achieved a net profit of Rs 23 million and, as of year-end 2001, has invested USD 100 million in its extensive rollout, which included infrastructure building and the creation of its own Internet services.

Technical Assistance

Technical assistance is provided mainly for officers of regional development banks to enhance their project appraisal and follow-up skills in promoting the formulation of viable projects. NDB also trains bank officers in credit approval policies. Recently, NDB has conducted seminars and trainings for companies seeking specialized loans under the E-Friends program. Companies seeking financing under the E-Friends program are eligible for interest-free technical assistance loans.

Equity Investments

NDB operates funds through NDB Bank as the result of the acquisition of all of ABN Amro Sri Lanka's operations and through Eagle Insurance, NDB's insurance arm. Eagle NDB operates mutual funds that contain 3-, 6-, and 12-month treasury bills issued by the Sri Lankan government; 2-, 3-, 4- and 5-year government bonds; investments from the corporate money market, such as commercial paper, corporate debt and asset-backed notes; and a combination of any of the 232 stocks listed on the

Colombo Stock Exchange. The three main funds offered include the Edged, containing only government securities; Fixed-Income, containing a mix of government securities as well as fixed-income instruments such as corporate debt; and Growth, which invests exclusively in shares for long-term growth stakes in SMEs and may provide management input. The main objective of these funds is to gain capital through a fund ranging from USD 20 million to USD 30 million. The fund is usually high-risk and requires substantial gains from a few successful investments. Ayojana, a joint venture between NDB and Auerous Capital of the UK, is a venture capital company that provides equity to listed and unlisted companies.

III. ELIGIBILITY AND APPLICATION PROCESS

Small- and Medium-Enterprise Funding

Companies seeking loans under the SMILE II program must have fixed assets that do not exceed Rs 14 million. Companies are expected to finance 25 percent of the project cost, with NDB providing loans for up to 75 percent of the cost. Loans are considered for economically viable projects that contribute economic benefits such as local raw material usage and labor intensity and that have market competitiveness, managerial capabilities, experience, technical feasibility, integrity, and profitability. Enterprises in the following sectors are eligible to receive financing under SMILE II:

- Food processing
- Textiles
- Garments
- Metal products
- Construction materials
- Rubber products
- Wood and leather products
- Plastics
- Printing and paper products
- Chemical products
- Agro-industries
- Fisheries
- Animal husbandry
- Construction
- Transportation

For more information on eligibility and application information, contact NDB headquarters.

IV. CONTACTS

Headquarters:
National Development Bank
40 Navam Mawatha, Colombo 2
Sri Lanka
Tel: 94 1 437701, 437350, 323966
Fax: 94 1 341044, 440262
Telex: 21399 NDB CE
Internet: www.ndb.org
Email: info@ndb.org

Director, General Manager
N. S. Welikala
Tel: 94 1 4488889

SMI and Branches, Corporate Banking
A. L. Somaratne, Assistant General Manager
Tel: 94 1 440175

R. D. Abeywardena, Unit Head of SMI Direct Lending
Tel: 94 1 440178

Corporate Banking, Privatization and Infrastructure
N. I. R. de Mel, Assistant General Manager
Tel: 94 1 440177

A. Wickramaratne, Unit Head
Tel: 94 1 347912

Ayojana Fund Management
R. Wijesieghe, Director
Tel: 94 1 074510505

Eagle Insurance
W. J. Churche, Director
Tel: 94 1 310300

Citi National Investment Bank
S. K. Wickremesinghe, Director
Tel: 94 1 300385(9)

Terms

(Italicized terms are also defined in this section.)

A/B Loan: Syndicated *loan* where commercial banks and other investors provide their own funds and take commercial risk, while an MDB remains the lender of record. B lenders benefit from implicit political risk protection because host governments are less likely to *expropriate* or limit the foreign currency available to an MDB-supported project.

Acquisition Financing: Funds obtained for buying existing companies or projects, as opposed to *greenfield* financing. Traditionally, MDBs have only provided acquisition financing to the extent that the sponsor undertakes a major program of expansion or rehabilitation. Privatization projects are generally likely to be supported more actively than private sector mergers and acquisitions.

Additionality: MDBs are often explicitly prohibited from competing with ("crowding out") private sector financial institutions. The additionality test performed early in the screening of a project is meant to assure the MDB that the private sector is not ready to fund the project on "acceptable terms." For *ECAs*, additionality can be satisfied if there is keen and *ECA*-financed foreign competition for a contract.

Bilateral: Direct assistance from a donor country to a recipient country, as opposed to *multilateral*. Examples of bilateral agencies include OPIC, FMO, and AfD.

Bond: A negotiable note or certificate that evidences indebtedness. It is a legal contract sold by one party, the issuer, to another, the investor, promising to repay the holder the face value of the bond plus interest at future dates. Bonds are also referred to as "notes" or "debentures." The term "note" usually implies a shorter maturity than the term "bond." Some bond issues are secured by a mortgage on a specific property, plant, or piece of equipment. In an emerging markets context, project finance bonds may carry *PRI* from an MDB or an insurer. Additionally, MDBs may provide parallel lending facilities or liquidity reserves in support of a bond issuance. Finally, MDBs may guarantee specific commercial and political risks, such as extending the maturity of the bond beyond what the market can do by itself.

Breach of Contract: Violation of any terms or conditions in a contract, such as a power purchase agreement without legal excuse, or failure to make a payment when it is due. This is one of the basic *PRI* coverages provided by insurers such as MIGA and OPIC.

Bretton Woods Institutions: Founded in 1944 and named after the village of Bretton Woods, New Hampshire, the Bretton Woods Institutions were a culmination of international negotiations between 44 nations. It was here that the World Bank and the International Monetary Fund (IMF), collectively known as the Bretton Woods Institutions, were established in order to direct and manage the world economy after World War II.

Buyer Credit: A financial agreement in which a bank or *ECA* makes a *loan* directly to an overseas purchaser to import goods and services. Disbursements may be made either directly to the exporter or to reimburse the buyer for previous payments already made.

Capital Markets: An all-encompassing term that includes tradable debt, securities, and *equity,* as separate from private markets or banks. MDBs have recently become more active in assisting *emerging markets* borrowers and projects to access the international *capital markets.*

Co-Financing: Two groups of lenders (such as *ECAs* and MDBs) agree to a common legal structure that presents the buyer with one financial package rather than a series of separate deals (e.g., there is only one loan agreement that is backed proportionately by each *ECA's* guarantee according to each country's national share of the export).

Commercial Cover: These covers apply to the financial loss incurred by an insured party as the result of the actual reported insolvency and/or partial or total default on payments by a private partner in a contract. Typically, *ECAs* provide commercial cover, while public sector insurers do not.

Commercial Interest Reference Rates (CIRR): The official lending rates of *ECAs*, calculated monthly and based on government *bonds* issued in the country's domestic market for the country's currency plus a spread. For example, the USD CIRR for long-term loans over 8.5 years is based on the 7-year U.S. Treasury bond yield plus 1 percent.

Commercial Risk: Risk of nonpayment on *export credit* by a buyer or borrower due to bankruptcy, insolvency, protracted default, and/or failure to accept goods shipped by the terms of the supply contract. Typically, *ECAs* cover commercial risks, while public sector insurers (OPIC, MIGA, etc.) do not.

Commitment Fee: The fee charged by a lender to compensate for committing funds, based on undisbursed balances.

Commitment Letter: A formal offer by a lender making explicit the terms under which it agrees to lend money to a borrower over a certain period of time.

Completion: The point after which the project's cash flows become the primary method of repayment. It occurs after a series of completion tests (technical, financial, and legal) are satisfied. Usually, completion occurs months after the project is actually built and commissioned. Prior to completion, the primary source of repayment is usually from the sponsors or the turnkey contractor.

Completion Support: The contingent *guarantees* provided by the project sponsors and contractors before "completion." These can take the form of corporate guarantees, surety bonds, letters of credit, and others. The lenders are entitled to call on these guarantees at any time before completion to cover cost overruns, ramp-up failures, and so on.

Comprehensive Coverage: Insurance or *guarantee* cover that combines both commercial risk coverage and *PRI* coverage. Typically provided by *ECAs*.

Consultant Trust Funds: A financial and administrative arrangement between an MDB and an external donor, under which the donor entrusts funds to the MDB to finance a specific development-related activity. Consultant Trust Funds finance the cost of services by MDB consultants engaged to support operational work. Typically, donors are rich countries and grant agreements often stipulate the use of consultants from the donor country.

Corporate Finance: The practice and philosophy of the ways firms select and finance their investments, choose between debt and *equity* instruments, and disburse cash back to shareholders. Technically, *project finance* is part of corporate finance. As a shortcut, corporate finance is often used to mean "on-balance sheet" rather than "off-balance sheet" financing of projects.

Currency Inconvertibility and Transfer Cover: A form of *PRI* that protects investors against possible losses from financial crises, hard-currency shortages, or political actions that result in a failure of the host country to allow the conversion or transfer of its own currency into foreign currency. This type of insurance does not cover currency depreciation or devaluation.

Delegated Authority: Authority granted to commercial banks or exporters to approve insurance/guarantees without specific approval from the *ECA*. Typically, the *ECA* gives this approval based on previous experience with the bank/exporter.

Development Finance Institution (DFI): Financial institutions created by governments to stimulate and mobilize private investment in private sector projects in developing and emerging economies. DFIs can be *bilateral* or *multilateral.*

Development Impact: The economic and social consequences of a project supported by an MDB. It is usually measured by the amount of incremental GDP growth stimulated, employment, infrastructure improvements, technology transferred, schools and hospitals funded, and so on.

Direct Loan: Loan from an *ECA* or an MDB to a borrower without the intermediation of another bank. It is the opposite of a *guaranteed loan.*

Eligible Costs: The sum total of the bona fide project costs that includes personnel, durable equipment, subcontracting, travel and subsistence, consumables, allocated overhead costs, and other specific project costs. Costs are eligible only when they are necessary for the project and are provided for in project contracts. For *ECAs*, eligible costs are associated with exported goods and services plus a small (15 percent) component for "local" costs.

Emerging Markets: Lesser-developed countries experiencing rapid economic growth and liberalization of government restrictions on free commerce. The term has almost completely replaced the terms "developing countries" and "second" and "third world."

Environmental Impact Assessment (EIA): Method of identifying the environmental effects of a project. Most MDBs and *ECAs* follow the World Bank *EIA* guidelines.

Equity: Net worth; assets minus liabilities. The stockholder's residual ownership position in a company or project. Some MDBs are willing to provide equity for projects, but *ECAs* do not.

Export Credit Agency (ECA): A government-owned or -sponsored financial agency offering *loans, guarantees,* credit insurance, or financial *technical assistance* to support exporters.

Export Credits: Financing provided to an exporter or foreign buyer from a commercial bank or *ECA* during pre- or post-shipment operations.

Exposure: From the perspective of a lender or an insurer, the potential loss in the event of nonpayment by a borrower or counter-party of the insured entity.

Exposure Fee: A fee that protects lenders against possible defaults by borrowers. Exposure fees are the primary pricing mechanism by *ECAs* for direct and *guarantee* loans and export credit insurance. Exposure fees are based on several factors, including country risk, tenor of the loan, and type of borrower (sovereign vs. private enterprise). Exposure fees are usually considered an eligible project cost.

Expropriation: The official seizure by a government of private property. Any government maintains this right according to international law as long as prompt and adequate compensation is given. This risk is one of the basic *PRI* coverages.

Facility Fee: Up-front payment made by a borrower to a lender for arranging a *loan*. Usually, it is paid out of the proceeds from the first disbursement of funds.

Financial Guarantee: A commitment or assurance that in the event of nonpayment of an export credit by a foreign borrower, the *ECA* will indemnify the financing bank if the terms and conditions of its *guarantees* are fulfilled.

Foreign Direct Investment (FDI): Investment in a foreign company or foreign joint venture. The investment is normally made in cash but sometimes in the form of plant and equipment or know-how. As defined by the OECD for statistical purposes, FDI is investment in at least 10 percent of voting stock of a foreign company. FDI is typically a *long-term* investment in unlisted companies or projects, as opposed to a *short-term* portfolio investment in listed securities.

Grace Period: An interval of time allowed to the borrower by the lender after *loan* proceeds are disbursed and before repayment of principal begins. The grace period usually covers the construction period plus 6 to 12 months.

Greenfield: A new capital investment as opposed to an acquisition of existing assets. Typically, the *project finance* loans provided by MDBs are for greenfield investments or major expansions.

Guarantee: Used generally to denote any assurance of payment or compensation given to the entity financing an *export credit*, which is to be honored in the event of default or nonpayment by the primary obligor.

Insurance: Cover that indemnifies the insured from loss due to a specified type of contingency or peril. Insurance in project finance is commercial, political, or comprehensive.

Lender: Investor who provides (senior) debt to a company or project. Typically, lenders are MDBs and commercial banks, but can also be institutional investors, corporations, and similar entities.

Letter of Interest (LI): A pre-export marketing tool. An LI is an indication of willingness to consider financing for a given export transaction that can be used to assure counterparties of the availability of financing. However, the existence of an LI does not imply a commitment to finance.

LIBOR: The London Interbank Offered Rate of interest on deposits traded between major banks. There is a different Libor rate for each deposit maturity and currency (e.g., Euro Libor).

Loan: A senior debt instrument that is typically held privately rather than easily traded (a *bond*).

Loan Guarantee: A partial or comprehensive assurance of repayment provided by an *ECA*, MDB, or other entity to a lender.

Long-Term: Repayment terms greater than 5 years. OECD Rules limit the tenor that can be offered to borrowers. For *project financing*, *ECAs* are limited to an average loan life of 7.25 years, which is equal to 14 years of level repayment or 12 years of mortgage-style repayment.

Medium-Term: Repayment terms usually ranging from 181 days, 365 days, or up to 5 years. Based on the *OECD* Arrangement for *ECAs*, the range for medium term is 2 to 5 years.

Multilateral: Agreements or arrangements that involve more than two countries, as opposed to *bilateral*. *Multilateral* banks include the World Bank and UNDP.

OECD Arrangement: Agreement adopted in 1978 by members of the Paris-based Organization for Economic Cooperation and Development (OECD) to limit credit competition among member governments in officially supported *export credits*. The OECD Arrangement superseded the OECD Consensus.

Organization for Economic Co-Operation and Development (OECD): A group of 30 (mostly wealthy) member countries sharing a commitment to democratic government and the market economy. OCED also produces instruments, decisions, and recommendations to promote the rules of the game in areas where multilateral agreement is necessary for individual countries to make progress in a global economy.

Partial Risk Guarantee: Used typically in the context of a *capital markets* financing. An MDB may issue a *guarantee* that covers specific risks (e.g., devaluation) in support of a locally or internationally placed *project finance bond.*

Political Risk Insurance (PRI): Insurance or *guarantee* cover that protects the exporter or financing bank from nonpayment by the buyer or borrower because of political events in the buyer's country or a third country through which either goods or payment must pass. The four basic PRI covers offered by insurers include inconvertibility and transfer restrictions (but not devaluation), *political violence cover,* and war, *expropriation,* and *breach of contract.*

Political Violence Cover: A form of *PRI* that covers loss of assets or income due to war, revolution, insurrection, or politically motivated civil strife, terrorism, or sabotage.

Premium Rate: Cost of insurance per dollar of cover, usually calculated on the gross invoice value for *short-term* sales or on the financed portion for *medium- and long-term* sales. *PRI* providers often distinguish between the current rate and a lower standby rate, which is similar to the commitment fee of a *loan.*

Private Equity: Investment in the unlisted stock of a privately held company or project. *Venture capital* refers to early-stage investments, while mezzanine capital refers to the later-stage investments when the company is up and running but not quite ready for a public offering. Private equity is often used to denote later-stage investing in established companies, including the context of management buyouts.

Project Financing: A *loan* structure that relies for its repayment primarily on the project's cash flow with the project's assets, rights, and interests held as secondary security or collateral. It is a form of "off-balance sheet" financing from the perspective of the sponsoring entity.

Quasi-Equity: This type of financing is usually considered debt for tax and other purposes but maintains the characteristics of *equity* such as flexible repayment, higher rates of return, and lack of a security package. It typically refers to funds employed in a business that will remain in a business as permanent capital.

Recourse: The right of a financial institution to demand payment from the guarantor of a *loan,* if the primary obligor fails to pay. *Project financing* is often referred to as limited recourse financing because the lender cannot force the sponsor to repay the debt after the completion date.

Refinancing: Repaying existing debt and entering into a new *loan*, typically to meet some corporate objective such as the lengthening of maturity or lowering the interest rate. MDBs typically do not provide refinancing loans but may include limited refinancing as part of the eligible project costs.

Reinsurance: One insurer (e.g., MIGA) fronts the entire cover while agencies (e.g., private sector insurers) provide reinsurance. Reinsurance is used to expand the available capacity for any single project or country.

Repayment Style: Can be level of repayment of principal, mortgage-style (equal payments of principal and interest), or tailored.

Repayment Term: The term (or tenor) of the *loan*, e.g., "20 semi-annual installments."

Risk Capital: Usually synonymous with *equity* or seed funding.

Secured Debt: Senior debt that has first claim on specified assets in the event of default. *Project finance loans* are usually secured with all assets and pledge of sponsor shares.

Short-Term: *Repayment terms* generally of up to 180 days, or exceptionally up to 365 days. Berne Union *OECD* guidelines for *short-term ECA* insurance refer to repayment terms of up to 2 years depending on the product and the size of transaction.

Subordinated Debt: All debt (both *short-* and *long-term*) that, by agreement, is subordinated to senior debt. Often, subordinated debt is considered a type of *quasi-equity*. MDBs offer this type of debt, but *ECAs* do not.

Supplier Credit: Financial arrangement in which the supplier (exporter) extends credit to the buyer to finance the buyer's purchases. Normally the buyer pays a portion of the contract value in cash and issues a promissory note or accepts a draft to evidence the obligation to pay the remainder to the exporter. *ECAs* can then insure or guarantee the draft or promissory note.

Technical Assistance: Transfer or adaptation of knowledge, practices, technologies, or skills that foster economic development. Financing for this type of assistance is generally granted in order to contribute to the design and/or implementation of a project or program in order to increase the physical capital stock of the host country.

Tenor: Total repayment period of a *loan*. Also referred to as the "term." Door-to-door tenor refers to the *grace "construction" period* plus the repayment period. *OECD* rules limit the tenor of the loans that can be extended by *ECAs*.

Tied Aid Program: Tied aid is provided by agencies of the rich-country governments, sometimes in conjunction with their national *ECAs*. Tied aid differs from typical *export credit* terms offered by *ECAs* in that it usually involves concessionary terms: total maturities longer than 20 years, interest rates equal to one half to two thirds of market rates in the currency of denomination, or large grants.

Venture Capital: *Risk capital* extended to start-up or small, going concerns. Venture capital is a form of *private equity*.

Working Capital: Cash required to fund inventories and accounts receivable. Accounting definition is current assets less current liabilities. MDBs can fund start-up working capital as an eligible project cost.

The World Bank Group

OVERVIEW

Founded in 1944, the World Bank is one of the world's largest sources of development assistance. It provided USD 19.5 billion in loans to its client countries in fiscal year 2002, and is now working in more than 100 developing economies, bringing a mix of finance and ideas to improve living standards and eliminate the worst forms of poverty. For each of its clients, the World Bank works with government agencies, nongovernmental organizations, and the private sector to formulate assistance strategies. Its country offices worldwide deliver the programs in countries, liaise with government and civil society, and work to increase understanding of development issues.

The World Bank is owned by more than 184 member countries whose views and interests are represented by a Board of Governors, and a Washington DC-based Board of Directors. The World Bank uses its financial resources, highly trained staff, and extensive knowledge base to individually assist developing countries onto paths of stable, sustainable, and equitable growth. The primary focus is on assisting the poorest people and the poorest countries, but for all its clients the World Bank emphasizes the need for

- Human Capital—investing in people, particularly through basic health and education
- Economic and Social Development—focusing on social development, inclusion, governance, and institution-building as key elements of poverty reduction
- Improving Governance—strengthening the ability of governments to deliver quality services, efficiently and transparently
- Environmental Protection
- Private Business Development

- Economic Reform—promoting reforms to create a stable macroeconomic environment, conducive to investment and long-term planning.

The World Bank's products support a broad range of programs aimed at reducing poverty and improving living standards in the developing world. It also helps countries strengthen and sustain the fundamental conditions needed to attract and retain private investment. With World Bank support—both lending and advice—governments are reforming their overall economies and strengthening banking systems. Their investments in human resources, infrastructure, and environmental protection, enhance the attractiveness and productivity of private investment. Assistance in fiscal year 2001 to developing countries in recent years was geared toward the following:

ACCELERATED DEBT RELIEF

Significant progress has been made to provide deeper, broader, and faster debt relief to some of the world's poorest countries, many of them in Africa, under the enhanced Heavily Indebted Poor Countries (HIPC) Initiative framework. As of June 30, 2002, 26 countries were receiving debt relief under this framework, expected to amount to USD 41 billion over time. After HIPC (and combined with traditional) debt relief, these 26 countries will witness a two-thirds reduction in total debt, increase social expenditures, and reduce spending on debt service.

SUPPORT IN THE FIGHT AGAINST HIV/AIDS

The HIV/AIDS epidemic now poses a paramount threat to sub-Saharan Africa. In collaboration with partners, the Bank launched in September 2000 the Multi-Country HIV/AIDS Program (MAP) for Africa—the first of its kind. Under the MAP, flexible and rapid funding will be committed, on International Development Association (IDA—the Bank's concessional lending window) terms, to individual HIV/AIDS projects developed by countries.

MULTIDIMENSIONAL SUPPORT FOR POVERTY REDUCTION

The Bank's World Development Report 2000/2001 emphasized opportunity, empowerment, and security as keys to reducing multidimensional poverty. To this end, support for education is emphasizing access, quality, and equity; working toward a cleaner, healthier environment has entailed extensive global consultations to inform its new environment strategy; and a fast-growing area of support is focused on law and justice. World Bank focus has evolved from specific law reform to encompass legal education for the public, anticorruption programs in the judiciary, indigenous dispute resolution mechanisms, and legal aid for poor women.

IMPROVED DEVELOPMENT EFFECTIVENESS

The number of projects considered "at risk" in the World Bank's portfolio has been cut in half over the past 5 years and is now the lowest it has been in many years. The quality of project appraisal and supervision has also improved substantially; a similar trend is emerging with respect to nonlending services.

Headquarters—General Inquiries
The World Bank
1818 H Street, NW
Washington, DC 20433
Tel: (202) 473-1000
Fax: (202) 477-6391

ARMS OF THE WORLD BANK GROUP

The World Bank Group consists of five closely associated institutions, all owned by member countries that carry ultimate decision-making power. As explained below, each institution plays a distinct role in the mission to fight poverty and improve living standards for people in the developing world. The term "World Bank Group" encompasses all five institutions. The term "World Bank" refers specifically to two of the five, IBRD and IDA.

The International Bank for Reconstruction and Development (IBRD)
Established: 1945
Members: 184
Cumulative lending: USD 360 billion
Fiscal 2002 lending: USD 11.5 billion for 96 new operations in 40 countries

IBRD reduces poverty in creditworthy developing countries. Products offered include loans, guarantees, and technical assistance.

The International Development Association (IDA)
Established: 1960
Members: 162
Cumulative lending: USD 135 billion
Fiscal 2002 lending: USD 8.18 billion for 133 new operations in 62 countries

IDA allows the World Bank to serve countries which have little or no capacity to borrow on market terms. IDA assistance helps provide these countries with better education, heath care, sanitation, and water access. IDA aims to increase productivity and improve employment opportunities.

The International Finance Corporation (IFC)
Established: 1956
Members: 175
Committed portfolio: USD 21.6 billion (includes USD 6.5 billion in syndicated loans)
Fiscal 2002 commitments: USD 3 billion (includes syndications, USD 2.7 billion for own account) in 204 companies for 75 countries

IFC supports economic development through programs directed at the private sector providing loans, guarantees, risk management products, and advisory services. Projects are encouraged in regions underserved by private investment, and looks to improve market opportunities.

The Multilateral Investment Guarantee Agency (MIGA)
Established: 1988
Members: 157
Cumulative guarantees issued: USD 10.34 billion
Fiscal 2002 guarantees issued: USD 1.36 billion (includes USD 136 million leveraged through the Cooperative Underwriting Program)

MIGA provides political risk insurance to projects in developing countries in order to improve foreign investment opportunities. Insurance protects against noncommercial risks, such as expropriation, currency inconvertibility and transfer restrictions, and war and civil disturbances. MIGA also provides technical assistance and investment dispute mediation services.

The International Centre for Settlement of Investment Disputes (ICSID)
Established: 1966
Members: 134
Total cases registered: 103
Fiscal 2002 cases registered: 16

ICSID provides facilities and resources for the conciliation and arbitration of investment disputes, in order to improve relations between host countries and foreign investors. ICSID also provides research and publications in the area of arbitration and foreign investment law.

National Development Finance Institutions (NDFIs)*

Region	Country	Organization	Address	Phone
Africa	Algeria	Algerian Bank for Development	12 Bd du Colonel Amirouche Algiers, 16000 Algeria	213-263 88 95 to 99, 273 8950, 274 52 53 and 54
Africa	Algeria	Bank of Agriculture and Rural Development	17, Bdda Colonel Amirouche Algiers, Algeria	213-273 40 25, 264 72 64, 264 73 22
Africa	Algeria	Local Development Bank	5 Rue Gaci Amar Staoueli, 42000 W. Tipaza Algeria	213-239 28 06
Africa	Botswana	National Development Bank	Development House, Plot 1123 The Mall, Gaborone	(09267) 352801
Africa	Egypt	Principle Bank for Development and Agricultural Credit	110 Qasr Al-Aini Street Cairo Egypt	(0020 2) 3563873
Africa	Ethiopia	Development Bank of Ethiopia	Josip Broz Tito Str., P.O. Box 1900, Addis Ababa	(00251 1) 511188/9
Africa	Gabon	The Gabonese Bank of Development	Alfred Marche Street Box 05 Libreville Gabonese Republic	241 76 24 89 241 76 24 29

GOV—Institution is government-owned.
L/G—Loans and guarantees are available.
EQ—Equity is available.
Ins—Insurance is available.
TA—Technical assistance is available.

*This list is not meant to be all-inclusive. Institutions where information was scarce or unavailable were not included.

Email	Web	Year	Gov	L/G	EQ	Ins	TA
	www.geocities.com/ CapitolHill/1078/ banks.html						
	www.geocities.com/ CapitolHill/ 1078/banks.html						
	www.geocities.com/ CapitolHill/1078/ banks.html						
	www.bankofbotswana. bw/ndb.htm						
		1931	X	X			
		1970	X	X			
infos@bgd-gabon.com	www.bgd-gabon.com	1960		X			

Region	Country	Organization	Address	Phone
Africa	Ghana	Agricultural Development Bank	Cedi House Liberia Road P.O. Box 4191, Accra	661118, 662762, 780319/20
Africa	Libya	Agricultural Bank	P.O. Box 1100 Tripoli Libyan Arab Jamahiriya	(00218) 21
Africa	Mali	Banque Nationale de Development Agricole	Immeuble CCA, Quartier de Fleuve Bamako Mali	(00223) 226464, 226611, 226633
Africa	Maurituis	Development Bank of Mauritius	Port-Louis (Head Office) Chaussée	(230) 208 0241/2/3, (230) 208 3081/2/3
Africa	Morocco	Caisse Nationale de Credit Agricole	12 avenue d'Alger B.P. 49 Rabat	(00212 7) 725920, 732555, 732580
Africa	Nigeria	Nigerian Agricultural and Co-operative Bank Ltd.	Yakubu Gowon Way PMB 2155 Kaduna Nigeria	(00234 62) 234957
Africa	Seychelles	Development Bank of Seychelles	Independence Avenue P.O. Box 217 Victoria, Mahe Seychelles	(248) 224 471
Africa	South Africa	Development Bank of South Africa	1258 Lever Road, Headway Hill, Mirand South Africa	011-313-3911

GOV—Institution is government-owned.
L/G—Loans and guarantees are available.
EQ—Equity is available.
Ins—Insurance is available.
TA—Technical assistance is available.

Email	Web	Year	Gov	L/G	EQ	Ins	TA
adbweb@ africaonline.com.gh	www.adbghana.com	1965	51%	X			
		1957	X	X			
		1981	X	X			
dbm@intnet.mu	www.dbm-ltd.com/ html/home.html	1964			X		
		1961		X	X		
		1973			X		
dbsmd@seychelles.net	www.dbs.sc/ Pages/dbs.htm	1977	50%	X			
webmaster@dbsa.org	www.dbsa.org	1983		X	X	X	

Region	Country	Organization	Address	Phone
Africa	Sudan	Agricultural Bank of Sudan	P.O. Box 1363 Khartoum Sudan	(00249 11) 777432, 770973
Africa	Sudan	Farmers Bank for Investment and Rural Development	Gasr Street P.O. Box 11984 Khartoum Sudan	(00249 11) 774960
Africa	Swaziland	Central Bank of Swaziland	P.O. Box 546 Mbabane Swaziland	268 404 3221/5
Africa	Uganda	Centenary Rural Development Bank Ltd.	Plot 7, Entebbe Road P.O. Box 1892, Kampala, Uganda	(00256 41) 251276, 251277
Asia	Armenia	Armenian Development Bank	21/1 Paronyan Str., 375015 Yerevan, Republic of Armenia	(374 1) 538930, (374 1) 533233
Asia	Bangladesh	Bangladesh Krishi Bank	83-85 Motijheel Commercial Area Dhaka, Bangladesh	880-2-9560031-5 PABX, 880-2-9560021-5 PABX
Asia	China	China Development Bank	Rm 3307-08 One International Finance Ctr 1 Harbour View St Central Hong Kong	8610 68307304

GOV—Institution is government-owned.
L/G—Loans and guarantees are available.
EQ—Equity is available.
Ins—Insurance is available.
TA—Technical assistance is available.

Email	Web	Year	Gov	L/G	EQ	Ins	TA
agric-bank@yahoo.com		1957	X	X			
		1998		X			
info@centralbank.org.sz	www.centralbank.sz/cbs.html	1974		X			
		1983		X			
info@armdb.com	www.armdb.com/start.htm	1990		X			
bkb@citechco.net	www.krishibank-bd.org/index.htm	1973		X			
	www.cdb.com.cn	1994		X	X		

Region	Country	Organization	Address	Phone
Asia	India	Industrial Development Bank of India	IDBI Tower Cuffe Parade Bombay 400005 India	(91 22) 218-9111
Asia	India	Industrial Investment Bank of India	19, Netaji Subhas Road Calcutta 700001 India	220-9941, 220-9911
Asia	India	Small Industries Development Bank of India	10/10 Madan Mohan Malviya Marg Lucknow – 226 001 India	2209517-21
Asia	Indonesia	Bank Mandiri	Plaza Mandiri 22nd Floor Jl. Jend. Gatot Subroto Kav. 36-38 Jakarta 12190	(62-21) 524 5577
Asia	Japan	Development Bank of Japan	9-1, Otemachi 1-chome, Chiyoda-ku, Tokyo, Japan 100-0004	03-3244-1900 03-3244-1770 (International Department)
Asia	Kazakhstan	Development Bank of Kazakhstan	Samal 12, Astana Tower, 16-18 Floors, Astana 473000, Republic of Kazakhstan	7 (3172) 580260

GOV—Institution is government-owned.
L/G—Loans and guarantees are available.
EQ—Equity is available.
Ins—Insurance is available.
TA—Technical assistance is available.

Email	Web	Year	Gov	L/G	EQ	Ins	TA
	www.idbi.com	1964	Over 51%	X	X	X	
iibiho@vsnl.com		1956	X	X	X		X
	www.sidbi.com	1990		X	X		X
	www.bankmandiri.com	1997	X	X	X		
	www.dbj.go.jp/english/	1999		X			X
info@kdb.kz	www.kdb.kz/index.php	2000	X	X			

Region	Country	Organization	Address	Phone
Asia	Korea	Korea Development Bank	16-3, Youido-dong, Yongdeungpo-ku, Seoul 150-973 Korea	82-2-787-7407
Asia	Maldives	Bank of Maldives		
Asia	Mongolia	Trade and Development Bank of Mongolia	Khudaldaany gudamj-7, Ulaanbaatar-11, Mongolia	(976-1)-321171
Asia	Nepal	Agricultural Development Bank Nepal	Agricultural Development Bank Ramshah Path Kathmandu Nepal	977-1-262885/262596
Asia	Philippines	Development Bank of the Philippines	Sen. Gil J. Puyat Avenue corner Makati Avenue, Makati City, Philippines	(632) 815-0904/818-9511
Asia	Russia	Russian Regional Development Bank	129594 Moscow, Sushchevsky Val, 65	095-933-03-43
Asia	Singapore	Development Bank of Singapore	DBS Bank 6 Shenton Way, DBS Building Singapore 068809	65 6327 2265

GOV—Institution is government-owned.
L/G—Loans and guarantees are available.
EQ—Equity is available.
Ins—Insurance is available.
TA—Technical assistance is available.

Email	Web	Year	Gov	L/G	EQ	Ins	TA
	www.kdb.co.kr	1954	X	X	X		X
	www.bankofmaldives.com.mv/index.html	1982	X	X			
tdbank@tdbm.mn		1990	70%	X			
info@adbn.gov.np	www.adbn.gov.np/introduction.html	1967	X	X			X
info@devbankphil.com.ph	www.devbankphil.com.ph/dbpage/DBPage.htm	1947		X			
bank@vbrr.ru	www.vbrr.ru	1996	X	X	X		
	www.dbs.com/	1968		X			

Region	Country	Organization	Address	Phone
Asia	Sri Lanka	National Development Bank	40 Navam Mawatha Colombo 2 Sri Lanka	94 1 437701
Asia	Syria	Agricultural Cooperative Bank	Al Naanaa Garden P.O. Box 4325 Damascus Syria	(00936 11) 215132, 2213461
Central America and Caribbean	Antigua and Barbuda	Antigua and Barbuda Development Bank	27 St Mary's Street, Box 1279, St John's Antigua	(268) 462 0838
Central America and Caribbean	Bahamas	Bahamas Development Bank	Cable Beach, West Bay Street P. O. Box N-3034 Nassau, Bahamas	242 327-5780-6
Central America and Caribbean	Dominica	National Commercial Bank of Dominica	NCB Head Office 64 Hillsborough Street Roseau	1 767 448 4401/2/3/4
Central America and Caribbean	Mexico	BANCOMEXT	Camino a Sta, Teresa 1679 Delegación Alvaro Obregón 01900 México, D.F.	55-5481-60-00
Central America and Caribbean	Mexico	National Financiera	Av. Insurgentes Sur 1971 Col. Guadelupe Inn 01020, Mexico, D.F.	01 55 53 25 64 00

GOV—Institution is government-owned.

L/G—Loans and guarantees are available.

EQ—Equity is available.

Ins—Insurance is available.

TA—Technical assistance is available.

Email	Web	Year	Gov	L/G	EQ	Ins	TA
info@ndb.org	www.ndb.org/	1979	G	X		X	
		1888	G	X			
grodgers@bahamas developmentbank.com	www.bahamas developmentbank. com/main.php	1974	G	X		X	
chairman@ncb.dm	www.ncbdominica. com/about/bank.htm	1978		X			
privatesector@adb.org	www.bancomext .com	1937	G	X		X	
info@nafin.gob.mx	www.nafin.com	1934	G	X	X	X	

Region	Country	Organization	Address	Phone
Central America and Caribbean	Panama	Banca de Desarrollo Agropcuario	Av. 4 de Julio y Calle L Apartado Postal 5282 Zona 5 Panama	(00507) 2620140
Central America and Caribbean	Puerto Rico	Government Development Bank for Puerto Rico	P.O. Box 42001, San Juan, PR 00940-2001	(787) 722-2525
Europe	Czech Republic	Czech-Moravian Guarantee and Development Bank	110 00 Praha 1, Jeruzalémská 964/4	420 255 721 111
Europe	Hungary	Hungarian Development Bank	1051 Budapest, Nádor u. 31., Levélcím: 1365 Budapest, 5. PF. 678 Hungary	428-1400, 428-1500
Europe	Poland	BRE Bank	Ul. Senatorska 18 00-950 Warszawa, Poland	(0 22) 829 00 00
Europe	Romania	Romania Development Bank		
Middle East	Cyprus	Cyprus Development Bank	Alpha House, 50 Makarios III Ave., P.O. Box 21415, CY-1508 Nicosia Cyprus	357-22846500

GOV—Institution is government-owned.
L/G—Loans and guarantees are available.
EQ—Equity is available.
Ins—Insurance is available.
TA—Technical assistance is available.

Email	Web	Year	Gov	L/G	EQ	Ins	TA
		1973	G	X			
gdbcomm@ bgf.gobierno.pr	www.gdb-pur.com/ GDBEng.htm		G	X			
info@cmzrb.cz	www.cmzrb.cz	1992		X	X		X
bank@mfb.hu	www.mfb.hu/	1991					
redakcjaportalu@ brebank.com.pl	www.brebank.com.pl	1986		X	X		
	www.brd.ro english						
info@cdb.com.cy	www.cdb.com.cy/ index_fie.shtml	1963		X	X		

Region	Country	Organization	Address	Phone
Middle East	Iran	Agricultural Bank of Iran	129 Patrice Lumumba Street Jalal-Al-Ahmad Expressway P.O. Box 14155/6395 Tehran 14454 Iran	(0098 21) 825 2246
Middle East	Israel	Industrial Development Bank	Asia House, 4 Weizman St., Tel Aviv 61334 Israel	972-3-6972772
Middle East	Jordan	Agricultural Credit Corporation	P.O. Box 77 Amman Jordan	(00962 6) 661105, 661108
Middle East	Oman	Oman Development Bank	P.O. Box 309 Muscat - Oman	(968) 738021
Middle East	Pakistan	Agricultural Development Bank of Pakistan	1 Faisal Avenue P.O. Box 1400 Islamabad Pakistan	(0092 51) 202 009, 209 006, 202089
Middle East	Turkey	Development Bank of Turkey	Development Bank of Turkey Izmir cad. No. 35 Kizilay–Ankara Turkey	90 312 418 1515
Middle East	Turkey	Development Bank of Turkey	Türkiye Sınai Kalkınma Bankası A.Ş. Meclisi Mebusan Caddesi No. 161, 80040 Fındıklı-Istanbul	(212) 334 50 50

GOV—Institution is government-owned.
L/G—Loans and guarantees are available.
EQ—Equity is available.
Ins—Insurance is available.
TA—Technical assistance is available.

Email	Web	Year	Gov	L/G	EQ	Ins	TA
info@agri-bank.com	http://www. agri-bank.com/	1980	G	X			
	www.dbank.co.il/ pv2/index_site2.asp? mainUrl=Mkteng1.htm	1957	G	X			
		1959	G	X		X	
adbp@isb.paknet .com.pk	www.adbp.org.pk/	1961	G	X			
tkbhaberlesme@ tkb.com.tr	www.tkb.com.tr	1975	G	X		X	
info@tskb.com.tr	www.tskb.com.tr/ index_eng.htm	1950		X			

Region	Country	Organization	Address	Phone
Middle East	Yemen	Yemen Bank for Reconstruction and Development	P.O. Box 541 Sana'a— Republic of Yemen	967 1 270481 /270483
North America	Canada	Business Development Bank of Canada	BDC Building 5 Place Ville Marie, Suite 400 Montreal, Quebec H3B 5E7	1 877 BDC BANX (232-2269)
Oceania	Fiji	Fiji Development Bank	Kings Road, P.O. Box 317, Nausori	679 347 7277
Oceania	Samoa	Development Bank of Samoa	P.O. Box 1232, Apia, Samoa	(685) 22 861
Oceania	Solomon Islands	Development Bank of Solomon Islands	P.O. Box 911 Honiara Solomon Islands	(00677) 21595/96
South America	Brazil	Brazilian Development Bank	Av. República do Chile, 100-Centro 20031-917 Rio de Janeiro-RJ	(21) 2277-7447/6978
South America	Honduras	Banco Nacional de Desarrollo Agricola	Apartado Postal 212 Tegucigalpa Honduras	(00504) 2373790

GOV—Institution is government-owned.
L/G—Loans and guarantees are available.
EQ—Equity is available.
Ins—Insurance is available.
TA—Technical assistance is available.

Email	Web	Year	Gov	L/G	EQ	Ins	TA
info@ybrd.com.ye	www.ybrd.com.ye	1962	52%	X			
info@bdc.ca	www.bdc.ca/en/home.htm	1944		X	X		
isoa@fdb.com.fj	www.fijidevelopmentbank.com	1967		X			
falefal@dbsamoa.ws	www.dbsamoa.ws/	1974		X	X		X
dbsi@welkam.solomon.com.sb		1978	G	X	X		X
	www.bndes.gov.br/english	1952	G	X	X		X
vpresid@netsys.hn		1980	G	X			

Selected Government-Backed Equity Funds

Agen.	Fund	Fund Manager
EBRD	AIG New Europe Fund	AIG-CET Capital Management
EBRD	AIG Silk Road Fund	AIG Capital Partners
EBRD	Argus Capital Partners	AIG Capital Partners
EBRD	Danube Fund	Alpha Group
EBRD	DBG Osteuropa Holding	DBG Eastern Europe
EBRD	Dexia-FondElec Energy	FondElec Group
EBRD	EIF Central and Eastern	IEF UK Management
EBRD	Environmental Investment	PP Investments

Address	Geography	Size (Million USD)	Short Description
Ul. Chopina 5A, Flat 20 00-559 Warsaw, Poland Tel: 48 22 583 7000	Central and Eastern Europe	320	Enterprises within the region
175 Water Street, 23rd Floor New York, NY 10038 Tel: 212-458-2156	Central Asia		
4th Floor Culters Court 115 Houndsditch London, EC3A 7BU, United Kingdom Tel: 44 20 7398 2001	Central and Eastern Europe	172	Small and medium size enterprises
8 Merlin Street 10671 Athens, Greece Tel: 30 1 362 7710	Central and Eastern Europe	30	Diverse, small enterprises
Jungmannova 34 11000 Prague 1, Czech Republic Tel: 420 2 2409 8400	Central Europe	100	Regional investments for small companies
Stamford Harbor Park, 333 Ludlow Street Stamford, CT 06902, United States of America Tel: 203-326-4570	Central and Eastern Europe	150	Energy and emissions-related industries
Duke's Court, 32-36 Duke Street St James's London, SW1Y 6DF, United Kingdom Tel: 44 20 7766 7162	Central and Eastern Europe	250	Small and medium enterprises involved in power and generation projects
Bank Center (Citibank Tower) Szabadsag ter 7 1054 Budapest, Hungary Tel: 36 1 474 8146	Central and Eastern Europe	22	Regional environmental projects

Agen.	Fund	Fund Manager
EBRD	EuroMerchant Balkan Fund	Global Finance International
EBRD	European Renaissance Capital	Renaissance Partners
EBRD	Innova/98 L.P.	Innova Capital
EBRD	New Europe East Investment Fund	Capital International
EBRD	Technologieholding Central and Eastern European Fund	3TS Venture Partners
EBRD	TPG Co-Investment Fund	TPG Aurora
IFC	The Private Equity/ Venture Cap Fund	Quadriga Capital Russia
IFC	Bancroft II	Bancroft Group L.P.
IFC	Darby-BBVA Latin American Private Equity Fund	Darby Overseas Investments

Address	Geography	Size (Million USD)	Short Description
Bd. Aviatorilor nr. 60-62, Apt. 1, Sector 1 70401 Bucharest, Romania Tel: 40 1 231 7571/7573	Central and Eastern Europe	68	Industrial small to medium enterprises
Blanicka 28 12000 Prague, Czech Republic Tel: 420 2 2225 2407	Central and Eastern Europe	39.5	Diverse small and medium enterprises
Aurum Building, ul. Walicow 11 00-865 Warsaw, Poland Tel: 48 22 583 9400	Central and Eastern Europe	125	Regional small and medium enterprises
25 Bedford Street London, WC2E 9HN, United Kingdom Tel: 800 243 38637	Central and Eastern Europe		Small and medium enterprises
Andrassy ut. 11 Budapest, Hungary Tel: 36 1 411 2310	Central and Eastern Europe	80	Small to medium enterprises in communications technology and industrial electronics
14-1 Tverskoy Boulevard 103009 Moscow, Russia Tel: 7 095 797 5737	Central and Eastern Europe	185	Media, telecommunications, IT, and distribution
Tel: 202-473-0696 Email: sandrews2@ifc.org	Primarily Russia	140	Diversified manufacturing, financial and service industries.
251 Brompton Rd. London SW3 2EP United Kingdom Tel: (44) 207 823 9222 Email: martin@ bancroftgroup.com	Central and Eastern Europe	Euro 250	Diversifies companies with focus on later-stage business
1133 Connecticut Avenue, NW Suite 400 Washington DC 20036 Tel: 202-872-0500	Latin American	250	Export/cross-border oriented companies and domestic market/consolidation oriented companies

Agen.	Fund	Fund Manager
IFC	Advent Latin American Private Equity Fund II	Advent International
IFC	China Private Equity Fund	China International Capital Corporation
IFC	South Africa Junior Mining Fund	Decorum Capital Partners
IFC	Korea Corporate Governance Fund	Zurich Scudder Investments, Inc.
IFC	Futuregrowth Empowerment Fund	Futuregrowth Asset Management (Pty) Limited
IFC	AfriCap	AfriCap MicroVentures, Ltd

Address	Geography	Size (Million USD)	Short Description
75 State Street Boston, MA 02109 Tel: 617-951-9788 Email: wbalz@ adventinternational.com	Latin America	250	Later stage businesses with limited exposure to fast growing telecommunications
28/F, China World Trade Tower 2 1 Jian-guo-men-wai Ave., Beijing, China Tel: (86) 10 6505 8165	China	100	Established companies with substantial operations in China
Tel: 27 11 644-2458	Southern and Central Africa	250	Invest in pre-feasibility stage (after the resource has been identified), feasibility study stage, and early stages of production in junior mining projects
345 Park Avenue 16th Floor New York, NY 10154	Korea	150	Medium-sized Korean companies seeking to implement the highest standards of corporate governance
Tel: (27-21) 659-5418 Email: jdebruyn@ futuregrowth.co.za	South Africa	54	Targeted at black empowerment and developmental investment opportunities in South Africa
365 Bay Street, Suite 600, Toronto, Ontario, Canada M5H 2V1 Tel: (416) 362-9670 Email: sharpe@ calmeadow.com	Africa	15	Make investments in the form of equity and quasi equity in about 10 well-performing MFIs in calmeadow.com Africa

Agen.	Fund	Fund Manager
IFC	Colombia Capital Growth Fund	TCW/Latin America Partners, LLC
IFC	Turkish Private Equity Fund	Turk Venture Partners LLC
IFC	Brazilian Corporate Governance Fund	Bradesco Templeton Asset Management
IFC	Baring Vostok Private Equity Fund	Baring Vostok Capital Partners
IFC	SEF Central Asian Small Equity Investment Fund	Small Enterprise Assistance Fund .
IFC	IndAsia Fund	IndAsia Fund Advisors AMP Asset Management
IFC	Thai Equity Fund	Lombard/Pacific Partners

Address	Geography	Size (Million USD)	Short Description
Email: LSilva@ifc.org	Colombia	225	Investments in Colombian middle market companies that are strategically placed and in need of risk capital
Email: igen@ifc.org.	Turkey	40	A diversified portfolio in industries driven by growth, exports, and deregulation
Av. Brig. Faria Lima, 1461-10 Andar 01 481-900, Sao Paolo, Brazil Tel: 55 11 3039 3721 Email: stephen@ bradesco-templeton.com.br	Brazil	100	Mid-sized Brazilian companies committed to implementing the highest international standards of corporate governance
10 Uspenski Pereolok, Moscow, Russia 103006	Primarily Russia	150	Investment in private sector infrastructure and natural resource development
1100 17th Street, NW Suite 1101, Washington, DC 20036 Fax: 202-737-5536	Central Asia	20	Specifically at small and medium-sized enterprises, strong focus on agribusiness and agricultural processing
3, Scheherazade, Justice Vyas Road, Colaba Mumbai-400 005 India	India	100	Companies that have developed under the protected domestic environment and now need help to adapt to the more liberalized environment
600 Montgomery Street 36th Floor San Francisco, CA 94111 Tel: 415-397-5900	Thailand	425	Companies and financial institutions that are in need of financial restructuring

Agen.	Fund	Fund Manager
IFC	SEAF Trans-Balkan Fund	Small Enterprise Assistance Fund
IFC	Central America Growth Fund	Provident Group
IFC	The AIG Emerging Europe Infrastructure Fund	Emerging Markets Partnership (EMP)
IFC	Capital Alliance Private Equity Fund	Africa Capital Alliance
IFC	Maghreb Invest Fund	Maghreb Invest Gestion
IFC	TCW LA Fund	TCW/Latin American Partners LLC
IFC	Macedonia SEAF	Small Enterprise Assistance Fund
IFC	Africa Infrastructure Fund	Emerging Markets Partnsherhip

Address	Geography	Size (Million USD)	Short Description
20-22 Zlaten Rog St., Floor 5th kv. Lozents Sofia 1407, Bulgaria Tel: (359-2) 917 4950	Balkans	25	SMEs with demonstrated growth potential in the Balkan region
Armando Gonzalez Tel: 212-601-2400 Email: agonzalez@ provident-group.com	Central America	50	Target medium-size enterprises with long-term growth and capital appreciation potential
43-45 Portman Square London WIH 9TH 44 (0) 207-886-3600	Central and Eastern Europe	1000	Infrastructure-related industries
P.O. Box 55955 Northlands 2116, South Africa Tel: (011) 27-11-268-6911	Nigeria	30–40	Joint venture investments with foreign companies seeking to establish or re-establish operations in Nigeria
Tel: (202) 473-7711 Fax: (202) 974-4384	Morocco	30	Small- and medium-sized companies to support their expansion and diversification, including restructuring
Gary Ritelny (212) 707-1216	Latin America	100	Latin American middle-market private companies
Vladimir Pesevski Metropolit Teodosij Gologanov 28 1000 Skopje, Macedonia Tel: 389 2 137 178	Macedonia	12.5	Supporting viable SME equity investments
Paul V. Applegarth 2001 Pennsylvania Avenue, NW Suite 1100 Washington, DC 20006 Tel: 202-331-9051	Africa	500	Infrastructure projects and infrastructure-related industries

Agen.	Fund	Fund Manager
IFC	Baring Mexico Private Equity Fund	Baring Private Equity Partners
IFC	Croatia Capital Partnership	CCP Ventures Ltd.
IFC	South Africa Private Equity Fund, L.P	Brait Capital Partners Limited
IFC	Hambrecht & Quist Korea Growth and Restructuring Fund	H&Q Asia Pacific
IFC	Black Sea Fund	Global Finance
IFC	Advent Central and Eastern Europe II	Advent International Corporation
IFC	Tuninvest Private Equity Fund	SIPAREX
IFC	Patagonia Fund	Merchant Bankers Asociados S.A.(MBA), and Elektra Fleming

Address	Geography	Size (Million USD)	Short Description
Homero No. 440 9 Piso Desp. 901-901 Col. Polanco 11560 Mexico, DF Tel: (5255) 52 54 32 80	Mexico	50–60	Minority equity stakes in unlisted Mexican middle-market enterprises
Mr. Ante Cicin-Sain Pantovcak 104c 10000 Zagreb, Croatia Tel/Fax: (385)1-48-22-304	Croatia	25–30	Small- and medium-sized enterprises
Private Bag X1 Northlands 2116 Johannesburg, South Africa Tel: 27(11) 507-1000	South Africa	350	Growth companies
156 University Avenue Palo Alto, CA 94301 Tel: 650-838-8088	Korea	140	Small- to medium-sized enterprizes ("SMEs"), with a focus on technology-related firms
14 Filikis Eterias Square, 10673 Athens, Greece Tel: 30-210 7208 900	CIS	50	Medium-sized enterprises in the Black Sea region
75 State Street Boston, MA 02109 Tel: 617-951-9788 Email:wbalz@ adventinternational.com	Central and Eastern Europe	150	Medium-sized enterprises in the region
139, rue de Vendome 69477 Lyon, France Tel: (33) 04 72 83 23 23	Tunisia	25	Unlisted Tunisian companies
c/o Patterson Belknap Webb & Tyler LLP New York, NY 10036 Tel: 212-336-2000	Argentina	55	Mid-sized Argentine companies

Agen.	Fund	Fund Manager
IFC	ZN Mexico Capital Growth Fund	ZN Management Ltd
IFC	Icatu Equity Partners	Banco Icatu
IFC	Renewable Energy and Efficiency Fund	Energy Investors Funds, Environmental Enterprises Assistance Fund, and E & Co
IFC	TCW/ICICI India Private Equity Fund	TCW/ICICI Investment Partners, L.L.C.
IFC	Scudder Latin American Power Fund	Scudder, Stevens and Clark
IFC	Mexico Partners Trust	Grupo Financiero Inbursa and Lazard Freres & Co
IFC	Terra Capital Fund	Dynamo Administracao de Recursos Ltda.
IFC	Proa Fondo de Inversion de Desarrollo de Empresas	Moneda Asset Management S.A.

Address	Geography	Size (Million USD)	Short Description
320 Park Avenue New York, NY 10022 Tel: 212-508-9400	Mexico	50-75	Mexican small and medium-sized enterprises (SMEs) with sales no greater than USD100 million
Av. Presidente Wilson, 231 10. Andar Rio de Janeiro 20030-021 Tel: (21) 3804 8500	Brazil	200	Influential minority equity positions in Brazilian mid-sized enterprises
K. R. Locklin 727 15th St., NW 11th Floor Washington, DC 20005 Tel: 202-783-4419	Global	110 Equity, 100 Debt	Renewable energy (both grid-connected and off-grid) and energy efficiency projects in developing countries
Raheja Plaza, 4th Floor, 17 Commissariat Road, D'Souza Circle, Bangalore - 560 025 India	India	125	Unlisted equity or equity-related securities issued by medium-size, later-stage, and some early-stage companies
	Latin America	150–250	Private sector power projects located in several countries
	Mexico	250	Help Mexican middle-market enterprises restructure
	Latin America	20–30	Unlisted private companies undertaking sustainable uses of biological diversity
Av. Isidora Goyenechea 3621, Piso 8 Santiago 6760412, Chile Tel: (56-2) 337 7900	Chile	50	Medium-sized unlisted Chilean companies

Agen.	Fund	Fund Manager
IFC	All Asia Growth Ventures - I	Asian Venture Capital Managers, and All AsiaCapital Managers
IIC	Aureos Central America Fund	AUREOS Capital Limited
IIC	Central American Banking Growth Fund	Darby Overseas Inv. Ltd.; The Netherlands Dev. Bank; Central American Bank for Economic Integration
IIC	The Cori Capital Partners Fund	Violy, Byorum & Partners Holdings; CDPQ Capital International
IIC	CEA Latin American Communications Partners Fund	Communications Equity Associates (CEA)
IIC	The Central America Growth Fund	Provident Group Limited
IIC	Latin American Private Equity Fund II	Advent International

Address	Geography	Size (Million USD)	Short Description
7th Floor, All Asia Capital Center 105 Paseo De Roxas, Makati City 1200, Philippines Tel: (63-2) 818-3211	Phillipines	70	Investments in early development companies and those with fairly clear prospects of going public in the short term
Erik Peterson General Manager Tel: 506 211 1511 Fax: 506 211 1525 Email:epeterson@ aureos.com	Central America, Panama and DR		Later-stage SMEs
BBVA Bancomer Montes Urales 620, 3 Piso Col. Lomas de Chapultepec Mexico, D.F. 11000 Tel: (5255) 5325-8054	Central America and Panama	60	Financial sector
712 Fifth Avenue New York, NY 10019 Tel: 212-707-1200 Email: contact@vbp.com	Latin America	300	SMEs in industries undergoing regional and/or global consolidation
101 East Kennedy Blvd., Suite 3300 Tampa, FL 33602 Tel: 813-226-8844	Latin America and Caribean	100	Small and middle market media and telecommunication companies
45 Broadway, 23rd Floor, New York, NY 10006 Tel: 212-742-4900	Central America and Panama	50	Retailing; food and beverage processing; manufacturing; media and telecom; tourism; differentiated export products
75 State Street Boston, MA 02109 Tel: 617-951-9788	Brazil, Argentina, Mexico	500	Middle market growth-oriented companies

Agen.	Fund	Fund Manager
IIC	Multinational Industrial Fund	Wamex, S.A.
IIC	Negocios Regionales Fondo de Inversión Privado	
IIC	The Caribbean Investment Fund	ICWI Group Limited
OPIC	Africa Growth Fund	Equator Overseas Services Limited
OPIC	Africa Millennium Fund	Savage Holdings LLC
OPIC	Agribusiness Partners International	Agribusiness Management Company, LLC
OPIC	AIG Brunswick Millennium Fund	American International Group/ Brunswick Capital Mgm
OPIC	Allied Small Business Fund	Allied Capital Corp.

Address	Geography	Size (Million USD)	Short Description
	Mexico	80	Mexican companies entering into joint ventures with foreign companies to generate exports
	Chile	23.5	Small- and medium-size enterprises
28 Barbados Avenue (5), Jamaica Tel: (876) 926-2925	Caribbean Region	150	Small- and medium-size enterprises
45 Glastonbury Boulevard Glastonbury, CT 06033 Tel: 860-633-9999	Sub-Saharan Africa	25	Mining, manufacturing and financial services
1414 Avenue of the Americas, Suite 1804, New York, NY 10019 Tel: 212-750-7400 Email: fsavage@ savageholdings.com	Sub-Saharan Africa	350	Equity or quasi-equity securities of companies that work in the Infrastructure Sector and that operate in countries eligible for investment in sub-Saharan Africa
America First Companies, 11004 Farnam Street, Omaha, NE 68102 Tel: 402-930-3060 Email: bpetyon@am1st.com	NIS/Baltics	95	Agriculture, food firms, infastructure projects, privatizations, food storage and distribution facilities
175 Water Street, 24th Floor New York, NY 10038 Tel: 212-458-2156	Russia, NIS and Baltics	288	Large infrastructure projects, including power, transportation, natural resource development, and related industries
1919 Pennsylvania Ave. NW, Washington, DC 20006-3434 Tel: 202-973-6319	All OPIC countries	20	Basic manufacturing and service industries sponsored by qualifying U.S. small business

Agen.	Fund	Fund Manager
OPIC	Aqua International Partners Fund	Texas Pacific Group
OPIC	Asia Development Partners	Olympus Capital Holdings (Asia)
OPIC	Asia Pacific Growth Fund	Hambrecht & Quist Asia Pacific
OPIC	Bancroft Eastern Europe Fund	Bancroft UK, Ltd.
OPIC	Emerging Europe Fund	TDA Capital Partners, Inc.
OPIC	Global Environment Emerging Markets Fund I	GEF Management

Address	Geography	Size (Million USD)	Short Description
345 California Street, Suite 3300, San Francisco, CA 94104 Tel: 415-743-1570 Email: jsylvia@texpac.com	All OPIC countries	237.75	Operating and special purpose companies involved in the treatment, bulk supply, and distribution of water in emerging market countries
153 East 53rd Street, 43rd Floor, New York, NY 10022 Tel: 212-292-6531 Email: dmintz@zbi.com	Southeastern Asia	150	Telecommunications, consumer products, and financial services
156 University Ave Palo Alto, CA 94104 Tel: 650-838-8098	Southeastern Asia	75.25	Light manufacturing, financial, construction, high tech, and telecom services
7/11 Kensington High Street, London W8 5NP Tel: 44-20-7368-3347 Email: martin@ bancroftgroup.com	Central Europe/ Baltic republics	90.85253	Distribution networks, basic manufacturing, consumer goods, and related service networks
15 Valley Drive, Greenwich, CT 06831 Tel: 203-625-4525 Email: jhapler@ templeton.com	Central and Eastern Europe	60	Sustainable development industries
1225 Eye Street NW, Suite 900, Washington, DC 20005 Tel: 202-789-4500	All OPIC countries	66.7	Environment-oriented sectors relating to the developing, financing, operating or supplying of infastructure relating to clean energy and water

Agen.	Fund	Fund Manager
OPIC	Global Environment Emerging Markets Fund II	GEF Management
OPIC	India Private Equity Fund	Indocean Capital Advisors
OPIC	Inter-Arab Investment Fund	InterArab Management, Inc.
OPIC	Modern Africa Growth and Investment Fund	Modern Africa Fund Managers LLC
OPIC	New Century Capital Partners	NCH Advisors
OPIC	Newbridge Andean Partners	ACON Investments, LLC

Address	Geography	Size (Million USD)	Short Description
1226 Eye Street NW, Suite 900, Washington, DC 20005 Tel: 202-789-4500	All OPIC countries	120	Environment-oriented sectors relating to the developing, financing, operating or supplying of infastructure relating to clean energy and water
Oppenheimer Tower, World Financial Center, New York, NY 10281 Tel: 212-667-8190 Email: michele.buchignani@ us.cibc.com	India	140	Consumer goods, basic manufacturing, banking, computer, and related industries
National Securities Building, P.O. Box 941430, Amman 11194, Jordan Tel: 962-6-566-2481	Jordan, West Bank/ Gaza, Oman	45	Basic industries that create intra- and inter-regional synergies
1100 Connecticut Avenue, NW Suite 500, Washington, DC 20036 Tel: 202-887-1772 Email: SDCASHIN@aol.com	Sub-Saharan Africa	117	Focus on manufacturing, telecommunications, and natural resources
712 Fifth Avenue 46th Floor New York, NY 10019-4018 Tel: 212-641-3229	Former Soviet Countries	250	Diversified manufacturing, consumer products, financial and service industries
1133 Connecticut Avenue, NW, Suite 700, Washington, DC 20036 Tel: 202-861-6060 ext 103	South America	160	Diversified manufacturing, financial and service industries

Agen.	Fund	Fund Manager
OPIC	Poland Partners	Landon Butler & Company
OPIC	Russia Partners A	Sigular Guff & Co.
OPIC	Russia Partners B	Sigular Guff & Co.
OPIC	Soros Investment Capital Ltd.	Soros Private Funds Management LLC
OPIC	South America Private Equity Growth	Baring Latin America Partners LLC
OPIC	The Great Circle Fund, L.P.	Great Circle Capital, LLC

Address	Geography	Size (Million USD)	Short Description
700 Thirteenth Street, NW, Suite 1150, Washington, DC 20005 Tel: 202-737-7300	Poland	63.5	Manufacturing, consumer goods, distribution networks, merchandising, and related service networks
630 Fifth Avenue, 16th Floor, New York, NY 10111 Tel: 212-332-5108	Russia	105	Natural resource-related companies, telecommunications, light manufacturing, and consumer products and services
631 Fifth Avenue, 16th Floor, New York, NY 10111 Tel: 212-332-5108	Russia	50	Natural resource-related companies, telecommunications, light manufacturing, and consumer products and services
888 Sixth Avenue New York, NY 10106 Tel: 212-333-9727	Balkans	200	Provide equity capital to Southeast Europe as part of the international recovery effort
230 Park Ave., New York, NY 10169 Tel: 212-309-1795	South America	180	Diversified manufacturing, financial and service industries
2039 Palmer Avenue Larchmont, NY 10538 Tel: 914-834-7000 Email: Rburke@ GreatCircleCapital.com	All OPIC countries	200	Equity and quasi-equity investments in companies operating in the maritime transportation, logistics and services industries that are new, expanding, or in the process of being restructured or privatized

Agen.	Fund	Fund Manager
OPIC	ZM Africa Investment Fund	Zephyr Management LP

Address	Geography	Size (Million USD)	Short Description
320 Park Avenue New York, NY 10022-6815 Tel: 212-508-9410	South Africa	120	Diversified manufacturing, financial and service industries

Public and Private Political Risk Insurance (PRI) Providers

This section details public and private PRI providers that are not listed in other chapters of the book. Many of the public institutions described in the book also offer this type of insurance.

PUBLIC

MIGA

The Multilateral Investment Guarantee Agency is a member of the World Bank Group that provides political risk insurance to investors and lenders in order to encourage foreign direct investment in developing countries. MIGA has issued more than 650 guarantees since its inception in 1988 and has members in 163 countries.

MIGA is willing to cover a variety of investments including equity, shareholder loans, and shareholder loan guarantees, as well as offering technical assistance, management contracts, and franchising and licensing agreements. Equity investments can be covered up to 90 percent, and debt up to 95 percent. Coverage is typically available for up to 15 years, but may be extended for as long as 20 years in some cases. MIGA generally guarantees up to USD 200 million.

Contact: Roger Pruneau, VP Underwriting
Tel: (202) 473-6168
Email: Rpruneau@worldbank.org

1818 H Street, NW
Washington, DC 20433

Tel: (202) 473-6167
Fax: (202) 522-2630
Internet: www.miga.org

PRIVATE

AIG GLOBAL TRADE AND POLITICAL RISK

The AIG companies offer a broad range of insurance and risk-management programs through a network of offices in 130 countries and jurisdictions.

Commercial Credit Insurance Coverage provides insolvency risk insurance, credit-risk insurance, and comprehensive export credit insurance. Political Risk Only Insurance Coverage provides contract-repudiation insurance, political risk insurance for exporters and importers, and on-demand bond insurance.

Contact: Stephen Kay
Tel: (212) 770-8633

70 Pine Street, 12th Floor
New York, NY 10270
Tel: (212) 770-8109
Fax: (212) 269-3387
Email: AIGGlobal.NY@aig.com
Internet: tradecredit.aig.com

ATRADIUS

Atradius, formerly Gerling NCM, is the second-largest credit insurer worldwide. They are located in all major economic markets and provide commercial credit and political risk coverage to mid- and large-sized companies. They offer an extensive range of classic credit insurance products and innovative risk management concepts. They have a premium volume of more than USD 1.3 billion and must maintain an "A" rating from Standard and Poor's.

Contact: Eileen Jackson
Email: eileen.jackson@gerlingncm.com

5026 Campbell Blvd.
Baltimore, MD 21236

Tel: (410) 931-9441
Fax: (410) 246-5532
Internet: www.gerlingncm.com

AXIS CAPITAL

Through its Global Insurance group, Axis offers insurance coverage for "specialty risks" that cover terrorism, marine and aviation war risk, and political risk. PRI generally provides protection against sovereign actions resulting in cross-border impairments.

Contact: John Kuhn, EVP Financial Insurance Solutions
Email: john.kuhn@axiscapital.com

106 Pitts Bay Road
Pembroke HM 08, Bermuda
Tel: 441 296 2600
Fax: 441 296 3140
Email: info@axis.bm
Internet: www.axis.bm

CHUBB

The Chubb group of insurance companies has 130 offices in 31 countries. They have political risk specialists in three global offices in London, Melbourne, and New Jersey. Available products include confiscation, expropriation, and nationalization (CEN); wrongful calling of guarantee; and contract frustration to help protect lenders, trading companies, exporters, and companies with assets in emerging markets. Political risk products have a capacity of up to USD 75 million and contract frustration and wrongful calling of guarantee, each of which has a capacity of up to USD 37.5 million. Chubb insurance protects against political violence, currency inconvertibility, and cross-border war.

Contact: Keith Dunford
Tel: (908) 572-4691
Email: kdunford@chubb.com

15 Mountain View Road
Warren, NJ 07059
Tel: (908) 903-2000
Fax: (908) 903-2027
Internet: www.chubb.com

EXPORTER'S INSURANCE COMPANY (EXPORTER'S)

Exporter's is a group captive insurer offering political risk and credit insurance to its members or their designees. The company was started in 1990 and now has 91 active members with over USD 52 million in capital and a portfolio of USD 2.4 billion outstanding. Political risk insurance covers losses due to nonpayment, currency inconvertibility, expropriation, political risk violence, appropriation deprivation, contract repudiations, and wrongful calling of guarantees.

30 Woodbourne Avenue
Hamilton HM 08, Bermuda
Tel: 441 296 1745
Fax: 441 292 8682
Email: exporters@efsgroup.com
Internet: www.exporters.bm

FCIA CREDIT INSURANCE

FCIA Management Company, Inc. (FCIA), is a wholly owned subsidiary of Great American Insurance Company of Cincinnati, Ohio, the flagship insurer of American Financial Group, Inc. FCIA provides credit insurance that protects both export and domestic sales. It specializes in offering flexible coverage options against nonpayment risks, whether resulting from commercial or political events. Its coverage is available to U.S. businesses on their customers worldwide. For an insured resident in many countries outside the United States, coverage can also be arranged through a European insurance group with which FCIA has a cooperation agreement. FCIA makes its products available exclusively through brokers and independent agents, many of whom are specialists in credit insurance and related financial products.

FCIA Credit Insurance
125 Park Avenue
New York, NY 10017
Tel: (212) 885-1500
Fax: (212) 885-1535
Email: service@fcia.com
Internet: www.fcia.com

LLOYD'S OF LONDON

Lloyd's of London provides specialty insurance services to businesses in over 120 countries. In 2003, 71 syndicates underwrite insurance at Lloyd's. The company maintains an "A" rating from Standard and Poor's. Lloyd's is a leading provider of PRI to companies across the globe.

One Lime Street
London EC3M 7HA
Tel: 44 (0) 20 7327 1000
Email: market.services@lloyds.com
Internet: www.lloydsoflondon.co.uk

SOVEREIGN RISK INSURANCE LTD. (SOVEREIGN)

The company depends on its financial strength to provide greater flexibility than other insurers. Sovereign is the only underwriter in the private political risk market that is not dependent on reinsurance for its underwriting capacity. It can issue policies for individual political risks on a stand-alone basis for limits of up to USD 125 million and terms of up to 15 years. Coverage is available up to 100 percent on a loan or investment. It does not require two or more coverages to be purchased together as a package. War coverage is available for noncancelable terms of up to 15 years and can also be written on a stand-alone basis. Currency Inconvertibility Coverage can be written for the full amount of the exposure.

Contact: Christina Westholm Schroder
Tel: 441 296 4279, ext. 15
Email: Christina.Westholm-Schroder@ace.bm

45 Reid Street, 5th Floor
Hamilton, HM12 Bermuda
Tel: 441 296 4279
Fax: 441 296 4281
Internet: www.sovereignbermuda.com

TRADE UNDERWRITERS AGENCY

Trade Underwriters Agency's trade credit insurance policies provide coverage of short-term (up to one year) trade credit transactions, both domestic and international. Coverage is available on a comprehensive, commercial-only or political-only basis. Generally, credit periods are less than 90 days. Policies are offered in two basic formats: multi-debtor and single-debtor. The multi-debtor policy provides coverage for a portfolio of an insured's trade. Eligible debtors include private debtors and government-controlled debtors. Maximum coverage under the multi-debtor policy is generally 95 percent. The single-debtor policy provides coverage for an insured's trade with one specific debtor, whether private or government controlled. Coverage under the single-debtor policy is generally not more than 90 percent. Higher or lower percentages of cover may be considered, depending on the circumstances of a specific case.

410 Jericho Turnpike, Suite 201
Jericho, NY 11753
Tel: (516) 681-2191
Email: info@tuagroup.com
Internet: www.tuagroup.com

UNISTRAT CORPORATION OF AMERICA

Unistrat Corporation of America is a subsidiary of the French entity Unistrat (a market leader in continental Europe) and specializes in the coverage of political risk. Based in Paris, Unistrat covers commercial contracts and assets in more than 170 countries for its clients. Unistrat offers a complete range of products, including coverage of commercial risk. Its two shareholders are the COFACE and SCOR groups.

Contact: Bernard Labadie
Tel: (212) 389 6470
Email: blabadie@unistratusa.com

444 Madison Avenue, 24th Floor
New York, NY 10022
Tel: (212) 390 5401
Fax: (917) 322 0430
Internet: www.unistrat.com

XL CAPITAL, LTD.

Initially founded in 1986 as EXEL by 68 of the world's largest global corporations, XL Capital Ltd has grown and diversified far beyond its early insurance foundations. XL Capital offers unparalleled vision and expertise in blending traditional insurance and reinsurance techniques with capital market financial engineering. XL Capital offers political risk insurance through XL London Market in the United Kingdom and financial guarantee services through XL Financial Assurance. Their customer segments range from USD 50 million to over USD 500 million. XL Capital provides political risk insurance over Africa, Asia, Australia, Europe, and the Americas.

Contact: David Wright, War & Political Risk Class Underwriter
Tel: 44 (0) 20 7648 1177
Email: david.wright@xlinsurance.co.uk

XL London Market Ltd
Fitzwilliam House
10 St. Mary Axe
London EC3A 8NL
Tel: 44 (0) 20 7648 1000
Fax: 44 (0) 20 7648 1003
Internet: www.xlinsurance.com

THE ZURICH EMERGING MARKETS

ZEMS provide political risk insurance and credit insurance to protect investors against exposures when operating in emerging markets. ZEMS focuses on risks facing emerging markets investors (for trade and project finance, equity investments, and capital markets transactions). To date, ZEMS has written policies covering risks in 70 developing countries in Latin America, Asia, Africa, Middle East, and Eastern Europe.

Capacity for political risk insurance policies is up to $100 million per risk with a maximum term of coverage of 15 years. Coverage includes: policy terms between 1 and 7 years, capacity up to USD 70 million per transaction, absence of restrictions regarding the customers' nationality, coverage available for a wide variety of transactions with emerging markets.

Nathan Younge, Senior Underwriter–Americas
Email: nathan.younge@zurich.com

1201 F Street, NW, Suite 250
Washington, DC 20004
Tel: (202) 525-3100
Fax: (202) 628-2216
Internet: www.zurichna.com

General Outline for Information Memorandum

I. EXECUTIVE SUMMARY
Key Facts
Introduction
The Project
Participants
Project Budget & Financing Plan
Projected Cash Flow

II. PROJECT DESCRIPTION
Project Scope and Description
Project Cost, Financial Plan, and Proposed Financial Structure
Projected Financial Statement and Return on Investment
Technology
Technical Considerations and Feasibility Study
Marketing and Distribution
Permits, Licenses, and Authorizations

III. THE COMPANY AND PROJECT SPONSORS
History and Business of Sponsors, Including Financial Information
Proposed Management Arrangement with Names and CVs

IV. INVESTMENT CONSIDERATION
Developmental Benefits
Benefits to the Project Country
Environmental Issues

V. MARKET
Market Overview
Market Demand
Market Supply and Competitive Position
Pricing
Market Trends

VI. PROJECT ECONOMICS
General Assumptions
Tax Assumptions
Financing Assumptions

Additional Information

This appendix includes other sources that may be useful in locating organizations, completing applications, or pinpointing products and services. Informative websites, magazines, and other publications are included.

INTERNET

GENERAL INFORMATION

Overseas Private Investment Corporation (OPIC)—Great source for research and general information.
Internet: www.opic.gov/

- Country Links connect you with more than 15,000 documents and other non-OPIC sources of economic, business, political and social data for all of the countries and areas in which OPIC can currently do business
- OPIC's State Links can take you to web sites in your state sponsored by state government agencies and other organizations that can be helpful in international investment and trade
- OPIC's General Links database can connect you with various federal agencies and other organizations that can be helpful in international investment and trade
- OPIC's Investor Information Gateway contains links to country, regional, and business information resources provided by selected U.S., state and local government agencies, and quasi-government and private organizations. Resources include economic, political, and investment climate data; travel information; important contacts in the U.S. and abroad; and much more
- OPIC's Investor's Information Gateway Country Link Database connects you with more than 10,000 documents

and other sources of economic, business, political, and social data for all of the countries and areas in which OPIC can currently do business

International Finance Corporation (IFC)—Excellent Source for Articles
Internet: www.ifc.org

Lessons of Experience: The Environmental and Social Challenges of Private Sector Projects: IFCs Experience
Internet: www.ifc.org/publications/pubs/loe/loe8/loe8.html

Impact, Private Sector Partners: Infrastructure in Focus
Internet: www.ifc.org/publications/pubs/impact/issue2/issue2.html

Small and Medium Enterprise Department (SME): Review of Small Business Activities 2002
Internet: www.ifc.org/sme/jp6328_SME_Lo.pdf

Results on the Ground: The Private Sector and Development
Internet: www.ifc.org/economics/pubs/results.htm

Paths out of Poverty: The Role of Private Enterprise in Developing Countries
Internet: www.ifc.org/publications/paths_out_of_poverty.pdf

Project Finance in Developing Countries
Internet: www.ifc.org/publications/ifc_catalog/Untitled_Stacked_Page/untitled_stacked_page_30.html

Center for International Development, Harvard University—Great links to the world of Development Finance
Internet: www.cid.harvard.edu/cidlinks/internat.htm#International%20&%20Regional%20Development%20Organizations

UN and Aid Programs
Internet: global.finland.fi/english/publications/annual/1999/text4b.html

The Association of European Development Finance Institutions (EDFI)
Internet: www.edfi.be/

PROJECT FINANCE

Comprehensive Project Finance Links
Internet: members.aol.com/projectfin/project_finance_
links.htm

Project Finance Portal
Internet: www.hbs.edu/projfinportal

The Directory of Project Finance Investors, Lenders and
Advisors
Internet: www.infocastinc.com/pfdir.html

POLITICAL RISK

Political Risk Insurance for Private Infrastructure Projects:
A Key Ingredient for Successful Transactions in Developing
Countries
Internet: www.privatizationlink.com/feature/feature.cfm

Political risk key concern for global business in 2003; Global
Credit and Political Risk Map reveals top threats for businesses
Internet: www.aon.com/about/news/press_release/
pr_005058B9.jsp

Political Risk Management Tools and Insurance Solutions
Internet: www.aon.com/us/busi/risk_management/risk_
transfer/trade_credit/political_risk/tools_and_solutions/
default.jsp

EXPORT CREDIT

ECA Watch
Internet: www.eca-watch.org

PUBLICATIONS/ARTICLES

PROJECT FINANCE

Project Finance Magazine
Internet: www.projectfinancemagazine.com/contents/
publications/pf

Project Finance Monthly
Internet: www.pfmonthly.com/

The Journal of Project Finance
Internet: www.cmsinfo.com/ZIIJPF.html

Institutional Investor
Internet: www.institutionalinvestor.com

POLITICAL RISK

International Political Risk Management
Internet: www.miga.org/screens/pubs/iprm/order.pdf

EXPORT CREDIT

Trade Finance Magazine
Internet: www.tradefinancemagazine.com/contents/
publications/tf

BOOKS

* See beginning of book for listing of other titles by William A.
Delphos.

PROJECT FINANCE

Culpeper, Roy. *Titans or Behemoths.* Canada, Renouf Publishing
Co., 1997.

Dollar, David, and Paul Collier. *Globalization, Growth, and Poverty:
Building an Inclusive World Economy.* Oxford Press, World Bank,
2001.

Glen, Jack D. An *Introduction to the Microstructure of Emerging
Markets.* World Bank, 1994.

Gutner, Tamar L. *Banking on the Environment: Multilateral
Development Banks and their Environmental Performance in Central
and Eastern Europe.* Cambridge, MA, The MIT Press, 2002.

Hallberg, Kristin. *A Market-Oriented Strategy for Small and Medium
Scale Enterprises. World Bank,* 2000.

Morrison, Rod. *Project Finance International.* IFR Publishing,
2000.

Pinto, Brian, and Jack D. Glen. *Debt or Equity? How Firms in
Developing Countries Choose.* World Bank, 1994.

Sullivan, Ronald F. *International Project Financing,* 3rd Edition, New York, Juris Publishing Inc., 2002.

Yaron, Jacob, and Mark Schreiner. *Development Finance Institutions: Measuring Their Subsidy.* World Bank, 2001.

Yescombe, Edward. *Project Finance.* Sutton Technical Books, 2003.

POLITICAL RISK

Glossary of Insurance and Risk Management Terms. International Risk Management Institute, 2001.

Moran, Theodore. *International Political Risk Management: Exploring New Frontiers.* World Bank, 2001.

Wagner, Daniel. *Political Risk Insurance Guide.* International Risk Management Institute, 1999.

EXPORT CREDIT AGENCIES

Johnson, Thomas. *Export/Import Procedures & Documentation.* New York, American Management Association, 2002.

Stephens, Malcolm. *The Changing Role of Export Credit Agencies.* International Monetary Fund, 1999.

INDEX